"As the man who created U.S. homeland security in the post-9/11 era, [Tom Ridge] is also the man who can most authoritatively recount how it happened, where we are now, and what still needs to be done. In a candid voice, he does all of that in *The Test of Our Times*. This is a book that lets the political chips fall where they may. Ridge also fills this important and readable account with pithy anecdotes, self-deprecating humor, compassion, and a critical eye to the personalities of those historical events that are still being played out in these very dangerous times."

—BARRY CASSELMAN, syndicated columnist and author of
  North Star Rising: Minnesota Politicians on the National Stage

"Every law enforcement officer, firefighter, medical responder, as well as all Americans, should read this book."

—LEROY D. BACA, sheriff, County of Los Angeles

"As the Canadian counterpart to Tom Ridge following 9/11, I quickly learned that he was one of those rare political leaders who was all about action rather than talk. A patriot and a public servant to his core, Tom is a pragmatic and practical problem-solver, a man whose word could be counted on and who truly made his country safer. His is a compelling story that shows that good people can make a positive difference through commitment to public life."

—JOHN MANLEY, former Deputy Prime Minister

THE
TEST
OF OUR
TIMES

America Under Siege . . .
And How We Can
Be Safe Again

TOM RIDGE

with LARY BLOOM

THOMAS DUNNE BOOKS | NEW YORK
ST. MARTIN'S PRESS

THOMAS DUNNE BOOKS.
An imprint of St. Martin's Press.

THE TEST OF OUR TIMES. Copyright © 2009 by Tom Ridge.
All rights reserved.
Printed in the United States of America.
For information, address St. Martin's Press,
175 Fifth Avenue, New York, N.Y. 10010.

www.thomasdunnebooks.com
www.stmartins.com

Book design by Mary A. Wirth

LIBRARY OF CONGRESS CATALOGING-IN-PUBLICATION DATA

Ridge, Thomas J.
   The test of our times : America under siege . . . and how we can be safe
again / Tom Ridge with Lary Bloom.—1st ed.
       p. cm.
   Includes index.
   ISBN 978-0-312-53487-5 (alk. paper)
   1. Terrorism—United States—Prevention.   2. Terrorism—Government
policy—United States.   3. United States. Dept. of Homeland
Security.   4. Emergency management—United States.   5. September 11
Terrorist Attacks, 2001.   6. War on Terrorism, 2001–   I. Bloom,
Lary.   II. Title.
   HV6432.R53 2009
   363.325'170973—dc22

                                                              2009016740

First Edition: September 2009

10 9 8 7 6 5 4 3 2 1

*To the men and women of the Department of Homeland Security
whose names may not appear on these pages but who,
against considerable odds and with immeasurable
personal sacrifice, worked to protect us from
harm and to preserve our liberties.*

Contents

Preface

Congressional leaders and pundits are stuffing [Tom Ridge] into the Beltway meat grinder: Either he'll fail because he has no money and authority to pummel bureaucracies into line, or he'll fail because some disaster will occur, or he'll fail for giving out too much information, or not enough information or conflicting information. Or he'll fail because he can't possibly succeed. He has the scariest and most difficult Washington job you could possibly imagine.

— ANN GERHART,
The Washington Post, November 12, 2001

In the days and weeks after I packed the boxes and left the job as the country's first secretary of homeland security, the question came up and again and again. "Will you write a book?" The interest was understandable. Until January 2005 I had filled a new post in the federal government with unprecedented responsibilities; as Senator Joseph I. Lieberman put it, "Building an ark after the flood started." I saw how the power plays of official Washington sometimes bumped up against the needs of the country from a singular perspective during a time of widespread anxiety. Even so, the answer to the question about writing a book was a resolute "maybe." There were compelling reasons to reject the idea. For one, the genre of books written by former administration members, once a rare business that focused primarily on policy and was loath to include criticism of the president or his administration, has greatly expanded. In many of those that have been recently published, a "get-even" quality has become the baseline, and, in more than a few cases, they became exercises in self-aggrandizement while evading responsibility. My ego is as healthy as anyone's inside the Beltway, but using a book to promote my own ambitions had limited appeal. Nor did I think it a good idea to write simply a blow-by-blow account (called a "tick-tock" by journalists) of my days in the department—"and this happened and then this happened"— because I thought that task would be better left to historians. In addition, in the days after I left my post, I felt as I had when I came back from the war in Vietnam many decades earlier: I was a soldier there, and there had been thousands of soldiers. I became a congressman, and there had been thousands of those before me. And a governor, many have served. To put it in the technical terms of memoir, who cares?

As reluctant as I had been, the idea of writing something about the years following 9/11 never fully disappeared. I realized I couldn't possibly identify all the key players and important moments, but hopefully I could portray the capability and commitment of those with whom I worked and the environment within which we sought to secure America. I thought my fellow citizens and public officials needed to know about what happened, what ought to have happened, and what we must do in the future to secure America and to raise the issue of security well above politics.

As I write, we are no longer as breathless as we were in the immediate aftermath of 9/11. We have an opportunity to adjust to new realities just as we did, in reasonable ways, during the cold war. Back then, we accepted a different international environment. We supported approaches necessary to reduce the risk of nuclear war. As we accepted the new norm of nuclear confrontation, we continued to advance important economic and social interests. The civil rights movement flourished, there were great strides in medicine, Silicon Valley sprang up and became the international leader in technological innovation, and we built the strongest and most diversified economy in the world—all under a constant nuclear threat. Perhaps, I reasoned, I could contribute in some way to a new set of national expectations and responsibilities. In fact, the urge to do this—as I saw what was happening—became stronger as time went on.

As I thought about this, I realized there were two distinct possible outcomes for our efforts within the department. On the one hand, we could be successful. This would mean that residents of the United States would enjoy business (and life) as usual. They could go about their routines and pursue their dreams without undue fear of boarding an airplane or driving across a bridge. In communities with tall buildings, office workers could press the elevator button for the fortieth floor without wondering whether, just to be safe, they should apply for a job in the exurbs. And when they got home at night, they could open their mail without worry that white powder would spill out and their lungs would fail them. If that sense of well-being happened in the wake of 9/11—and, obviously, that was our goal—there would be no televised black-tie events that celebrated our achievements, no credits doled out. We would retire with the sufficient reward of knowing we did our jobs well.

On the other hand, if a terrorist attack occurred on American soil—and this was highly anticipated by all of us—I and my newly forged network of 180,000 federal employees imported from twenty-two agencies would have failed with no authority over our major intelligence efforts or the Pentagon, and far less support from the White House than official pronouncements ever led the public to believe. We often felt we were swimming upstream. So we worked harder.

As I sat there that night in my far from palatial digs, what occurred to me was not what you might imagine. Certainly, images regularly came to mind that could frighten anyone, and certainly frightened me. As we were focused on starting an enormous enterprise from scratch or on the ever-elusive goal of interagency cooperation, we could be interrupted by, for example, a cargo ship approaching New York Harbor with a nuclear device. No need for a precise delivery system like the MX missile. No need for the perpetrators of Armageddon to avoid elaborate container inspections. No need to try to bribe port officials. No need to arrange for phony visas. Just stop several hundred yards from shore and then blow America's signature city to radioactive dust, using old technology (nuclear) and relatively new attitudes about life and death (suicide bombing). No, not a day went by without "noise" out there, reports of possible threats, and our collective imagination running wild.

But I also had—sitting in that dark and ill-equipped place—a great sense of awe. In this job I had the privilege of working with public servants whose names the public at large would likely never know—heroes and heroines who took America's security seriously, who didn't play political games with it, and whose job was to show up before the sun came up and stay as long as was required, trying to anticipate dangers and to affect public policy in a way that would secure the country, at the same time they read résumés of job applicants, drew up organization charts, and made late-night forays into other offices to "borrow" supplies.

These dedicated Americans didn't seek headlines for themselves, and, in many cases, they gave up lucrative positions in private industry to take on modestly paid, pressure-packed, and underappreciated posts that kept them from their families and put them squarely into high-risk situations. I wanted to tell some of their stories that would otherwise be lost in what was becoming obvious to me—the turf battles and political skirmishes among those who couldn't resist using the politics of terrorism for partisan advantage.

At the Homeland Security Department there were issues that needed to be seen from the inside in a way that could enlighten citizens—that might engage them at a higher and more effective level than the often destructive politics of Washington. And, to that end, it was always our fervent desire to keep our work above politics. We knew that if we lost the public's trust for any reason, our efforts would be in vain. If Americans saw us as simply carrying out a political agenda they would not respond to our effort to engage the federal, state, and local governments, as well as private industry—and the man and woman and child on the street—in a new way of thinking about mutual cooperation and the satisfactions of pitching in for the common good. In short, the kind of national camaraderie and unifying sense of national mission we have not experienced since the days of victory gardens and Rosie the Riveter.

This was a delicate balance: How were we to inspire and motivate cooperation in an atmosphere where many were seen as using American security for political leverage? This was a new and different kind of leadership and organizational challenge. We would plan a national strategy to combat this new threat to our way of life and then build a department to execute it. The strategy and the department were designed to engage government at all levels; the corporate, nonprofit, and academic worlds; and all citizens. It was a massive undertaking having a global reach, but limited authority and resources.

No, the reading public didn't really need another book about Washington infighting, though some of those tales are instructive, as the patient reader will see. It doesn't need another tome that settles scores and argues that the book's hero is smarter than everybody else. In my many years serving as a congressman, governor, and cabinet secretary, I always made it a point to settle differences privately and, wherever possible, in collegial fashion, not by being the guy who speed-dialed a favored reporter to make certain his side of the story got out first.

Even so, I knew as time went on that I had a duty to put down the circumstances as I saw them; otherwise, as a nation we would not learn from our successes and, more pertinently, from our mistakes. Why, for example, was Attorney General John Ashcroft calling a press conference to tell Americans that the threat of an attack was imminent as I was saying, from a different podium, that all was well and not to worry so much? How was it that the commitment to build an office in the White House was not matched with the support to do it right? And why did Congress turn national security into yet another political sideshow? I also knew I wanted to use such experiences and incidents to express how things ought to be, for that need has become clearer and clear to me since I left official Washington.

The aftermath of Hurricane Katrina was heartbreaking. That monstrous storm had the capacity—no matter how effective the preparations or the response—to cause widespread heartbreak. But that devastation should not have been compounded by the

governmental impotence that followed, and by ignoring the policies we had so painstakingly set in place for just such events. Like
all Americans, I felt a sense of devastation in the days following.
But my outrage had a slightly different tinge to it. I knew it did not
have to be.

As this book will explain, real security is never a black-and-
white issue, while in politics, those sorts of phenomena tend to be
reduced to the lowest common denominator, the subject of dema-
goguery and worse: Black or white. Right or wrong. You or me. To
understand what has happened in this world, and America's position in it, requires an open mind, a sense of the true global picture,
and a willingness to put aside a hard-line political view long enough
to consider complex but sensible alternatives. In short, a mind-set
that seldom appears inside the Beltway.

In the years since I left the post at DHS, I have often been
asked about how security, politics, and citizens interact, or ought
to interact. These requests come from universities, communities,
corporations, foreign countries, and other entities to whom the subject of national security was, just a few years ago, a matter of little
importance.

But over the years yet another reason emerged for speaking up.
In the years since I left that post, I have seen a sense of public complacency creep in. I was (understandably) satirized when I suggested years ago that Americans ought to have duct tape in their
houses, that it would be useful in the case of an attack. And the
same was true when we introduced color codes. One of the joys of
writing this book was reviewing the monologues of David Letterman, Jay Leno, Conan O'Brien, and any number of others who made
hay (and much more) out of what we did. (Have you heard the one
from Craig Kilborn? "Tom Ridge says we don't have to run out and
put plastic sheeting over our houses. Great. Tell that to my dead
parakeet.") A sense of humor and the need for a thick skin come
with the territory.

Now the jokes have faded and I continue to worry about growing public complacency, which is as dangerous as it is false. I have
a certain wariness that as we move farther in time from the mind-

set of 9/11 we will have lost our edge, and not be prepared psycho-logically or physically should disaster happen.

Much political advantage has derived from hard-line attitudes about American security. There is not much I can do about that. But I will be successful in this endeavor if I can accomplish a few goals in the storytelling and recommendations that follow.

I hope to convince you to take the ongoing threat of terrorism seriously. And, at the same time, I will argue that we can live with that threat, and prepare for it, and, if and when terrorism strikes, recover physically and psychologically. I want to persuade you to become a partner in a new kind of America, more alert and more willing to pitch in for the common good, but also more resilient. I want to convince you we can manage these risks more effectively every-day, but we cannot eliminate them. I want you to understand that in this long-term struggle there are potential trade-offs between security and convenience, risk and freedom. To do this, I am obliged to tell a few tales from the inside. Some of them, on their own, may in no way reassure you about the ability of the government to protect us. But the point here is, if I can paint the picture honestly and with pertinent detail, the prescription for America that I provide at the end will seem to you a natural response to an unprecedented situation. The threat, certainly, is real, but on balance, given our culture, our value system, and our technological capacities, we can preserve our freedom and emerge from this a stronger, more confident, more secure America.

1

TO THE FIELDS OF SHANKSVILLE

Most people in counterterrorism were talking about the likelihood of a doomsday scenario involving germ warfare or nuclear weapons. We feared that something would happen on a terrifying scale, but not that it would be done with conventional tactics—hijacking—that is reminiscent of the 1970s.

—JULIETTE KAYYEM,
National Commission on Terrorism

On the morning of September 11, 2001, as governor of Pennsylvania, I was unaware of the drama playing out in the cloudless sky overhead. I did not know that the Pennsylvania State Police were looking for me. I was tending my garden, removing the dead stems and leaves from the daylilies, cannas, and roses in one of several raised beds I had built around our house in Erie, the working-class city of my youth. As always, whenever I escaped the capital in Harrisburg for home, I lost myself in the rocky soil and earthy details.

Three hundred miles northwest of the governor's residence—where more than a full schedule awaited my return later in the day—I once again felt the gardener's sense of renewal. Public service was in my blood. I loved being governor of the Commonwealth of Pennsylvania and still had much to accomplish before my second and final term ended. But the garden was another matter altogether: It was mine to create. There was nobody pulling on my coat sleeves and no political compromises in the doing, except the bargains forged with Mother Nature for suitable weather. I love the varieties and textures of plants and the cycle of garden life. They offer lessons and comfort—the planting, the blossoming, the withering away, the rebirth the following spring. In that cycle the garden mirrors the capacities of human beings. Indeed, I love the sense of optimism gardening inspires: If I plant in the spring, flowers will bloom through the summer.

Early that morning I had visited my mother at St. Vincent Hospital, where she was recovering from surgery. She suffered from a variety of ailments, but she remained a source of strength to me. No bigger than a minute—with ankle weights, coming in maybe at 105 pounds—Laura Ridge was never a complainer. When I brought jelly donuts to her room, I asked how she felt. Although eighty-one at the time and obviously frail, she quoted in answer the classic American folk tune: "The old gray mare, she ain't what she used to be."

I'd return to the hospital, I thought, once my gardening duties were completed, and still have plenty of time before the state plane, a King Air turboprop, would be sent from the capital to take me back to Harrisburg. Once there, I'd get back to the business of governing. The last thing on my mind was terrorism.

What I didn't know that morning was plenty. The state police called the troopers assigned to me, and they gave me the startling, incomprehensible news that two commercial airplanes had flown into the Twin Towers in New York City.

I was pulling into my driveway at the time. I went into the house, turned on the television in the master bedroom, and picked up the phone. I talked to Mark Campbell, my chief of staff, as I watched horrifying images repeated over and over: passenger jets were crashing into office towers, smoke was billowing, unimaginable horrors were occurring inside.

"What do you know?" he asked.

"I know what you know," I replied. Which was very little beyond what I was watching through the lenses of network cameras.

I said, "I don't know if there are more planes in the air and other attacks coming." I thought, well, Pennsylvania has its own share of tall buildings and historic structures, and who the hell knows where this enemy, whoever it was, could be headed. I asked Campbell to ramp up operations at the headquarters of the state's emergency operations center outside of Harrisburg. When I hung up, I watched a report from the Pentagon by NBC correspondent Jim Miklashevski. He was reviewing what the Department of Defense knew about what had happened in Manhattan. Suddenly, there was a loud explosion behind him. He ended his report, saying he needed to find out what had happened. It was, of course, the third civilian airplane turned into a missile—a direct hit on America's military headquarters. And soon there would be a fourth, the one that would hit, quite literally, home.

In the time that has passed since that day, I have often pictured myself as a passenger in the cabin of United Airlines Flight 93. With the chances of survival slim to none, I have wondered what I would have done.

The sky above Pennsylvania was in the typical flight plan of United 93. It had originated at New Jersey's Newark Airport, then flown due west toward San Francisco en route to its ultimate destination, Tokyo. The Boeing 757-200 had rolled down the runway at 8:42 A.M., about twenty-five minutes later than usual. That the flight was late taking off due to heavy airport congestion meant that its fate, though tragic, would differ from that of the three other passenger jets hijacked that morning by a well-rehearsed team of nineteen men intent on killing themselves while carrying out their stunning assault on America.

It appeared to air traffic controllers that United 93 was flying according to plan until 9:28 A.M., near the Ohio border, when the craft unaccountably went into a brief descent—seven hundred feet—and then: "Mayday" and "Hey, get out of here! Get out of here! Get out of here!" was heard and recorded at the FAA's Cleveland Center facility.

By that point, it was clear that our country was being attacked by an enemy that used a far different strategy than any we had ever faced or even contemplated. This enemy hadn't gone to the trouble of outfitting itself with ground troops equipped with mortars and supported by tanks, helicopters, and an aircraft carrier battle group. They had the ingenious and horrific idea of turning passenger planes, filled with humanity and thousands of gallons of jet fuel, into weapons of mass destruction.

By 9:15 A.M. American Airlines Flight 11 and United Flight 175, both out of Boston, had already hit the upper floors of the World Trade Center in Lower Manhattan, and another plane, American Flight 77, out of Washington Dulles International Airport, was headed for the Pentagon. The attack had by then brought destruction, death, and a state of national shock on a scale that immediately invited comparisons to that "date which will live in infamy," December 7, 1941.

Passengers on those three planes had been unaware that the hijackings were intended for a much different purpose than those they'd read about or seen on the news. Since the 1960s, when the phenomenon began with flights being diverted to Cuba, hijacking was used primarily as a bargaining tool. The hijackers held those aboard as hostages for ransom to secure the release of comrades held in prison, or other similar purposes. That was the era before the widespread phenomenon of the suicide bomber.

But to passengers aboard United 93, it appeared that a suicide bomber was aboard. Of the four men seated in the first-class section—Saeed al-Ghamdi, Ahmed al-Nami, Ahmad al-Haznawi, and Ziad Jarrah—who conspired to take over the cockpit by using their box cutters and knives, one also had a device strapped to his body. From the cockpit, Jarrah, the native of Lebanon who sat in the pilot's seat after the attack on the cockpit crew, told the thirty-seven passengers over the intercom, "Ladies and gentleman, ladies and gentlemen. Hear the captain. Please sit down, keep remaining seating. We have a bomb on board, so sit." The other three hijackers on United 93—as were most of the nineteen involved that morning—were Saudi Arabians. But to the passengers flying over Pennsylvania, such distinctions were pointless.

Soon all aboard knew the deadly intentions of these men, if not their ultimate destination. Planners of the hijackings, it became clear in the days that followed, intended for the planes to hit their targets within minutes of each other. But United 93's delay in taking off from Newark had meant there was a lag time—time enough for the news of the hijackings of earlier flights to reach the cockpit and the passenger compartment.

As the flight progressed—as Jarrah turned the plane south and then southeast over Pennsylvania and toward the nation's capital—many aboard made emergency calls to relatives and friends using cell phones or the Verizon Airfones stored on the back of seats. In these emotional conversations passengers gave blow-by-blow descriptions, and they revealed at least three people had been killed: the captain, the first officer, and a flight attendant. The passengers learned about the attacks on the Twin Towers and the Pentagon and so knew that they were aboard what had become a deadly weapon. They may have concluded that it was headed for Washington. They certainly were aware that if they didn't act, another key target would be hit. (Later evidence indicated it likely would have been the White House or the U.S. Capitol.)

One of the passengers in first class, Tom Burnett, called his wife and said, "Don't worry. We're going to do something." Another in coach, Todd Beamer, tried to make a credit card call and was given the customer-service representative, who heard him say the words that became the American rallying cry: "Are you guys ready? Let's roll."

Armed with information after calling their loved ones, discovering what had transpired, and knowing their fate was all but certain, they decided their deaths wouldn't be in vain. In spite of the absolute horror and fear—what a monstrous emotional hurdle to overcome—they harnessed the energy, the commitment, and the will to fight back.

The black box, ultimately recovered, revealed that it is likely the passengers never were able to reach the cockpit. But as they were breaking down the door, Jarrah rolled the airplane to the left and right, attempting to knock them off balance. Then, sensing that the passengers were about to attack him, Jarrah, shouted in Arabic, "Allah is the greatest! Allah is the greatest!" and put the plane into a steep dive. When United 93 hit the Pennsylvania countryside outside of the town of Shanksville, only twenty minutes from its Washington, D.C., target, it was descending at a forty-degree angle and traveling at 580 miles per hour.

The Erie airport was uncommonly quiet. No aircraft were taking off because the FAA had ordered every plane out of the air. By the time I got to the small terminal that serves private flights, I learned there could be a long wait. That induced a great sense of frustration. In telephone conversations, I heard some of the basics about the four doomed flights from staff members. Tim Reeves, my press secretary, told me what he knew about United 93, that it had gone down outside of Shanksville. But even as a governor of a state involved in all this, I didn't know any more than an average citizen watching television. And I wondered what else was to come. How many hijackings in all and what other attacks had been planned or might be underway? These questions were on the minds of every government official, at every level, at that moment.

I reviewed a mental catalogue of potential targets in my state, including the historical icons of Philadelphia, such as Independence Hall, Pittsburgh's skyscrapers, and the capital's leafy campus of government buildings. I obviously needed to get back to Harrisburg, and my staff was working with authorities to try to get an exception to the FAA ban. At 9:00 A.M., there had been 3,900 civilian aircraft in U.S. airspace. Two hours later, there were none. Only one large aircraft was aloft, Air Force One, carrying President George W. Bush from Strategic Air Command in Nebraska, where he had been taken as a precautionary measure, back to Andrews Air Force Base. However, by that time, there were more than a hundred military aircraft deployed in the effort to protect large metropolitan areas.

I've never considered myself a control freak, but I always crave information. I learned another expression for it later—situational awareness. The staff back at the capital was doing its best to keep me informed, and I knew that our emergency response team, the Pennsylvania Emergency Management Agency (PEMA), was already at work. That gave me some comfort because I had seen this team perform many times. The agency was composed of professionals extensively trained in emergency preparedness, response, and recovery. Most of the experience had come from extreme weather— blizzards, tornados, and floods. We had periodic exercises around different emergency events, but never a terrorist attack. PEMA had always responded quickly and with great efficiency because it always erred on the side of overpreparation. In addition, PEMA officials were connected; they had forged bonds with local officials all around the state, as well as with key figures in business and industry. It was the model for an emergency response plan that I later tried to advance in Washington. But of course, on that beautiful late summer morning in 2001, I saw that our vulnerability as a country extended beyond any limits we had ever anticipated.

To that point, like most Americans, I was naïve and relatively uninformed about terrorism dangers. The bombs that had gone off in the World Trade Center's garage in 1993 and outside the federal building in Oklahoma City two years later seemed like aberrations in an otherwise orderly society, not a sign of things to come. The authorities arrested and convicted a blind sheikh, and most Americans, including me, thought this was the individual act of an isolated fanatic, not part of a larger and longer, threat. Similarly, Timothy McVeigh was arrested and convicted. His was the act of a twisted and demented mind. But as we learned later, even American citizens are quite capable of joining a network that specializes in horror.

Yet in all my conversations with fellow governors over the years at our semiannual meetings I don't recall a single session devoted to domestic terrorism or to Sheikh Omar Abdel Rahman (the man behind the 1993 World Trade Center bombing), radical Islam generally, or Al Qaeda in particular. As we later learned, we were not alone in our ignorance or dismissal of this developing, malignant force. Information that emerged after 9/11 revealed the Central Intelligence Agency had tried to get the threat of imminent terrorism on the agendas of the White House and the FBI, with limited success. Neither the term "Al Qaeda" nor the name bin Laden was widely known until after the 1993 attack. (Indeed, Richard

A. Clarke, former national coordinator for security and counterterrorism wrote in his memoir *Against All Enemies* that most administration officials hadn't heard of Al Qaeda at the time of the four hijackings.) Apparently, by the night after the attack some members of the Bush counterterrorism team had already begun to question Al Qaeda's ability to execute such a sophisticated attack and suggested that it had to be state sponsored. That investigative path led to a dead end. What history doesn't record is whether the mind-set led to other conclusions that affected our ability to kill or capture bin Laden.

As governors, we of course knew of deadly attacks on ordinary citizens in other countries. The most frightening for those of us who had taken oaths to protect the health, safety, and welfare of our citizens was the attack on the Tokyo subway system in 1995 when domestic Japanese terrorists used sarin gas to kill a dozen commuters and severely injure many more. But that incident, as well as the 1998 bombings of U.S. embassies in Tanzania and Kenya, as well as the attack on the USS *Cole* in Yemen in 2000, seemed far away. And they were, geographically. We did not comprehend at the time that the latter two were literally attacks on America. Our collective anxieties were usually limited to a crumbling infrastructure or chaos and danger to residents in the wake of blizzards, tornados, or floods, and the threats posed by career criminals—and not those who take their own lives and those of a vast number of innocents in quest of eternal reward from Allah.

But I also thought back to an omen, and my last visit to the World Trade Center, in December 2000. On the weekend of the annual Pennsylvania Society gathering (a tradition begun by Andrew Carnegie and the Mellon family), I held a luncheon for my supporters at Windows on the World, the celebrated restaurant on the 107th floor of the North Tower. After greeting the guests, I walked the perimeter of the room and looked out over the city. What a stunning view it was, in all directions! And yet, a dark vision emerged. My internal governor's voice asked, "What will happen if the elevators don't work, and there is an emergency? How would people get out? It would be a real life-and-death version of

Towering Inferno. I told a couple of staff members to take one last look around because this would be the final ingathering for us in this place; the next time we assembled it would be somewhere much closer to the ground. Even so, I had never imagined the frightful images that every American remembers from that second date of infamy.

After two hours of waiting in the Erie airport, I learned that the state police had finally received permission from the FAA to carry me back to Harrisburg in one of their helicopters. I knew that as soon as I got to Harrisburg the people of Pennsylvania would expect me to be in front of the cameras. In fact, Tim Reeves, my communications director, had scheduled a press conference even as he and other members of the staff were making plans for all of us to get to the site of the crash.

Press conferences were, of course, nothing new to me. As governor, and as a congressman before that, I had participated in or presided over many, usually without trepidation. However, as any person in public office will tell you, these events can be, in a word, uncomfortable. Reporters often ask tough questions that have no easy answers, and afterward sound bites or written quotes are presented without proper context. This press conference would be very different. I'd be talking about events about which I knew virtually nothing not available to anyone else who had access to a television set. I was also carrying in my heart and head the same range of emotions that my fellow citizens were experiencing—shock, anger, disbelief, sadness. All the way back to my days in Vietnam, I had learned it is always important to be in control of your emotions. That's the only way to think straight and communicate with authority. It is the only way to reassure constituents—whether a squad of soldiers or the 12 million citizens of Pennsylvania, even if the official delivering the remarks needs his own reassurance. As it turned out at that press conference, I faced the most difficult question I'd ever had to answer.

"What," Rick Wagner, a television anchorman for a local ABC

affiliate, wanted to know, "should Pennsylvania parents tell their children about the events of today?"

I stood there stone-faced, but my insides were churning. I thought of my own kids, and thousands of other children, who had by then viewed those horrible images from the Twin Towers over and over. Many thoughts and images came to mind. I knew that, on the one hand, I had to acknowledge what had happened and how vulnerable we all felt, but on the other it was important to offer some sense of comfort, to affirm that in time we'd recover from this, and justice would be done. I stood silently in front of the cameras for about fifteen seconds—which in television terms is almost a lifetime. (Later aides told me that they thought they saw me tear up for the first time.) I responded, finally, more in terms of a dad than as a governor:

> It's pretty difficult to explain to your kids that there are people in the world who would kill innocent men, women, and children and subject them to the enormous terror associated with these events to advance a cause. There's nobody that's claimed, as I understand to date, responsibility for these acts. Whether they do or not, we will find them.

After this conference, I boarded another helicopter—a Chinook provided by the Pennsylvania National Guard—a model I'd flown in many times in Vietnam. As we descended at Shanksville, I looked out over the open hatch to the landscape. I had never before been to this rural community of 245 people, eighty miles southeast of Pittsburgh. I had never seen its downtown, with Beaner's Marine, Ida's Country Store (a gift and craft shop), the Shanksville Volunteer Fire Department, and Methodist and Lutheran churches. I had never seen what seemed to me a scene out of a Norman Rockwell illustration— flagpoles in front of every house in the rolling countryside. Yet it was a town that, like Lockerbie, Scotland, fourteen years earlier, the site of the crash of Pan Am Flight 103, would become notorious just for being where it is, and for what happened there beyond its control; indeed, beyond its comprehension.

United 93 had ended in a reclaimed strip mine just outside of town. On the way to the site, I thought of images from my past, including those from Vietnam as well as disaster sights I had seen as congressman and governor. I prepared myself to witness a scene that would more than remind me of those. Like most people, I had seen crash sites on television, with parts of the fuselage, debris, and carnage everywhere. I had also seen death on the battlefield. None of it prepared me for this encounter with tragedy and evil.

In the fields at Shanksville, there were no hints of an engine or plane part, no bodies—merely a large, smoldering hole. As Captain Frank Monaco of the Pennsylvania State Police observed, debris was limited to small pieces that appeared to be "junk, garbage." A Shanksville resident, Paula Pluta, who had called 911 to report the crash, told *The New York Times* that when she first got to the site along with members of the local fire department, she did not see any smoke or fire, merely bits of metal no larger than the small American flag she kept in a potted plant on her porch.

There were no bodies strewn about, no debris field. What was so striking and profound was how minimal it all appeared. It was as if the plane had headed straight down with the purpose of burying itself in the earth. It left me to contemplate the humanity that was lost in such a horrifying way.

By then the TV crews had arrived—from Washington, Philadelphia, and elsewhere, creating a semicircle in the middle of the field. I had never stood before so many cameras. I told the media that afternoon that what had happened there was "irrational, despicable, unconscionable, immoral—the dictionary is inadequate. There aren't enough words."

Privately, I was thinking, "Who did this? How could a heart be so leaden, so evil, that it would take a civilian passenger airplane and turn it into an instrument of war? What kind of enemy is this? How can we ever protect ourselves against such horrors?"

I had no idea as I stood in front of those reporters outside of Shanksville that those questions would take me on a much different course than my family and I had planned and that I would be thrust into the most thankless yet rewarding job in America.

2

THE PRESIDENT
CALLS

A sense of duty pursues us ever. It is omnipresent, like the Deity. If we take to ourselves the wings of the morning, and dwell in the uttermost parts of the sea, duty performed or duty violated is still with us, for our happiness or our misery. If we say the darkness shall cover us, in the darkness as in the light our obligations are yet with us.

—DANIEL WEBSTER,
"Argument on the Murder of Captain White," April 6, 1830

Six days after the attacks of 9/11, about two hundred relatives of the victims aboard United 93 gathered under a tent near the Shanksville crash site. Many had placed personal objects on the hillside: teddy bears, photographs, and baseball caps, along with sprays of asters and mums, and, saddest of all, single red roses.

With First Lady Laura Bush, my wife, Michele, and I went down the ranks of first responders, thanking firefighters, police, and emergency medical technicians. Later, my wife confided, "They looked so young and so shell-shocked and so dazed." As were we all. By that time, images of the burning and crumbling Twin Towers had been repeated so often on television they made many Americans, including Michele, physically ill.

The national sense of America's vulnerabilities had risen to unprecedented levels. It was different from Pearl Harbor, which, after all, was a surprise attack on a naval base, not the civilian population.

Mrs. Bush huddled with a woman who had lost two daughters

in the crash. And we all watched as relatives lit candles in memory of the victims. These were soon blown out by an unsympathetic, but not ill, wind.

The media had been barred from the service, but one of the dignitaries, Red Cross president Bernadine Healy, later told a reporter there was "a certain peace, a certain beauty" to the service. She said Shanksville was "a kind of Gettysburg for the first heroes of the war against terrorism."

As the afternoon progressed, I thought of another mass memorial five years earlier. TWA Flight 800 had exploded off the coast of Long Island over the Atlantic Ocean, killing all 230 aboard, including dozens of students from Montoursville High School, in north central Pennsylvania. They had organized car washes and bake sales to finance a class trip to France. When called upon to speak at that service, I could not offer the families of those lost much beyond acknowledging the tragedy that occurred and the pain that family and friends would have to endure forever.

In the case of United 93, there was another dimension. It was by no means a stretch of the imagination or hyperbole to observe that these passengers and their actions would inspire Americans to be empowered, not feel helpless, in the face of evil. Their actions had saved hundreds, maybe thousands, of lives. In her remarks, Laura Bush expanded that message. She told the families: "America is learning the names, but you know the people. And you are the ones they thought of in the last moments of life. You're the ones they called, and prayed to see again. You are the ones they loved."

After the service, I said to Mrs. Bush, "I don't know what any of us can do here to help you and the president—but name it." I meant this, but also knew it was the sort of comment often heard during times of crisis. I certainly didn't think anything would come of it.

The following afternoon I was making notes at the governor's residence in my favorite work space. The library features subdued lighting, comfortable high-back chairs, a working fireplace, a fourteen-foot ceiling, and hundreds of books that document Pennsylvania's early history. There are biographies of William Penn and Benjamin Franklin, descriptions of Quaker settlements, histories of the state's sixty-seven counties, including references to the revolutionary period when York and Philadelphia briefly served as our nation's capital cities, and the period novels of James Michener, who grew up in Doylestown. The shelves also hold accounts of the wars in which our state provided classic battlegrounds: Valley Forge and Gettysburg. The library was for me the Harrisburg equivalent of my gardens in Erie, a private place of solitude away from the demands of the political world.

Like all Americans, I had been trying to digest the events of 9/11. On September 12, I appeared on WITF, a public television station in Harrisburg, to take questions called in by viewers. Pennsylvanians needed reassurance that their state was on high alert and that their law enforcement agencies, firefighters, and emergency response teams were prepared for any similar event. During the question-and-answer period, I spoke to many anxiety-ridden callers. One made a lasting impression. The following transcript tells the story:

HOST NELL ABOM: We have on the phone right now a 12-year-old boy, Brian?

BRIAN: Um, hello.

GOV. RIDGE: Hello, Brian.

BRIAN: Where in Afghanistan is this guy?

GOV. RIDGE: Brian, you ask a wonderful question. The guy you referred to is bin Laden. Bin Laden is a master of disguises. We know that the Taliban government for the past several years, and that's the government in Afghanistan, has been harboring him and supporting him. It is reported that he may move his location almost on a daily basis. I don't believe that the intelligence community of this country or anybody else has been able to pinpoint his location. It's a question that you ask in a very simple, straightforward way and I'll tell you, that's a question that the intelligence community not just in the United States but in a lot of the free world has been asking for several years: Where is this guy? We'll find him, one of these days.

BRIAN: And I have one more question.

Gov. Ridge: That's alright. Please.

Brian: Are we going to retaliate, then? Are we gonna nuke him, or something?

Gov. Ridge: Well, the uh . . . Your question about retaliation I think is very important particularly since you're a young man and you've got a lot of young people your age. My son's only a couple years older than you. And uh, my daughter is 15 and they've asked the same questions. This is a different kind of war that is being fought against America. I don't know, uh, you probably have some family members, perhaps your grandpa or other relatives that fought in either World War II, or Vietnam or Korea, or in the Gulf, whatever. And that was a time when we knew who our enemies were and we were able to send our soldiers in against military. This is a different kind of war that we're fighting now. These people, Brian, are . . . they consider themselves martyrs. We view them as cowards. They are combatants but they don't fight our soldiers. They don't have the courage or the guts to fight our soldiers. That's not their mission. They take . . . they fight our civilians. And then they run and hide and some other things. I think the president will respond in a military way. I think it will be forceful. I think it will be appropriate. We will all be united as Americans behind him.

"Cowards" seemed the right characterization at the time. However, along the way I have learned more about these zealots and could now offer a more thoughtful answer. The Blind Sheikh was prepared to kill others at the first World Trade Center bombing in 1993, but not himself. Timothy McVeigh drove a truck to the federal courthouse and ran for cover. Bruce Ivins, who the FBI ultimately charged with the anthrax murders, obviously had taken measures to protect himself.

Some of these terrorists, not all, have an entirely different view of themselves and their role in advancing the jihadist cause. Simply put, they don't care if they live or die. More to the point, they embrace death. They want to die. I should have explained to Brian that this is what makes stopping them so hard to do.

During the broadcast, I also pointed out the need for those in public service to press on and tackle the critical, as well as the mundane, matters of the state. Yes, we had to pause to digest what had happened to us. Notwithstanding the need of public officials to deal with the consequences of 9/11, we also had to continue to govern.

Around the time of the attacks, we had been negotiating on the hottest political issue in Pennsylvania, the state's attempt to take over Philadelphia's public schools. The Commonwealth's largest system was clearly in crisis—dreadful test scores, high dropout and pregnancy rates, and other ills. We were pouring more money than ever into a system that was obviously broken.

Education is the ultimate tool of empowerment, but when a school system becomes a scandal, what sort of empowerment is possible? I had hoped to convince the legislature that the way to reverse the hopelessness in urban neighborhoods was through dramatic educational reform, including charter schools, vouchers, and other measures that would give parents options for, and an investment in, their children's futures.

I often thought back to my own childhood—the earliest years in veterans' public housing, as the son of working-class parents who nevertheless managed to scrape up tuition for St. Andrew School. There at the corner of Sixth and Raspberry Streets, Sister Alice Marie felt compassion for an oversized seven-year-old who, in reading, was a notable underachiever. Without her patience and persistence, I never would have succeeded in school, would never have dreamed of a career in public service. My dream was for every child in our state to have a Sister Alice Marie in his or her life.

As I made notes to myself about the issue, I received a phone call from a member of the state police executive detail at the residence. "Governor," the sergeant said, "the president's chief of staff, Andy Card, is on the line."

I had seen Card on a number of occasions, including an event in Washington two months earlier. For July 4, the president and first lady had invited our family to stay at the White House and to watch fireworks from the Truman Balcony. A few weeks later, Card and I were in the Rose Garden crowd when the president introduced Robert Mueller as the new FBI director. I assumed that Card was calling me now because he needed to know something about Shanksville. The president was scheduled to address the nation on terrorism the next night. But what's that expression? Never assume.

President Bush, Card told me, was considering ways to respond to what happened, including a new high-profile federal job, "and he wants to talk to you about it later in the day." As I tried to digest what I had just heard, Card added, "By the way, the vice president is going to join me on the line."

I remembered the last time Dick Cheney called me with a request. Then, in the early summer of 2000, candidate Bush had turned to Cheney, who had been secretary of defense in the administration of George H. W. Bush, and later the chief executive officer of Halliburton, and charged him with finding a running mate. Cheney asked me if I would consider having my name added to the short list. I had said yes, but only for a brief period.

This time, Cheney said, "The president wants to do something differently in the White House to deal with the terrorist threat. It's a high priority. We're very serious about this, and he wants to talk to you about being a part of it." I stopped a moment just to think. Then he added, as if he'd anticipated the position he'd put me in, "Please keep an open mind."

But beyond that, neither Card nor Cheney could offer any detail, just that it appeared the country needed an antiterrorism czar. That may seem like an exalted position, but at the time there was no job description, nor would one be written until after I accepted the position. Nor would there be a specific promise of any staff. Instead, I was assured, I'd get the people and resources I'd need when I needed them. Card later told me that perhaps fifteen to twenty people could be spared, but he would be flexible. (Shortly before I retired I mentioned to the president that Andy had been "really" flexible. I had started with about a half dozen and finished with 180,000.) Even so, the White House callers needed to gauge my interest. Presidents don't want to be in a position of making requests of people who intend to turn them down.

As I listened to Card and Cheney, I asked myself unanswerable questions. "The president will be calling me to do *what*?" and "Why should I leave the job I love—governor of Pennsylvania—before it's done?" And "Why would he choose me for this enormous and seemingly impossible task?" Though I had been in the army and served on the ground in a war against a difficult and sometimes hidden enemy, I was certainly no expert on counterterrorism. President Bush could have chosen someone from the CIA or the Defense Intelligence Agency or some other intelligence agency that had been given the task of tracking Al Qaeda and could bring to the office instant credibility. On the other hand, I was a governor, and like the executive heads of each of our fifty states, had been involved often in emergency situations. I was also recognizable in Washington, a former congressman known, I believed, to be more interested in finding solutions than in scoring political points. This new job in Washington would require, no doubt, an unprecedented measure of tact and cajoling.

The president and I had long been friends. We met for the first time when we campaigned together for the Reagan-Bush reelection in 1984. We got to know each other better when we served as governors. It was during a visit to the family compound in Kennebunkport that he told me of his intention to run for the White House. He learned more when my name was added to his short list of vice presidential candidates, so he knew that during that time I had been loyal. Although that loyalty came at a significant personal cost to me.

Tempted by the prospect of the vice presidency, I submitted several folders of information responding to a wide range of personal and political questions. Shortly thereafter I decided to withdraw my name. Being governor of a large state whose constitution empowers you completely is more exciting and rewarding than most people can imagine. I was on the list, I think, mostly because my name might attract support from moderate Republicans and independents. (I've always been pro-choice and never thought we needed a constitutional amendment to define "marriage.") In the end, I decided there were things I wanted to complete as governor.

And then, perhaps, after a career in public service, I'd make full use of my law degree by returning to Erie and establishing a practice there or perhaps in Pittsburgh or Washington. I told Governor Bush that I was honored to be considered but I had to decline. He asked me to delay any discussion of my decision with the media. I presumed he needed time for political reasons, and so I agreed to stay silent on the matter. Regardless of the rationale behind the request, I thought it was important to honor it.

I believe elected officials have a responsibility to be accessible to the press and to speak as directly as possible to the issues raised. The First Amendment created and protects a healthy and often controversial tension between those who govern and those who report on the nature and effectiveness of that governance. My failure to disclose promptly my decision to withdraw my name from consideration tarnished, at least temporarily, my credibility with several Pennsylvania-based journalists. When I was finally free to speak publicly, journalists wrote some extremely negative stories, arguing that I hadn't been forthcoming, which was of course true. My credibility took a hit. But my first obligation, in this case, was to keep my commitment to my friend, the candidate.

A year and a half later, as I awaited a life-changing call, I suspected that in his quest to find someone to help him protect the country, George W. Bush's short list had only one name on it. I still had fifteen months to serve as governor in my second term, and I had assumed that whatever the change there would be afterward, the family and I could accommodate to it. Just another public official leaving public office, hanging up a shingle. Now, with a single phone call, that neat plan was shredded.

I had the same feeling in my gut that I had in the late 1960s when, as a student at the Dickinson School of Law (now the Dickinson School of Law of Pennsylvania State University), I received my draft notice. My father had worked hard as a meat salesman for Armour, and had moonlighted at grocery and shoe stores, so that I could become the lawyer he couldn't be. He was hugely upset when I received the letter from President Richard M. Nixon inviting me— under the threat of criminal prosecution should I decline—to appear for a military physical. He was disappointed there was no deferment for students who had started law school. I explained to him that I had always assumed that I would follow his example. He had served in the navy in World War II. The country had called him. He answered. So would I. I traded law books for army field manuals and classrooms for Vietnamese rice paddies. I never regretted that decision, and I had the same feeling about this new call to service.

On the afternoon of September 18, 2001, I told Card and Cheney that I would welcome hearing from the president. But I asked them to delay the conversation for a few hours so I could attend the wake of a friend and have some time to talk to my family.

I went to Michele's office at the residence. Because we didn't often visit each other during work hours, she instantly sensed I wasn't there to talk about the Community Partnership for Safe Children, which she chaired, or the upcoming walk to raise funds for breast cancer research.

She asked, "Is it your mother? Is she all right?"

"She's fine," I replied. "It's not about her. We need to talk, and we should do it upstairs." This was the part of the governor's residence that served as our private quarters. Michele sat on the club chair in our bedroom and watched as I paced the floor with nervous energy. I explained about the call from Card. I told her, "We don't know what the job is, really. The president and I are to have a conversation tonight when I hope to get a little more detail."

She said, "You can't say no, Tom." As the daughter of an army career soldier, Michele has a strong sense of duty, and was well aware that the attack on 9/11 meant a state of war. But she is a mother first. "There are two other people in this equation," she said. "How will we tell them?"

Our daughter Lesley, in particular, was in a groove. She was building an impressive academic record while playing clarinet in the high school marching band and vibes in the percussion band, singing alto in the choir, and playing first base and pitching on the softball team. Our youngest, Tommy, also a fervent athlete, was making progress in middle school, and comfortable with his classroom chums and his buddies at the governor's residence, including the state police, the maintenance staff, and the kitchen staff that taught him cooking.

In the full sweep of a global war these considerations may seem insignificant. But every parent knows how important it is for children to do well in those difficult years as adolescents.

"I know," I said. "They'll hate this."

There were other practical problems. For one, the only house we owned was in Erie, and that was too far from Washington to engage in weekend commutes. We'd most likely have to find an apartment in Harrisburg so Lesley and Tommy could complete their school year. It would be a snap to find a landlord who would be delighted to rent to a family with two teenagers and three oversized Labradors. For another thing, we owned no car. When I became governor we sold our cars partly because we were advised to do so by counsel and partly because under Pennsylvania law the state policemen drive the members of the first family wherever they want to go. Soon, we'd be investigating the mysterious world of minivans.

By coincidence, I had been scheduled to be in Washington the morning after Andy Card's call. The goal was to support Pennsylvania's quintessential industry, steel. Pittsburgh had always been Steeltown, U.S.A., but now our once behemoth companies were on their knees, struggling in the face of fierce (and, in the minds of many, unfair) global competition, particularly from Asia. I went to Washington to urge Congress to extend temporarily the tariffs on imported steel.

When I finished my testimony I went directly to the White House. My phone conversation with the president the night before had been brief—all business. He said, "We're in a war, obviously a different kind of war. And if we are attacked again I want to be able to pick up the phone and ask one person what's happening and what are we doing about it." He explained the new position would be an assistant to the president for homeland security.

As I later learned, nearly forty federal agencies had a role in protecting the homeland. Their competing agendas and missions caused confusion and misinformation and, as I later discovered, much worse. The president said he recognized that I still had an important agenda in Harrisburg, specifically mentioning my education agenda, but said that would have to be taken up by my successor.

At eleven o'clock on September 19, as we had arranged, I met Card in his office, where Vice President Cheney was already sitting. We chatted for a few minutes and then President Bush came in. After some small talk, he said, "Your office will be right next to mine, and there will be complete access to me. We need someone like you for this job, and you're the only you I know." He smiled, shook my hand, slapped me on the back, and left the room.

Card said, "So what do you think, Tom? The president's addressing a joint session [of Congress] tonight."

Now that I had a little more information, I told him, I'd like to return to Harrisburg to have a final discussion with family and a few intimate friends. I told him I'd get back to him within an hour or two. Shortly after I returned to Harrisburg, I called him and formally accepted the new assignment and asked for a month to conclude nearly seven years of governing. He called back and said, "The president wants me to thank you and tell you you've got two weeks. The president would like you to be in attendance tonight when he addresses the nation at the joint session of Congress."

Back in Harrisburg that afternoon, key staff members were incredulous, thinking I was making a mistake. Some tried to talk me out of taking the job. One said, in regard to attacks on the United States, that should none occur, I wouldn't get the credit, but if we had another 9/11 I'd certainly get the blame. Another counseled that whatever title was attached to my name would come with little power in the turf-protecting atmosphere of the nation's capital. And that while American citizens wanted to be told they were safe, there was no way to say that with any assurance. I knew all this, but also saw the larger picture.

I remembered a book I discovered as a kid while rooting through our musty basement in the house in Erie. *They Were Expendable,* by William L. White, was the gripping account of sailors aboard PT boats operating out of Manila in the immediate aftermath of Pearl Harbor. Their task was to defend the Philippines until the U.S. Navy recovered and regrouped, a desperate and ultimately fatal mission, but one that bought time for the cause. The book was about the hard realities of war, in which, in the end, some people are destined to be sacrificed. And if I suspected that my political career would be sacrificed, well, so be it: We are all expendable. Despite my reservations, I would take on this new assignment, and I would give it my best

That afternoon, I asked the state's lieutenant governor, Mark S. Schweiker, to come to the Erie Room in the governor's residence. Schweiker had been my running mate in both gubernatorial elections, but had no inkling of what had happened in the previous twenty-four hours. Or that, as a result, under Pennsylvania law providing for succession, he would soon become the forty-fourth governor of the Commonwealth. At that point, the only people who were aware of the developments, aside from key members of the Bush administration, were my immediate family and my closest aides. It had been important to keep it all under wraps because the announcement to the American people had to come from the president himself, not from news leaks.

I considered Schweiker an ideal successor. As former county commissioner and director of PEMA, as well as an experienced businessman, he had experience dealing with crises.

That afternoon, I said, "Mark, you've been a valued and trusted partner, and from my point of view you'd make a great governor, and that's a good thing, because as of October 5 you will be."

As I told him why, his reaction was subdued. He didn't show any sense of satisfaction or delight because of the sobriety of the moment. He shook my hand and wished me the best.

I still had to inform my cabinet, but there wasn't time before leaving for Washington. Since Reagan National Airport was closed as a result of fears of new attacks, we were obliged to land at Andrews Air Force Base. A driver took me directly to 1600 Pennsylvania Avenue. Once there, I was ushered to an office where I could make a conference call to cabinet members. I apologized for delivering the news on the telephone rather than in person. As soon as I hung up, I was summoned to the presidential limousine.

President Bush and the first lady sat in the backseat. I slipped into the seat facing the rear, next to a man I immediately recognized. The president said, "Tom, I'd like you to meet Prime Minister Blair." I had seen Tony Blair, of course, many times. On this night, I felt an even stronger sense of awe. In the days after 9/11, Britain had been our strongest ally, and Blair had flown to Washington just to stand with the president as a team against terrorism. I said to him, "Thank you, Mr. Prime Minister, for supporting my president and my country." I don't remember exactly what he said in response—I was too awestruck by the moment—except that he acknowledged the longstanding relationship between our countries, and that he should be there to show his support to the president and the United States.

President Bush then asked, "How did your family take the news?"

I didn't think, at that point, it was wise to get into the details, to tell him that, as I had expected, Lesley, in tears, pleaded: "Oh, Daddy, why do you have to do this?" I had made a little speech to an unwilling audience of one about the necessity of making sacrifices for your country. Such speeches—if I can draw broad conclusions from this instance—don't immediately register with teenagers. Lesley is a selfless and compassionate young lady, but I couldn't really expect her to understand why I was turning her world and her brother's world upside down on thirty seconds' notice.

Lesley was distraught, even when I told her that her mother and I had decided that she and Tommy could finish the school year where they were. And when I mentioned, "You can't say a word about this yet to anyone," she glared at me. Pleading my case, I said, "I can't even tell your grandmother or your Uncle David or Aunt Vikki." Michele, who calls Lesley "the queen of e-mail," had to almost literally sit on her to prevent her from informing everyone in cyberspace.

No, I couldn't really talk about any of this in the limo to the commander in chief. His question was more on the lines of "How are you?" So, I replied, simply, "Their heads are still spinning, Mr.

President. But they're relieved that I'll be able to commute to Harrisburg to see them on weekends." I thought to myself, I really don't think this is a Monday through Friday assignment.

He said, "You won't be driving yourself. The Secret Service will be doing that."

I thought, here I am in a limousine with the two most powerful men in the world. And here I am about to be introduced as the key figure in keeping our country safe. I never understood bungee jumping, and had never been tempted by it, but it seemed as if I was about to head off a cliff with a bungee that had not been properly measured.

At the end of the four-minute ride from the White House to the Capitol, a platoon of Secret Service personnel ushered us through the crowd, which parted much as the Red Sea had parted for Moses. The president went to his usual holding room. Mrs. Bush, the prime minister, and I were escorted upstairs to the seats traditionally set aside for the first lady. By then the chamber of the House of Representatives was filled with members of Congress (Republicans directly below and Democrats on the far side), ambassadors, the joint chiefs of staff, the justices of the U.S. Supreme Court, the cabinet, and members of the press corps. When the announcement came, "Mr. Speaker, the President of the United States," everyone stood, as customary, except for members of the press. (That tradition has always irked me. Can't they stand as a sign of respect for the office regardless of the occupant?)

In his speech (which has become known as the "We will not tire, we will not falter, and we will not fail" speech) the president laid out his plan to defeat Al Qaeda and its allies, and then went on to introduce the idea of a new position and the person who would fill it. "Our nation has been put on notice: We are not immune from attack. We will take defensive measures against terrorism to protect Americans. Today, dozens of federal departments and agencies, as well as state and local governments, have responsibilities affecting homeland security. These efforts must be coordinated at the highest level. So tonight I announce the creation of a cabinet-level position reporting directly to me—the Office of Homeland

Security. And tonight I also announce a distinguished American to lead this effort, to strengthen American security: a military veteran, an effective governor, a true patriot, a trusted friend— Pennsylvania's Tom Ridge. He will lead, oversee, and coordinate a comprehensive national strategy to safeguard our country against terrorism, and respond to any attacks that may come."

Every eye in the place was on me as I stood. At that moment, I thought of my dad, who had worked two jobs so I could get ahead. I thought of his lifelong support of me. The first time I ran for Congress, this lifelong Democrat went to the courthouse just before the Republican primary and changed his registration so that he could vote for me. (On the first day he was eligible to change it back, he did.) I wondered what my dad would have thought as the president introduced the son of Thomas Regis Ridge to the world. I hoped he would have been as proud of me as I have always been of him.

Oddly, during the applause, I felt something I had never felt in all of my years in that chamber as a congressman. In a city in which partisanship rules the days, where glad-handing and insincerity have been raised from a high art form to a religion, I was overcome by the warmth all around me. Everyone wanted me to be the guy who could make America safe and, perhaps in the process, hand over a gift box that contained the head of Osama bin Laden.

And I thought, "I hope you'll still be applauding three years from now."

The next morning, *The New York Times* reported on my appointment. It quoted Al Neri, editor of the *Pennsylvania Report,* a political newsletter: "This is the culmination of twenty-two years of friendship. Bush is looking for someone he trusts. He's been looking for a high spot in which to put Tom Ridge. He couldn't put him on the ticket as vice president because of his position on abortion. He didn't give him secretary of defense because there was commotion from Cheney and [Christian Coalition head Jerry] Falwell. This time, the atmosphere was correct."

Ed Rendell, who as Democratic mayor of Philadelphia had

worked with me on several issues, told the *Times*, "Tom has great personal skills. This position will intrude on the F.B.I., the C.I.A., the Justice Department. You're going to have to get all these agencies on the same page, without turf wars. Tom can get everyone pulling on the same oar." Nevertheless, Rendell went on to say that the new post was "fraught with hazard." He didn't know the half of it.

Before I left office, I would speak one last time to the Pennsylvania legislature. But before I did that, I had some serious moonlighting to do: to become an expert on terrorism threats and radical Islam in the space of two weeks. I knew that the minute I stepped into the job, the president and every American would expect an authority who could answer any question from the media or public on the reasons for and the sources of danger and how to protect our cities and towns and repair the damaged psyche of America. I had much to learn, starting nearly from scratch, and not much time to learn it. In effect, I had to drink from a fire hose even as, during most daylight hours, I had to tend to the pressing affairs of the state.

For several nights at the governor's residence, I sat at the dining room table with scores of briefing papers from multiple sources—almost all of it new to me.

I had been the product of a good, if ethnocentric, education. Our histories in my school days centered largely on Western culture, and, of course, whenever it touched on religion, the focus was the development of Christianity. The Prophet Muhammad and the vast Islamic world were mere mentions in thick texts. Even as an adult and as governor of a state that was home to many Muslims, I knew almost nothing about Islam. I had met in the course of my work only a few people who were practicing Muslims. I had never been inside a mosque. I was far from alone in this.

As we saw happen directly after 9/11, a great deal of anti-Muslim sentiment arose in America. It had been, like a weak but acrid scent, in the air for many years, particularly after the attempt to destroy the World Trade Center in 1993. In the hours after the 1995 bombing of the Alfred P. Murrah Federal Building in Oklahoma City and the death of 168 people, the widespread rumor, gaining momentum with the media's help, was that Arab Muslims were responsible. There had been no evidence of that (and indeed, it was soon discovered that a decidedly non-Arab, Timothy McVeigh, had delivered the explosives). Americans in general are reflexively protectionist, and many are suspicious of a religion, no matter how widespread internationally, that remains a distinct minority in this country (about one percent of the population). You put those dynamics together and you have, *wham*, the scapegoating of an entire segment of society.

In a large way, the prejudice against those who followed Islam was a tragedy in itself. Like all prejudices, it relies on ignorance to spread. As I learned in my reading, it ignores the long history of Islam's contributions to world civilization. Islam seems enlightened and humane when compared to the extreme measures of Christian intolerance and savagery in the Middle Ages. For a great portion of 1,200 years, in parts of Europe, Christians and Jews had lived safely and had prospered under Muslim rule.

Such a legacy was obliterated in popular America media by what appeared to be an international conspiracy among Muslims to destroy western culture and Israel. This was oversimplifying the case by plenty, and resulted in the condemnation of one fifth of the world's population. But there was no doubt that at the heart of Al Qaeda (which had been founded in the 1980s by Osama bin Laden and the Palestinian who previously laid the ideological foundation for an international jihad, Sheikh Abdullah Azzam), nothing short of the destruction of the West was acceptable. Azzam migrated to Pakistan at the outset of the Soviet invasion of Afghanistan. He became a dominant and inspiring figure within the Muslim community worldwide as he rallied support for a violent jihad against the West and the restoration of the Muslim caliphate. Much of the financial support of his religious and paramilitary effort was provided by an individual who would succeed him as the most influential figure within the radical Muslim community—Osama bin Laden.

To us in America, this was a new kind of war, very different from what my generation grew up with—the threat of nuclear holocaust, a danger obvious to every schoolchild who ever practiced hiding under a desk during a "duck-and-cover" drill.

It was different, too, from the kind of war that I had come to know firsthand in the provinces of Vietnam. We faced an enemy not bound to or encumbered by the more traditional rules or means of military engagement. I recalled several scenes from my own tour of duty. In one we chased a group of Viet Cong which had ambushed us. They started running through a cane field. Some undoubtedly disappeared in a camouflaged hole. Others probably hid their weapons and blended into several groups of peasants cultivating nearby rice paddies. This should have taught us that we were facing a new kind of insurgency, a formidable force that didn't come in the form of traditional military divisions but from the population itself. You didn't know whether the person walking down the street in the daytime, smiling at you, and shouting, "GI Number One!" was the man who fired mortars at the company's compound after the sun went down.

The Al Qaeda insurgency was a cousin—a distant cousin—of that in terms of strategies and tactics. The nineteen men who conspired to attack America in passenger planes were smartly dressed, clean-shaven, and polite as they went through security and boarded the planes. They blended nicely into the crowd of travelers on the morning of September 11. That respectful ruse was a dramatic juxtaposition to the seething underneath. In the end, though, it was not that much different from a Viet Cong, feigning happiness, shouting "GI Number One!" on Highway One, the road that ran through Duc Pho, Vietnam, a place with which I had become familiar.

I wondered what had turned certain followers of a religion that preaches the idea of leading a virtuous life and that encourages others to do the same into killers who used the Koran as their justification?

I had a few days to become an expert on nearly fourteen hundred years of Islamic history, to learn how the split came to be between the Shia and Sunnis, to discover why Osama bin Laden pointed to events a thousand years ago that made him determined, in the twenty-first century, to seek vengeance and, in his view, justice. To understand, too, the nature and idea of the caliphate, the universal form of government that is their ideal, the direct opposite of our belief in the separation of church and state.

The ignorance of all of this was widespread. Who knew there are 1.3 billion Muslims in the world living in over fifty countries. Most Americans believed that the majority of Muslims live in the Middle East. Wrong. Indonesia, Pakistan, and Bangladesh have far more. If you spin the globe you will find significant populations in the United States, Canada, Europe, Africa, and even India. Although Muslims, they speak many languages and have different religious, economic, and political perspectives.

It's unlikely that most Americans understand that Muslims embrace five basic tenets of faith. There is no God but God (Allah) and Muhammad is his messenger. They are to pray five times a day and are obliged to make a pilgrimage (hajj) to Mecca during their lifetime. They are expected to use their income to support the less fortunate and to observe the rituals of the month-long feast of Ramadan.

I felt, of course, the responsibility of trying to assimilate it all. I have never had trouble sleeping. (Even later, when people asked me in Washington whether I slept well with all the danger out there, I replied in the affirmative: I slept well—but not as long.) The two weeks I was focused on state business and learning what I could about our enemies was the most restless period of my life. I was often awake at 3:00 A.M., studying everything from Sufism to the exploits of Saladin, who recaptured Jerusalem for Islam during the Second Crusade.

Warning signs aside, it is clear now that there was a consensus among many who focused on terrorism that the threats demanded that old government structures and assumptions be discarded. There was an apparent gap in our overall defense strategy. That conclusion may seem odd to Americans, because the federal government has so many agencies and resources. But not one agency had direct and total responsibility for defending our country from the inside. The Department of Defense, for example, is charged with protecting us against invasion by the forces of foreign nations, not by terrorists within, and is largely prohibited by federal law from being deployed domestically. The FBI, CIA, the Department of Justice, U.S. Customs and Border Protection, Immigration and Naturalization Service, and other agencies had their hand in domestic protection, but each was limited by its mission and resources and prevented from addressing critical issues raised by 9/11.

As the interval between being chosen for the job and showing up for work proceeded, I knew I had plenty to learn. Just how much became clear as the days went on.

Among my first visitors to Harrisburg was Admiral James Loy, who was then commandant of the U.S. Coast Guard. If I had expected that his motive was to lobby for more resources—something he certainly had a right to do considering that, among the services that stand at the ready, his is, from a budgetary point of view, the smallest—I would have been wrong. He was instead focused on two messages. First, explaining the traditional roles of the Coast Guard and how it had responded on 9/11, particularly in New York. Second, making it clear that he would do everything he could to support my efforts.

In 1790, Congress authorized the secretary of the treasury, Alexander Hamilton, to create a maritime service to enforce the customs laws of the newly formed government. Tariffs and duties were its major source of revenue and so Washington came to rely heavily on an organization variously called the U.S. Lighthouse Service, the Revenue Cutter Service, the Steamboat Inspection Service, and the Lifesaving Service. In 1915, President Woodrow Wilson officially designated the unit as the United States Coast Guard. Its multiple missions have resulted in its being part of several departments since its inception. In 2003, it was transferred from the Department of Transportation to the Department of Homeland Security.

Its motto, Semper Paratus (Always Prepared) underscores the commitment and duty of every "coastie." In war and peace, dealing with natural and unnatural disasters, every man and woman is driven to help. Little did I realize, during our first encounter, how essential Admiral Loy's experience and support would be to me and our country in the years ahead.

Loy, a veteran of many legislative battles, reminded me of lessons I had learned in Congress. There, and in the governor's office, change is necessary, and building consensus is at the heart of it. About all that I had a deep concern, but I also had confidence. After all, my political roots were not in stern orthodoxy but, from the very first days, in problem-solving compromise. As a kid, I sat at the kitchen table totally engrossed in my parents' conversation. It was a mixed marriage in that sense. My dad was a lifelong Democrat (except for that one day when he switched party affiliation so he could vote for me). My mother, on the other hand, was a committeewoman in the local GOP. I could see, in these discussions, a great regard for the other person's point of view. There was no animosity or belittlement—and a great amount of what has eluded too many Americans for too long—listening. I went into politics as a listener. Yet I knew in Washington that I'd have to do much more than listen. I had a country to help protect, and no clear definition of the staff and resources that would help me do it.

In between such visits I continued to absorb as much information as possible. I read the work of leading experts in the field. Bernard Lewis, the Princeton professor and author of *What Went Wrong?* argued that the emerging Muslim sense of victimhood had prevailed in a culture that had once produced scientists and physicians who made great contributions to western civilization.

In his book, *The Clash of Civilizations,* Samuel Huntington carried Lewis's argument to an extreme. He wrote that it isn't Islamic fundamentalism that we should fear but the dark capacities of the religion itself: "A different civilization whose people are convinced of the superiority of their culture and are obsessed with the inferiority of their power." That seemed to me a clear and dangerous overstatement. Nevertheless, it was a viewpoint that was growing in influence.

During the years I was in Congress, I had served on the House Banking Committee and the Veterans Affairs Committee. There was no shortage of troubling news from the Middle East then. In 1983, only a few months after I first sat in the House, extremists attacked the U.S. Marine barracks at the Beirut Airport. Early one morning a Mercedes-Benz truck, thought to be loaded with drinking water, drove toward the headquarters of the U.S. 2nd Marine Division. The driver crashed through a barbed-wire fence and a gate and barreled into the headquarters lobby, where in a dramatic act of suicide and terror, he set off 12,000 pounds of TNT. The building collapsed, killing 241 American servicemen and 58 French paratroopers.

This was shocking news to us and to the Reagan administration. At the time, we didn't recognize the consequences of what had happened. I remembered thinking, "They are deployed in a hostile environment. What the hell are they doing in a high-rise?" Even so, the incident had appeared to me, as to others, as tragic but something of an anomaly. After all, it was "over there." Much of the Middle East seemed to have little to do with us. There was work for me and others in Washington to do on matters that *directly* affected the United States. In hindsight, our naïveté and insularity seem shocking.

What members of the intelligence committees in Congress had been paying attention to the political movement that became Al Qaeda many years later?

I did not know about a martyr, Sayyid Qutb, an Egyptian scholar and activist, whose exploits had been well known in such circles. He had been arrested in the aftermath of an assassination attempt on the life of Gamal Abdul Nassar, president of Egypt, in 1954. His suffering from torture in prison became widely known in the Arab world.

Nearly three decades later, one of Qutb's protégés, Dr. Ayman al-Zawahiri, would suffer similar treatment in the days after the assassination of Anwar Sadat, Nassar's successor. Al-Zawahiri masterminded a plan to attack the Sadat funeral with the intent of killing key members of a government thought to be too friendly with the West, oppressive at home of its own Muslim citizens, and treacherous for having done the unthinkable: seeking peace with Israel. The result of torture in those Egyptian dungeons was, I think, predictable—a rage for revenge. (It is a point I think about whenever I am engaged in discussions about the effects of Abu Ghraib and Guantánamo.)

In the years that followed, an array of intertwined events acted like gasoline on a small but intense fire. In 1973, Arab nations decided to punish countries that had supported Israel during the Yom Kippur War with an embargo on oil supplies that produced a crisis in the United States. The crisis intensified the ties between the United States and Iran because the shah, though severely criticized in his own country for being too friendly with the West, promised an uninterrupted flow of oil. It was, as it turned out, a short-lived promise.

In the emergence of terrorism, 1979 was a seminal year and created all the impetus for Al Qaeda to form and strengthen. The Soviet invasion of Afghanistan became a rallying point for Muslim extremists. They saw the invaders as heathens in a righteous world. The consequences of the ultimate success of what amounted to a ragtag force against a mighty power was the demonstration that wars didn't have to be fought with conventional means; underdogs could wage them in their own ways on their own turf, defining new rules, or no rules, of engagement. The superpowers, in their view, were paper tigers who could be outsmarted and outlasted. If war was to be a test of wills, they believed they would prevail. After all, to bin Laden and his supporters, a few years or a few decades amount to nothing. Their view of the epic struggle of Islam goes back a long way. Indeed, after the United States invaded Afghanistan in the months after 9/11, bin Laden made reference to Muslims driven out of Spain in 1492.

The shah of Iran was overthrown in 1979. The country forged a template to create and to impose what was seen as a just Islamic theocracy through the force of arms. Pushing the Shia (as opposed to the Sunni) side of the equation, the Iranians wanted to export this model to other countries. This dictum was enshrined in the preamble of the country's 1979 constitution, which announced that the Islamic Republic's armed forces "will be responsible not only for safeguarding the borders, but also for accomplishing an ideological mission, that is, the Jihad [holy war] for the sake of God, as well as for struggling to open the way for the sovereignty of the Word of God throughout the world."

All the while, Ayatollah Ruhollah Khomeini, who had returned from exile in Iraq and France, was saying, "Death to the Great Satan, America." Though Khomeini's regime demonstrated its brashness by holding fifty-two Americans hostage for 444 days, to many in the United States he seemed more bothersome than dangerous. He did not have an arsenal of nuclear weapons, after all. And in those days, the threat was arsenals, not ideology.

A third major element was the backlash of the Camp David Accords—signed a year earlier by Anwar el Sadat and Menachem Begin after thirteen days of secret negotiations. It not only brought the Arab and Israeli leaders to agree on peace but also fractured any reasonable relationship between nationalists and fundamentalists. Compromise didn't suit the latter at all—and created a growing distance. From their perspective, Anwar el Sadat sold out to the Israelis. Such an act was punishable by death.

Also in 1979, the actions of Iraqi president Saddam Hussein drew the United States deeper into Middle East conflicts. His army invaded Iran with the intent of seizing oil fields, an act that set off a long war between the neighboring countries. At the point when the war began, U.S. relations with Iraq were strained because of its ties to the Soviet Union. However, Iran's revolution was, by comparison, a greater threat, a situation that slowly changed the equation and led, eventually, to U.S. support of Saddam's regime, at least for a few years.

The new Iranian government had a destabilizing effect on Lebanon, whose capital, Beirut, was known as the "Jewel of the Middle East." Lebanon had been friendly to America, but had fallen into a devastating civil war, with one side fueled by Syrian and Iranian support and influence. In response, President Ronald Reagan ordered an American armed force into that country—a move intended to protect our interests in the Middle East. A year later, however, with the deadly attack on the marine headquarters in Beirut, we would get our first deadly lesson in the determination and abilities of anti-American crusaders.

Lebanon should have taught us that the traditional hardware of war was becoming obsolete in a world in which enemies increasingly

utilized deception, guile, misdirection, and other guerrilla tactics—
not as an adjunct of traditional forces, but as a replacement for
them. In the end, Reagan ordered all military forces out of Lebanon.

To maintain a strong presence in the Middle East, we intensified our support for Israel. This development inflamed Arab radicals and provided them with a recruiting poster: The United States
was increasingly anti-Arab and pro-Zionist.

The cold war was nurturing a unique relationship. The United
States, through the CIA, was engaged in a major—if secret—
program to help Afghan tribesmen defeat the army of the USSR.

"The enemy of my enemy is my friend" (even for a little while).
The adage explains how the coalition of the mujahideen in Afghanistan, comprising Saudis, Egyptians, and others, could accept support from the United States to fight the Soviets. From within the
group emerged Osama bin Laden, a well-connected man from a
wealthy Saudi construction company, who later found an ally in the
leader of the Taliban, Mullah Omar. After the war ended with the
Soviet Union withdrawing, America left Afghanistan cold. Osama
bin Laden's influence grew and eventually resulted in an organization that, after the attacks on 9/11, would be well known to everyone
who had not, previously, been paying attention. Including me.

There was much more, of course, to the story of the development
of antiwestern feeling and then the development of Al Qaeda into a
force that, even without a significant arsenal of its own and without hundreds of thousands of troops, staged a devastating attack
on America.

On a fall day in 2001, I entered the Pennsylvania legislature for
the last time, and prepared to deliver my farewell speech. Before I
began to talk, I wrote four words in large print on a note card and
put it on the podium.

That morning, I reminded the legislators of the disastrous state
of urban schools and the need to keep Pennsylvania economically
competitive, and cautioned them not to resort to higher taxes in
times of austerity. But I also commented on an issue that had implications far beyond the state's borders—America's response to
what had happened on September 11.

Already there had been stirrings in Washington about suspending ordinary freedoms to gather information on suspected terrorists. I saw this as a troubling development. I recalled for the legislature the words that Benjamin Franklin told the Pennsylvania Assembly in 1775: "'Those that can give up essential liberty to purchase a little temporary safety, deserve neither liberty, nor safety.' Liberty is a precious gift."

I also worried aloud about an emerging phenomenon, the harassment of people of Arabian or Middle Eastern appearance: "All Americans are inheritors of a legacy of freedom and religious tolerance. To those Americans who would lash out at your fellow citizens simply because they worship differently or dress differently or look differently than you, there is a word for such behavior: terrorism. And it must stop."

Even so, I knew that it was important not to waver. Television captures every word and every expression. It was reasonable to think that our enemies would look for any sign of weakness in the person who in a few days would be responsible for protecting America against them. At that moment, I experienced a royal flush of emotion. After all, I was leaving the state I loved, a loyal staff, many friendships developed over a lifetime, as well as unfinished work, to head into the unknown and the undoable. In normal times, I might have shed a tear at such thoughts. But I was determined not to do so as I said my farewell. If I needed any reminding, I glanced down at the note I had written for my own counsel.

"The bastards are watching."

3

A POWDER KEG

The United States has a still uncertain terror death toll, a war, a new civil defense agency with a quaint name, a popular President, a recession pressing in, a run on car-borne flags that have begun to fray in the wind, an exalted New York mayor, better manners here and there, a score to settle, and touchy nerves.

—CALVIN WOODWARD,
Associated Press, October 11, 2001

A few hours before the president introduced me to Congress, five letters were dropped into a mailbox in front of 10 Nassau Street in Princeton, New Jersey, near the campus of the Ivy League university. The envelopes contained a highly refined and poisonous dry powder. Yet, because of the deliberate way a particular form of anthrax works on the human body, it took more than two weeks for the first evidence of this act of domestic terrorism to play out and a few days more to confirm it. The attack would demonstrate the devastation that could be delivered in a way that had nothing to do with expensive missiles, vast armies, or even hijacked airliners—threats against which our government had traditionally prepared or was now feverishly building defenses. The cost was minimal—postage stamps.

Yet if 9/11 caught us off guard because we didn't have the same imagination for horror as our enemies, bioterrorism was, in a sense, an anticipated line of attack. The evidence in New York City, Washington, and the Pennsylvania countryside put Americans on high alert for all possibilities.

In the days before I or anyone else in public office knew that anthrax had been employed as a weapon, *The New York Times* published a piece in which health officials made the case that the nation needed new vaccines, a stronger public health infrastructure, and doctors who were better trained to respond to bioterrorism attacks. It reported that states and cities still had a patchwork of plans and federal agencies that "cannot [even] agree on which biological agents pose the biggest threat." Even so, anthrax, a substance known mostly to scientists and farmers, had became a more common term, even if it was hard to get ordinary people, including a certain governor of the Keystone State, to pay attention to its grim possibilities as a biological weapon. In the late 1990s William S. Cohen, the secretary of defense in the Clinton administration, brought a bag of brown sugar to the ABC *This Week* television show. Holding it up for the camera and pointing to it, he said, "The next threat to America will look like this—and it will be anthrax." His message should have awakened us to how the world had changed since the most threatening days of the cold war, when nuclear missiles were the presumed agents of Armageddon. It also indicated, to the select circle of experts who were thinking about this, if anthrax is the new weapon, who is the new enemy, and how are we prepared to defend against it?

After 9/11, bioterrorism became a subject of widespread speculation and concern, so much so that references to it were seen even on newspaper feature pages. On September 21, well before the first news of anthrax appeared, Marylou Luther, editor of the International Fashion Syndicate, told the Associated Press. "If I were a designer, I would be working with NASA and perfecting clothes impervious to anthrax." To this day, I don't know what prompted that observation. Ironically, at about the same time, a survey of health officials, not fashion designers, indicated the nation was not equipped to deal with terrorist attacks using biological weapons. The big problem, one official said, was "lack of basic public health infrastructure and preparedness that could thwart a terror attack or limit its effects." On September 30, Secretary of Defense Donald Rumsfeld warned that he expected enemies of the

United States to help terrorist groups obtain chemical, biological, and possibly even nuclear weapons technology.

At the same time, other high-level officials were saying that it was unnecessary for the public to rush out and get prescriptions for Cipro, an antibiotic that is effective against anthrax. In fact, during an exercise called "Dark Winter" at Andrews Air Force Base, in June 2001, Secretary of Heath and Human Services Tommy Thompson said the administration was "very confident that we could act and react to any kind of bioterrorist breakout." Within four months, I learned just how wrong that was. Three days before I arrived at my new post, a meeting was called in the Roosevelt Room at the White House where it became obvious that, for all of our ingenuity and commitment to the common defense as a nation, we still had a lot to learn. We had built a new Maginot Line, with our sophisticated but traditional weapons facing east, whereas the culprits of terror, men or women without uniforms but on deadly missions, were maneuvering behind our backs, over our heads, and in our mailboxes.

The agenda in the Roosevelt Room was limited to possible bioterrorism attacks and the supplies and dependability of vaccines. Smallpox was covered, and anthrax as well. Even so, at that hour, the question of such peril appeared to remain theoretical. Nevertheless, these subjects drew an audience that included the president and vice president, because terrorism, a bearded man in a cave, and the prevailing sense of vulnerability had become the only matters worth discussing in Washington. Among the other participants: Condoleezza Rice, then the national security advisor, and her deputy, Stephen Hadley; John Ashcroft, the attorney general; Robert Mueller, the new FBI director; and Lisa Gordon-Hagerty, a scientist and counterterrorism expert on the NSC staff.

As the group immersed itself in its theoretical discussions, an aide interrupted with news that any sense of the theoretical was now in the past. Sixty-three-year-old Robert Stevens, who worked in the art department of the *Sun,* a supermarket tabloid headquartered in Boca Raton, Florida, had apparently been poisoned by anthrax spores and taken to a hospital.

Immediately, questions arose as this group tried to determine whether it was an isolated incident and how it happened. Was the source of the anthrax strain connected to Al Qaeda? To Iraq? One of the participants in the Roosevelt Room, hopeful that it was all an accident, suggested that perhaps Stevens had bought a rug from the Middle East that contained active spores. Lisa Gordon-Hagerty told me she thought, "You've got to be kidding me. Did the guy sleep in the rug?" Later, when it was learned that Stevens had recently returned from a visit with his family and a fishing trip to North Carolina, authorities wondered if the explanation could be found there. Speculation bordered on the absurd.

Anthrax can, and does, appear naturally on farms. Unlike polio or smallpox, many universities store anthrax for medical and agricultural investigations. Other academic institutions and independent laboratories—an unknown number—had it as well. Anthrax was not treated like nuclear material, which under the law had to be registered, so there was no single source that listed all of the government labs, schools, pharmaceutical companies, and individual scientists (or, for that matter, ag school students) who might have a supply. Also, anthrax was known to be internationally available on the black market.

When the FBI investigated the Florida incident, it found spores on Stevens's computer, and in the *Sun*'s mailroom. By that time, Stevens had succumbed to the poison—the first person to die in the United States from anthrax inhalation since 1957 and the first ever to die in this country as a result of a biological attack. Others in his office had been infected by the substance, and were already undergoing treatment.

The question in everyone's mind and on many people's lips was: Was the contamination the work of terrorists, and, if so, was it connected to 9/11? Was it a criminal act? Or did it have a more benign, natural explanation. Tommy Thompson suggested to the media that Stevens had been exposed to anthrax from spores on his clothes or drinking water from a creek. But an anthrax expert at Louisiana State University, Dr. Martin Hugh-Jones considered that hypothesis far-fetched, saying the evidence indicated intentional poisoning. John Ashcroft said, "We regard this as an investigation that could become a clear criminal investigation. We don't have enough information to know whether this could be related to terrorism or not."

What no one understood at that moment was that these conflicting messages would become a metaphor for a federal government facing an unprecedented situation, and that questions of credibility, turf, and the politics of terrorism would soon overtake Washington, adding to the confusion and anxiety that gripped the entire nation.

It seems appropriate—in hindsight—that my first day on the job in the White House had not a moment for the usual adjustments to a new environment. This was nothing like television's *West Wing*. For one thing, White House offices are cramped, not the lavish expanse of rooms that the long-running NBC series portrayed. For another, the atmosphere is muted—not a mile-a-minute frenzy. The tension is of a quieter variety, but it is most certainly there. There is a seriousness that permeates the building. It is all business.

Every morning in the driveway between the White House and the Old Executive Office Building there was a lineup of black Suburbans from Justice, the FBI, and the Pentagon carrying high-ranking officials coming in for briefings. People who are chosen to work in the White House are accustomed to arriving at work before breakfast and staying until bedtime. The comings and goings of visitors become little more than background noise.

My arrival on the first morning was perfectly timed, considering the job for which I had been selected. "Welcome to the White House—and, oh, by the way, we've just bombed Afghanistan." A few hours earlier, U.S. and British fighter jets hit targets in Kabul and Khandahar, among other places, in response to 9/11 and the Taliban's support of Al Qaeda. Indeed, Vice President Cheney had been moved to an "undisclosed location" in case the invasion prompted another Al Qaeda attack on Washington.

At 8:00 A.M. I had my first official meeting in the Oval Office with what became the usual cast of characters, including CIA director George Tenet, Ashcroft, and Mueller. I had heard, of course, about the friction between the FBI and CIA but was struck by how well Tenet and Mueller seemed to get along, as well as how deferential Ashcroft, a strong personality otherwise, seemed to be in this company. Cheney was almost always there, and invariably seemed engaged in the subject of national security, as was the president. I noticed the ease with which the president and vice president interacted. The conversation in the group was always fluid and natural. You knew who the president was but for the most part it seemed like a conversation among equals. And the conversation often got deep into the details, because of the wide array of threats we were addressing.

At home, America was almost at a standstill because of a fear of opening the mail. The news media pointed out possible terrorist targets: nuclear and chemical plants, the Sears Tower in Chicago and other skyscrapers, ports, water supplies, energy distribution systems, bridges and tunnels, the food supply, stadiums, and prominent government buildings. Some officials (almost looking for a target they could warn about) voiced fears of a "digital Pearl Harbor." The list of targets appeared to be endless, and so, too, it appeared, was the growing area of concern and worry. Planes were back in the air, but passengers weren't. Masks and gloves were issued by civilian employers to white-collar workers. Mailrooms and post offices became places of scrutiny and potential danger. About such a atmosphere, Jon Ronson wrote in the British newspaper *The Guardian,* "If September 11th had mangled America's psyche, this [the anthrax attacks] pulverized it." Nevertheless, as I would learn in a few days, some Americans looked at this horrifying situation as a perfect time to play practical jokes.

On the morning I moved my files into an office that had been occupied by two of Andy Card's assistants, I was reunited with Ashley Davis, with whom I had worked in Harrisburg and who had been a key staff member at the White House since the President's inauguration in January. As deputy director of management administration, Davis had been one of the few federal officials asked to stay in the White House during the 9/11 evacuation. Both of us had been used to working with many people. When I was governor, my general counsel sat behind the door to my right, my chief of staff the door to my left, my executive assistant through the middle door, and any number of aides beyond that. I could push a lot of buttons and delegate a lot of responsibility. All of a sudden the very accomplished staff that I was used to directing was reduced to an army of one. Fortunately, it was an extremely talented army. Davis was well connected, poised, perpetually cheerful, and organized.

Fortunately for both Ashley and me, the occupant whose office was to my left for nearly five years as governor, my chief of staff, Mark Holman, joined us as one of my first recruits. He volunteered. After years of service in my congressional and governor's offices, he had moved to Washington. His talent, enthusiasm, and style served him well as he launched a very successful private-sector career. The ink wasn't dry on my appointment before he called. I'll have to write another book about all those who volunteered to work with me during those challenging times. I will be forever grateful to each of them.

In short order, we had help across the driveway from the West Wing in the Executive Office Building, where the other original members of the new Office of Homeland Security had found modest work spaces. This small team, no larger than my team of advisors in Vietnam, was now charged with coordinating the effort to protect America, and none of us, with the exception of retired navy admiral Steve Abbot, who became my deputy director, could list experience with what we were doing on our résumés. Clearly, there was an immediate need for expertise.

On the morning of October 8, help upon which I would rely arrived in reluctant form. Lisa Gordon-Hagerty, in the company of her boss, Richard A. Clarke, met me for my first official briefing. Clarke, now special advisor to President Bush for cyber security, had served the Clinton administration as national coordinator for security and counterterrorism. As she remembers it, she didn't say a word, just glared at me. "I was afraid if I opened my mouth, I would say something I would regret." If looks could kill, as I remember it, I would have been six feet under.

Our "conversation" took place in the Situation Room, on the lower level of the White House, where all highly confidential matters are discussed. In my two-week cram course, I had learned something about our counterterrorism efforts, but I didn't know specifically of Gordon-Hagerty or her work. As a scientist with a specialty in nuclear physics, she held several key government positions over the years, and had trained with Delta Force and Seal Team Six on nuclear weapons disablement.

Now, she feared a new bureaucratic nightmare, with me at the heart of it—a governor whose counterterrorism knowledge could fit on the side of a cereal box.

When I mentioned perhaps we could work on bioterrorism vaccines, she thought, "Yeah, well, genius, we've been doing that for years." All she knew about me was that I was the governor who had called the FBI director after 9/11 when an FBI agent stationed in Harrisburg reported an allegation of a nuclear device at the city's railroad yard. Just one of many unsubstantiated reports of impending doom that day.

Gordon-Hagerty had argued through her chain of command that it wasn't wise to separate homeland security from national security and that authority for homeland decisions should remain as a staff function of the National Security Council. You might conclude she doubted the need for the new office or for me.

I had already been at work a few hours when I was summoned to a small room in the White House for my swearing-in ceremony. My family was there, and a few other folks, but that was all—a low-key affair, no balloon drop and no confetti. No television cameras recorded Justice Clarence Thomas asking me to put my left hand on the Bible and raise my right. Our "celebration" was lunch in the White House mess, after which I said goodbye to Michele and the kids and went back to my office.

By my second morning of work, I had established the routine that would endure throughout my year-plus in the White House. I arrived at about 7:00 A.M., after commuting from Annapolis, where

I had found temporary lodging. Ashley Davis had by then gathered an array of materials, including my daily briefing material. The White House staff provided news clippings from overnight. At 7:30, I walked the few steps to the Roosevelt Room, where the morning briefing regularly drew Dr. Rice, Andy Card, Karen Hughes, Karl Rove, and other key administration members, and where the conversation covered political, domestic, and international issues as well as key events scheduled for the day. As with everything else in the White House, these were concise meetings without a lot of small talk, particularly in the first days following the anthrax attacks and the new war in Afghanistan. The same was true of the meeting that routinely followed in the Oval Office.

Mueller, Ashcroft, and I waited in the anteroom for the signal from Card to enter. The president was there with, inevitably, Cheney and Tenet, who was often chomping on an unlit stogie. The three had already had conversations about international situations, involving Afghanistan, China, North Korea, Iran, and elsewhere and were now ready for us—the new domestic counterterrorism team. One of the significant characteristics of these meetings was the extent of the president's involvement. Often in the press, at least in the early days, he was portrayed as indifferent, or worse, when it came to complicated international issues. But these meetings proved otherwise. He asked hard questions and frequently probed for more details. Criticism was rare, encouragement frequent, and engagement constant.

During those first few days, Steve Abbot proved to be an ideal choice as my deputy. The former Rhodes Scholar and naval academy grad had been a pilot, the commander of an aircraft carrier, and then a battle group, and had been deputy commander of the U.S. and European troops during the war in Kosovo. His father was a navy pilot, and his son, too. I could see that he was highly organized, had a keen sense of how to identify and overcome obstacles, and was unflappable.

Abbot and I met with several members from the Gilmore Commission. This was the congressionally mandated task force chaired by the former Republican governor of Virginia Jim Gilmore that had just issued a 173-page bipartisan report filled with recommendations showing that, prior to 9/11, Congress had at least some sense that terrorism was a rising threat. Among the recommendations: that the Bush administration develop a way to share intelligence gathered domestically and abroad with local, state, and federal agencies—an idea which, as a former governor, I instantly embraced. There was another key aspect to the report: Even as intelligence proliferated and got more and more people involved, safeguards for protecting against abuses, such as unjustified spying on citizens, needed to be developed. Within days, that report and some of its recommendations emerged in a critical debate in Congress and around the country.

My first visitor on the second day in office was Gordon-Hagerty. She was more cordial than the day before, and as I learned over the next weeks, an informed and experienced authority on threats to America and always, despite her early reserve, committed to using all of her influence and considerable network of experts to support my efforts. And I surely needed the help with all the issues emerging around the anthrax crisis.

In a few days, I knew I'd have to go before the cameras and appear to be the authority on bioterrorism or at least on anthrax. At that point, my qualifications for doing so were merely what I'd read in the newspapers and what I remembered from high school chemistry class at Cathedral Prep in Erie, which is to say, almost nothing. So at that moment, I had fairly basic questions about anthrax. "What is it?" and "How can it kill you?"

I learned about the basic forms of the substance, and that some of it develops naturally in the soil as opposed to labs, which is why it has always been a threat to cattle. Indeed, just the year before, 147 animals had died on a North Dakota farm. Anthrax spores release their bacteria, which grow and excrete a toxin that affects the cow's immune system, causing shock and quick death. The effect on humans is different, showing up as either skin lesions or, when a highly refined version of it is inhaled, as a flulike illness that then becomes acute and possibly deadly. This is part of why it is initially hard to diagnose. (Inhalation of even low quantities has proven to be 90 percent fatal unless massive doses of antibiotics are quickly taken.) Scientists needed supplies of anthrax in their labs as they tried to develop antidotes to it. Indeed, Louis Pasteur worked, unsuccessfully, on developing a vaccine.

As I learned, anthrax has been around forever. There are references to it in the works of Homer and Virgil, and some biblical scholars say it was the specific disease of livestock that was the fifth plague in Egypt. If that was the case, God saw the devastating possibilities long before man. Its use as an agent of war began in the late nineteenth century. In World War I, German agents injected it into American cattle. In the 1930s, Japan tested anthrax as a weapon in Manchuria. By the 1950s, the United States, Britain, and the Soviet Union had built inventories of "weaponized" strains. There had been a proliferation since then. In 1995, Iraq admitted to having a stockpile of liquid anthrax. Later intelligence sources indicated that Al Qaeda was working on chemical and biological weapons in Tora Bora in Afghanistan.

During one of the press conferences I conducted between October and November 2001, an exchange occurred about the "weaponization" of the anthrax used. Since the first letter surfaced a week after the 9/11 attacks, the abundant speculation about its source included foreign governments and terrorists' laboratories. While the term "weaponization" conjured up political and scientific implications, it seemed to me they were meaningless to the families whose loved ones had died or been hospitalized.

Whether the anthrax spores had been separated from the nonlethal debris around them and become a purer, more highly concentrated dose was irrelevant to the victims. Highly refined, or not, they had been assaulted by a biological weapon.

Some thought Iran was at the root of the problem. Because the anthrax spores eventually discovered in our investigations had characteristics relating to the military strains, many in the administration jumped to a conclusion. "It must be Iraq." Others included the Taliban as a possible culprit. No one was saying out loud that there might be another Unabomber or Timothy McVeigh out there.

At the outset, the federal government's response was an uncoordinated cacophony of sound bites. In the way the federal government worked at the time, many of the agencies that had some hand in national security began advising Americans on what do, and how to protect themselves. Advisories came from the postmaster general, the FBI, the Department of Health and Human Services, two of its subagencies, the Centers for Disease Control and the National Institutes of Health, and even the Agriculture Department. They all had a stake in this, and, of course, all had traditionally called their own shots when it came to providing information to the public.

In the next few days anthrax and related topics overwhelmed the media and the public, especially after we learned the incident in Florida was not, as we had hoped, an isolated event. Senator Tom Daschle's office received a letter with anthrax spores. Dozens of staff members had to be examined afterward, and twenty tested positive for exposure. Another letter had been sent to Senator Patrick Leahy, but because the ZIP code couldn't easily be made out, it wound up in the hands of a postal worker, David Hose, who opened it and became infected.

Then we heard from the media itself. An assistant to Tom Brokaw (who was still anchoring the NBC Nightly News) had gone to the doctor, complaining of flulike symptoms. She was suffering from anthrax exposure. After *New York Times* reporter Judith Miller opened an envelope that contained white powder, the newsroom of the *Times* emptied and men in white protective suits appeared. (She and colleagues were put on Cipro, though the powder proved benign.) A letter sent to the *New York Post* was typical in terms of its contents. In addition to what appeared to be weaponized anthrax were the printed words:

THIS IS NEXT

TAKE PENICILLIN NOW

DEATH TO AMERICA

DEATH TO ISRAEL

ALLAH IS THE GREATEST.

As the days passed, the pressure and confusion intensified. Nearly two dozen people nationwide had been infected and a total of five would die. The last was a ninety-four-year-old woman in the rural town of Oxford, Connecticut.

Ottilie Pauline Wilkie Lundgren had lived through the 1918 Spanish flu pandemic, the Depression, the spread of polio, and two world wars. She had been something of a pioneer, choosing career over marriage at a time when, for women, such a decision was rare. She became a legal secretary and office manager, and earned enough to sail in 1946 to England on the *Queen Elizabeth*. She finally married Carl Lundgren at the age of fifty-two but outlived him, and, even in her nineties, still lived in their home, spending a good deal of time reading mystery fiction. She had one last request of friends: that at her wake she would be dressed in the pink peignoir Carl had given her. But after she was poisoned by a contaminated letter, there could be no wake. Not when the whole town and surrounding communities became crime scenes.

FBI agents and Center for Disease Control (CDC) personnel in protective white suits arrived at the Nu-Look Hair Salon, where Mrs. Lundgren had regular appointments. They went to Fritz's Snack Bar, where she often ate. They even scrubbed down her church, Immanuel Lutheran, and focused on the pew where she sat. They took some of her communion records. None of these measures yielded any useful evidence.

The same was true when in the neighboring town of Seymour agents rooted through the garbage outside the Criscualo family home. They did this because they learned the Criscualos and Mrs. Lundgren had used the same dry cleaner.

Chaos in the midst of grief was common during the anthrax incidents. Though beforehand there had been no shortage of official reports about bioterrorism threats, it became clear when the real thing happened that no government agency—federal, state, or local—was prepared.

In Washington, the Secret Service wanted to know what to do with mail that was coming into the White House. I was on the phone every day with Jack E. Potter, the postmaster general, who was doing everything he could to protect his employees and at the same time keep delivering the mail. He said, though, that his people were not getting enough information about the threats, even though we believed we were sending boatloads. We were sharing everything we knew about bioterrorism. Apparently, it wasn't very useful. We discussed the purchase of irradiation machines. They would kill the spores on a letter, but obliterate the contents. The ultimate good news, bad news approach.

We had gone from an airplane turned into a missile to an envelope as instruments of death—from the twenty-first century to the twelfth century. There was no textbook, no means of accurate early detection, no sense of where the next threat would be mailed from or to.

The same kind of primitive technology was available in the testing of powder for biological pathogens. The products we relied upon were notoriously unreliable—often yielding false positives. The technology of detection remains one of our greatest challenges even today! We couldn't consistently distinguish poison from baby powder. How could we get accurate field tests so that alarm buttons would be pushed only at the right time, not every time? The silly impression Americans get from popular television shows and movies about the discovery and identification of substances is misleading. Screen cops find a cache of white powder, taste it, and say, "This is the real stuff, high grade." If it had only been that easy and safe in the accurate detection of anthrax.

There was also a great deal of debate as to who should get Cipro and how it should be delivered. If the poison mailing proliferated, would we have enough of the antibiotic available? And if we did, how would we get it from where it was to where it needed to be?

Meanwhile, the public wanted answers and wanted them yesterday. You can imagine the speculation: Were the mailings part of a coordinated attack led by Al Qaeda? Was there a terrorist cell operating in the United States? Later I learned that as early as the evening of September 11, speculation in the White House Situation Room included the possibility of Saddam Hussein being involved.

One of the questions: Why couldn't we find out who had done this? The FBI was draining lakes and ponds to look for equipment used to refine anthrax, and was also dismantling laboratories in the search for hard evidence. Hundreds of agents were at work; millions of dollars were spent in the effort.

No matter the source, anthrax clearly remained a threat, and our work was severely complicated by red herrings. A call came in from Chicago indicating a large supply of white powder had been spotted. It turned out be lime, used to line a jogger's path. There were dozens of similar "sightings."

On top of this, there were dozens of hoaxes. People began sending letters filled with white powder to enemies. For example, in an act that was hardly one of a kind, a woman who was upset about the breakup with her boyfriend sent white powder as a measure of revenge. One man sent a letter to an insurance agent who had been rude to him. One woman cooked up a plot to frame two teenagers who had picked on her son. And so in the weeks that followed, taxpayers paid the bill for investigations that led to evidence lockers fully stocked with Cremora, powdered sugar, flour, and talcum powder. In October alone, there were about ten thousand reports of suspicious substances sent through the mail, some of them causing widespread alarm. One of these envelopes arrived bearing an Egyptian postmark at the admissions office of Mercyhurst College, a Catholic institution not far from where I grew up in Erie. Almost five hundred students had to be tested, and most were given Cipro as a precaution. After waiting the necessary twenty-four hours for the results in an atmosphere of high anxiety, all were found to be free of any toxin. Roughly the same situation occurred at 550 abortion clinics around the nation, after each received an envelope containing white powder—all sent from a single source.

During this time, we began also to record the international effect of this copycat phenomenon. In Germany, scientists tested a white powder sent to Chancellor Gerhard Schroeder. In Canada, officials were obliged to close government offices when a worker showed up with a rash after handling a package that contained powder. In France, school children were sent home after the discovery of suspicious letters. In Lithuania, the office of Vilnius's largest daily newspaper was evacuated after a package arrived with the word "Jihad" scrawled on it. None of those cases turned out to be anthrax, or any other dangerous substance. And yet these hoaxes contributed to the climate of fear that was clearly in the air, and showed the obvious complications of the copycat syndrome. I suspect some twisted minds found amusement in these hoaxes. But in the context of the time—in the wake of the tragedy of 9/11 and worry over how we are going to live as a society—they were anything but harmless jokes to us.

To create anxiety or fear, to compound the feelings of vulnerability Americans felt, and to trigger a waste of precious resources was unconscionable. It had been a long time since I had prosecuted a case, but it would have been a pleasure to send some of these people to jail for a long time. There were thousands of hoaxes following the September 19 mailings, and they consumed incalculable time for analysis, investigation, and protection.

Part of my new job was to try to calm fears. And yet there was a fine emotional and informational line I knew I had to walk. If I lost the public's trust, the game was over. What could I tell people? Until 9/11, the most likely danger of opening an envelope was a paper cut. Now, it was possibly lethal.

As a governor, I'd had to deal with the results of floods, tornadoes, prison breaks, and terrible accidents. As difficult as that was, there was always a clear way to proceed. Rule number one: Go there, and do what you can do to help. Identify with the suffering. There was a finality to other tragedies, but in this case, I wondered, "When will this end?" Moreover, the more I learned about the level of our preparedness as a nation, the more I understood the immense task ahead.

There were communities that took such threats seriously. San Jose, California, for example, a capital of cyberspace, had spent a good deal of money on antibiotics, training classes, and a secret operations center. But most cities and states remained ill prepared for such emergencies. I doubt there was a single state or community that had thought they needed to prepare for an anthrax attack.

The federal government continued to issue alerts, but there was no context to them. Nobody knew how to focus the data or

share information. Citizens were left scratching their heads, saying, "OK, what the hell am I supposed to do? What's the nature of
the alert? Should I open my mail?" Clearly, if I wanted to create a
culture of disclosure, to meet the goal of keeping citizens informed,
I had a lot of work to do. As Dana Milbank reported in *The Washington Post* on the morning of October 18, the administration and
Congress were often inconsistent in their accounts of the anthrax
investigation. He referred to the scene as the "anthrax muddle."
And I was to be the mechanism through which the White House
was planning to unify the government's public message.

On the morning of October 19, I held my first press conference
in the White House press briefing room. I had had a crash course
in anthrax the previous ten days. Although this was the nation's
primary fear at the time, it was also a period of many other terrorist-
related anxieties. The federal government had to respond in a
clear, consistent, and reassuring manner. Even at this point, none
of us had any idea the attacks were only a small portion of a larger
terrorist plan.

In the many months that followed, politics and turf would intrude on the homeland security message. We would fight to include
our state and local partners in the intelligence loop. We would resist
the impulse to discuss the threat publicly at the first sign of a potential problem. We would argue the public deserved more, not less
information. As the Patriot Act became law, and as the 2002 election season heated up, some in Washington were seen as playing on
fear as a campaign strategy. We had been attacked in an unimaginable way by a largely invisible enemy. What was next?

Early on, I saw the intersection of the partisan world with
mine. Politics-as-usual could have no part in what we did. There
are times and places in Washington where partisanship is required
or unavoidable. My office was not one of them. If we were going to
protect America, all of our citizens had to trust us. We couldn't
become just another office of spin doctors. But I knew that in an
atmosphere of highly charged politics, that wouldn't be a goal easily
reached. All I could do was pursue a policy of openness and can-
dor in a place where there had always been a tradition of secrecy,

and the need to know was limited to the innermost members of the in crowd.

When I went in front of the cameras on that October morning, however, there were certain challenges I knew I wouldn't talk about—the emerging struggles and the discouraging response to my pleas for more support. Even as we tried to identify sources of anthrax, I was doing a kabuki dance with Joe Hagen, deputy chief of staff, pleading for a dramatic increase in staffing and more space.

We were also having trouble, as I had been warned, getting federal agencies to share information and respect each other's problems. For example, the FBI was focusing on the criminal aspects of the anthrax attack—and that only. It didn't want its crime scenes disturbed. But the EPA had to make the post offices and other affected sites safe for employees. Health and Human Services as well as the Centers for Disease Control had to know as much about what was happening as anyone else because they saw their duty as advising the public on what measures to take. The DOD had accumulated a great deal of knowledge on bioterrorism, but that knowledge had to be disseminated. During the administration of President Bill Clinton, for example, there had actually been a training exercise involving the government's response to a germ warfare attack. What were the lessons from these, and how could they apply to the real-life drama playing out in front of us all? Interagency cooperation, never a fine art in Washington, was clearly wanting. Historically, that was always an issue, but the difficulties increased exponentially in 2001, when, in its savagery, an outside-of-the-lines enemy skirted conventional assumptions. And so it became our job, twice each day of the week (and once on Sundays), to hold secure video conferences (what is known in the capital as SVTS—pronounced siv-itz—everything is an acronym).

Before the press conference on the nineteenth, I spoke to the president aboard Air Force One. He seemed pleased with the plan to bring to our public presentations an array of high-ranking officials, including Tommy Thompson, Jack Potter, Robert Mueller, and the surgeon general, Dr. David Satcher. This would serve at least two purposes. It would give the media access to specific and technical information and also show a unity of effort.

We answered questions about criminality, health, and the other issues Americans were worried about. Potter said the postal service would send a postcard "to every American" with instructions on how to handle suspicious mail. Mueller gave details of a $1 million reward for information leading to the person or group behind the anthrax attack.

When questions were directed at me, I wanted to be sure to focus on facts, not speculation, though there were plenty of facts I didn't know. I got into a debate about the form of anthrax found in the attacks with one reporter. He pressed me on the subject of whether the powder had been ground down and refined to a high degree of weaponization. I said I didn't think so. Even so, we were playing a semantic game. The families of the deceased victims were not wondering whether what killed their loved ones was up to military standards or not.

Media accounts of that first press conference were largely positive, including the story in *The New York Times*. But in my mind the event had displayed our collective weakness—the inability to speak with a single voice. Despite assurances to the contrary, agencies had continued to send out anthrax advisories and public warnings on their own without going through the Office of Homeland Security. The public speculation that the anthrax had become weaponized, which required grinding it very fine and adding other substances that would greatly enhance its toxicity, led to the inevitable conclusion that it would take a foreign country, rather than someone working alone, to do this.

I guess that there were some in the administration who thought that if the anthrax attacks could be tied to extremists, it would be easier to secure support for military action in response to 9/11. However, we didn't have the luxury to speculate, and there was nothing at the time that could tie these attacks to a foreign source. It was clear to me that, regardless of the nature of the attack, America wanted and deserved the facts, pure and simple, and absent reliable information, it was better to say nothing. We knew that certain terrorists had experimented with anthrax on animals, but connecting those experiments to what happened in the United States, at least at this time, was fantasy.

Credibility, of course, arises from a combination of elements. One is to be square with people when you don't know something. Yes, I was supposed to be a counterterrorism expert in the public's mind—after ten days on the job. I was dealing in a highly classified and sensitive environment, so I had decided that homeland security required an uncommon openness, a view that in the coming months and years would cause more than a little controversy.

That morning, I told people what I knew and what I didn't. I passed along information I'd received about the Daschle anthrax incident—incorrect, as it turned out—that the strain found did not consist of a particularly powerful form. I also said, "My job is to step back from all of these different agencies, take a look at all their moving parts. Then I can see where there can be some refining, some strengthening, and some improvements."

I played down the perceived need for the drastic restructuring of government to respond to this new threat. Some, including Senator Joe Lieberman, had worried that my title would be bigger than my authority, and that there had to be legislation to make homeland security a cabinet-level agency in order for me to have any power. But I reminded reporters that I had direct access to the president, and, as security was his top priority, there was no problem.

I was asked many tough questions. Among them was whether the government's focus on anthrax left the nation open to other types of terrorism, such as attacks on nuclear plants. I explained that all agencies involved—the CIA, Nuclear Regulatory Commission, and others—had taken measures in anticipation of that possibility, and that local officials across the country had been advised to be especially vigilant and prepared.

I was doing fine—feeling confident. And then someone asked me if the president had been vaccinated for anthrax. I replied, "I don't know. I'll get back to you on that." In the back of the room, Lisa Gordon-Hagerty gasped. I still had a big learning curve when it came to my new job. I didn't know enough to go against my idea of openness, and to say, "That's not something we're going to talk about." I wanted to talk about everything.

It was in the days that followed that I learned my representation of the anthrax sent to Tom Daschle's office had proven inaccurate. It had been weaponized. I also learned that the lack of cooperation between federal agencies was causing not just perceived, but actual problems.

Officials in the Department of Health and Human Services complained that the FBI had not passed along its finding that the Daschle sample was more lethal than first thought. Of the known forms of anthrax, the highly toxic one called the Ames strain was the culprit. (It was named for a strain that had been worked on in the science department of Iowa State University, though the anthrax, it was determined early on, did not come from their laboratories.)

That the government agency most responsible for public health was kept in the dark, intentionally or not, demonstrated precisely what I faced in my new office. If I couldn't get agencies to work together, the new Office of Homeland Security couldn't possibly carry out its mission.

In response to the interagency charges of secrecy and the lack of coordinated public messaging I called a late-night White House meeting of all relevant agencies.

I had heard that Secretary Thompson was complaining about the lack of cooperation with the FBI. The White House was clearly displeased with the lack of a coordinated public message. By 8:00 P.M., the principals of every federal department were seated in the Roosevelt Room. It was both astonishing and reassuring to see the postmaster general, the director of Central Intelligence, the secretary of agriculture, the FBI director, the secretary of health and human services, the attorney general, and others at the same table on a couple of hours' notice.

Jack Potter, with whom I was having almost daily conversations, had thousands of postal employees and millions of customers at risk. Robert Mueller and George Tenet were scrambling to identify the source. There was no strategic plan or playbook to draw from. Everyone had questions, but we were all looking for answers. There was no finger-pointing. Everyone agreed that the Office of Homeland Security would be the focal point for future press conferences and that any problems regarding collaboration or information sharing would be brought to my attention.

We urged everyone to "play nice." As *The New York Times* later described it: "Mr. Ridge directed those in attendance to cooperate fully with one another, and, asserting his new authority as the President's point man on homeland defense, declared himself in charge of the government's public response to bioterrorism."

The next day, I appeared at my second press conference, reasonably confident that the public would understand where to turn for answers. But if I thought I had solved the problem of the way Washington works, or doesn't, I was to find I was merely deluding myself.

4

CULTURE OF SECRECY

Ridge Issues Japanese Balloon Bomb Alert
Ridge Warns Al-Qaeda Plans to Herd Nation's Cats
Ridge Announces Homeland Security to Patrol
    Borders With Icarus Wings
Ridge Introduces New Terrorist Reporting System
Ridge Issues Santa Claus Advisory
Ridge Issues Lynch Dawg Alert
Ridge Issues Guinea-Zilla Alert
Ridge Issues Rubber Ducky Alert
Ridge Issues Wienermobile Alert
Ridge to Issue Slinkys to All Americans

—*Internet Weekly*

By 6:30 every morning the daily threat matrix—compiled from various intelligence agencies and offering fearsome snapshots of all the possible dangers afoot—was delivered by a member of the U.S. Coast Guard. The Secret Service picked me up in a Lincoln Town Car. (How secret is *that*?) Sometimes the listing was modest and sometimes voluminous. Some of the threats seemed far-fetched, others plausible. Each entry required its own interpretation based on a variety of factors, including CIA, FBI, National Security Agency, and Office of Homeland Security assessments. The matrix did not contain an opinion relative to credibility or corroboration. Fortunately, once the Department of Homeland Security was established we had our own intelligence unit to gather these assessments and render our own opinions. I was always aware of which agency was generating the information, but I didn't usually know whether the source was human intelligence, electronic intercept, interrogation, or some other.

A resident of the Persian Gulf region was warning that a second wave of attacks on the United States was about to occur. Was the information reliable? And, if so, what form would that attack take? Elements of dozens of plots were examined by intelligence agencies, including one predicted by a man in Jordan who, on September 10, 2001, had posted a warning on the Web that said "zero hour" was approaching. Should this source be considered an Al Qaeda insider, or just someone who, knowing of the building anger toward the United States, in certain circles in the Middle East, had simply guessed right? And what of the so-called suitcase nuke—a dirty bomb of modest size developed by Moscow that could possibly be carried into Manhattan in a Louis Vuitton bag and detonated on Madison Avenue?

At the end of the cold war, Senators Sam Nunn (Democrat of Georgia) and Richard Lugar (Republican of Indiana) introduced a bill that authorized the United States to pay for the security of nuclear sites in the old Soviet Union. With the dissolution of the USSR there was great concern about who might gain access to these sites and about potential proliferation of the materials or weapons stored within them. Our inability to confirm or deny that access was the source of great anxiety.

In September 1997, former Russian national security advisor Alexander Lebed revealed that many suitcase nukes were lost following the dissolution of the Soviet Union. In an interview on *60 Minutes*, Lebed said: "I'm saying that more than a hundred weapons out of the supposed number of 250 are not under the control of the armed forces of Russia. I don't know their location. I don't know whether they have been destroyed or whether they are stored or whether they've been sold or stolen." This report was disputed by the Russian government, but no one could say for certain whether Lebed was telling the truth. There is still no confirmation of his story. There's never been any credible intelligence indicating Lebed was correct. But then, as I was often reminded in my job, you don't know what you don't know.

We didn't have to look abroad for sources of worry. Our own federal agencies were filling out our full agenda of nuclear anxiety.

The Nuclear Regulatory Commission issued a 119-page report

that indicated that a fully loaded Boeing 757 or 767 could pierce the thick concrete containment wall designed to protect a nuclear reactor, although it would not result in a nuclear explosion. William Beecher, the NRC's public affairs director told the media, "Given that the situation has changed in ways no one could have predicted—no one had envisioned airliners being used like kamikaze bombers—it does raise questions that had not been seriously looked at before." The report also said that as early as 1982, nearly two decades earlier, the federal government had known nuclear plants were vulnerable in this way.

Suddenly, this threat became the topic of the hour. When people hear the word "nuclear," they put two and two together and come up with a mushroom cloud over Three Mile Island which happens to be in Pennsylvania. At the time the media focused with great intensity but little factual accuracy on this potential threat. This topic was often raised when I made television appearances during my early days in the White House. David Letterman certainly took it seriously. During my appearance on *Late Night,* we spent two-thirds of the interview discussing prospects of a nuclear incident at the power plant a few miles from his house, hardly the usual stuff of late-night comedy.

In the public's fervent imagination, a jetliner aimed at Three Mile Island or Sparrow's Point (in Maine) would certainly result in a mushroom cloud to doom everyone downwind. It was an assumption many would jump to, but it was wrong. Even before the anxiety level of the general public was raised to near-panic levels because of the media focus on this story, the Nuclear Regulatory Commission (NRC) had already begun to model the effects of a commercial airliner on a nuclear power plant. I met with officials from the NRC and asked what computer models had been used to determine likely outcomes of such an event. The effects might surely have been dramatic, but a mushroom cloud was not one of them. A modest radiological leak would be more likely—the equivalent of a small dirty bomb in the neighborhood. The NRC made specific recommendations on how this could be avoided by beefing up the protection for our nuclear infrastructure, recommendations that were adopted. It turned out, in the end, to be a story that delivered rare good news: Our nuclear facilities were very well protected. Even so, the public's concern was certainly understandable.

In just a few weeks after 9/11, new prescriptions for antianxiety medications increased by nearly 10 percent. Although there is no evidence to support it, you might assume that hefty doses were in the possession of federal officers and bureaucrats.

The Washington Post reported that the possibility of a bioterrorist attack on the nation's food supply renewed a long-standing call to unify government food inspection efforts. Government Accounting Office officials, and some in Congress, had long advocated the creation of a single agency to handle food inspection or the consolidation of current efforts into one existing department. But the Department of Agriculture, the Food and Drug Administration, and other agencies had resisted, just as intelligence agencies had done, any reorganization.

At the American Enterprise Institute, a conservative think tank, former Speaker of the House Newt Gingrich delivered a speech that imagined a variety of horrors and suggested a simple division of humanity that would influence the administration and the rest of the world and the prosecution of this war: "The next time it will be a germ agent or gas or a nuclear weapon . . . we must plan for a coercive, not a consensual, campaign. . . . There are only two teams on the planet for this war. There is the team that represents civilization, and there is the team that represents terrorism. Just tell us which. There are no neutrals."

Richard A. Clarke was still warning of "a digital Pearl Harbor," a prospect he had talked about well before 9/11. He argued that the attacks showed the innovations of terrorists, and that they had to be considering the destruction that could be caused in cyberspace. The Internet has become the central nervous system for everything we do in this country. It takes no imagination to see the dire consequences of someone hacking into a computer that might affect water flow to New York City or dams in the west, the electrical grid, or air traffic control. If you hacked into New York City after a terrorist attack, you could cut off emergency communications.

"Prior to 9/11," Clarke said in an interview with *The New York Times,* "there were a lot of people who thought that the only thing the terrorists could do is what they had already done. Now we know they can do something really catastrophic. The worst case here is that we might not be able to communicate for essential government services. And it might happen at a time when we're at war. It might happen at a time when we're responding to terrorism." Moreover, every aspect of ordinary life could be affected, from personal banking to command and control systems, everything that relies on electronic communication.

If you want a basic example, think about the toilets that would not flush, food spoiling in the freezer, sump pumps not working, and security systems inoperable.

Clarke's concerns were echoed by many in the administration, including several who worked with me. The federal government as a whole was extremely limited in its capacity to anticipate, identify, or remedy cyber breaches. We began working with private sector groups and the academic community, including experts from Carnegie-Mellon University in Pittsburgh, in a collaborative effort to address these challenges. We soon developed an early-warning system that is part of the national cyber protection infrastructure. The national effort remains a work in progress.

By then, however, anticipated dangers were coming from all directions, including the Oval Office. My usual morning meeting there had a routine, even furniture-wise. The president and vice president sat in two armchairs in front of the fireplace. George Tenet, Condi Rice, and Andy Card sat on one of the facing sofas. Ashcroft and I became furniture haulers, moving two armchairs so that we could face the president. But on a morning in mid-October 2001 after a routine meeting, the president asked me to stay, along with Andy Card, to discuss one more issue, and I took a seat on the sofa.

The subject was our land borders. There had been a huge cry to effectively close off access there, dramatically reducing the threat of terrorists simply walking in from Canada or Mexico. In the hours immediately after 9/11, with all the uncertainty as to whether other attacks were in the works and the form they might take, we closed our borders, north and south. For several weeks, the normal flow of goods and people was reduced to a mere trickle. Security was priority one. As a result, commerce was adversely affected and in many instances came to a screeching halt.

It became much harder to cross into the United States, even for people who had been doing it regularly and had never been suspected of crime. Delays were interminable everywhere. Since the inception of the North American Free Trade Agreement (NAFTA), trade with Canada and Mexico had tripled, yet the infrastructure (bridges, tunnels, etc.) needed to move the goods had not been expanded or improved. With the tightening of rules and the intensifying of inspections, the natural result was a crushing blow to commerce. Lettuce wilted in the field while the men and women who would harvest it waited in long lines at a southwestern border point. Critical parts for the automobile plants in Michigan sat on the Ambassador Bridge that runs from Windsor to Detroit.

There were human costs that couldn't be measured in dollars. Two children who lived in El Paso, Texas, fell asleep in the camper of their parents' pickup truck, as the family waited to return to the States from a visit to relatives in Mexico. In the combination of the intense desert heat, the long line of vehicles waiting to get through the clogged checkpoint, and the carbon monoxide from exhaust fumes that filled the camper, Ericka Valenzuela, thirteen, and her brother Daniel, six, suffocated.

The Valenzuela family had been typical of those seeking greater advantages for their children in America, a country that much more than any in the world built itself on the riches of diversity and immigration. The natural reaction of 9/11—*keep everyone out*—was neither realistic nor desirable for our own security or prosperity, nor that of the rest of the world. We are inextricably linked by the economic, diplomatic, and cultural forces of globalization, and the ties that bind us need protection and preservation.

This dimension is well known, and treasured, in our system of higher education. We have benefited greatly from foreign students who have come to America to study—a segment of the national student body that is highly motivated and usually does excellent work. We have produced in our colleges and universities many political and business leaders who have gone back to their home countries to live and prosper, and they have retained strong cultural ties to the United States. We had not understood that we had no way to track these students once they entered, and hadn't the foggiest idea whether they were studying Renaissance poetry or nuclear physics. We had no idea whether they were still here and if they were, where they were living or what they were up to. The department later developed SEVIS (Student Exchange Visitor Information System) and with the enthusiastic support and cooperation of the higher education community, facilitated entry and confirmed attendance at colleges and universities throughout the country. Even so, it was commerce that had caught the president's attention.

"We've got to find a better way, Tom," he told me. We had to keep commerce flowing at the same time we secured borders. I said, "Yes, sir, Mr. President. I'll take care of it." I knew there were thousands of miles of land borders, dozens of entry ports, and billions of dollars of commerce involved. We had just opened shop. The staff may have been cranked up to fifteen people, and I was about to engage our counterparts in Canada and Mexico in developing a smarter and more secure border. Some people had worried that I'd be given a great deal of responsibility but no authority or resources to go with it. That had come to pass.

I knew, as I left the Oval Office, that another crucial point had come early in my tenure. I had to persuade people who didn't work for me to do the right thing. The conversation with the president led to an intense and sustained effort over the next eighteen months with Canada and Mexico to build what we called Smart Border Agreements. The challenge in reconfiguring how we provided security along our northern and southern borders was complicated by the need to keep the flow of people and goods at pre-9/11 levels. It was the first and most dramatic lesson for me that some obvious and defensible measures could easily impede commerce and threaten our economic competitiveness. Rob Bonner at the U.S. Customs

Service and my counterparts in Canada, John Manley, and Mexico, Santiago Creel, were eager to help.

As the days progressed, the vulnerability of the rest of our travel infrastructure became obvious. We had beefed up security at our 416 commercial airports, but that left the thousands of private airports with minimal security. There was no real way to prevent a small plane from taking off with a cargo of high explosives and heading for a government building. About a week after the terror attacks, undercover police officers snuck a knife and a pocketful of bullets past the metal detectors at Boston's Logan International Airport. Passengers said they had been able to get through security with such banned items as corkscrews, scissors, and cigarette lighters. A friend of mine forgot to take a knife out of his pocket as he went through security at Reagan. He recognized it when he got to Atlanta and called his wife to ask what he should do. She said, "Hang up the phone and throw the damned knife away!" And these were just the cases we knew about.

The media itself was similarly engaged in probing the security at our airports and along our land borders. Newspapers trying to win prizes and television stations trying to drive up their ratings sent reporters on missions to test security measures all around the country. They were often able to show breaches, and when they couldn't they were not so eager to broadcast or write about it. The truth is, we didn't need their help. As a matter of policy, security measures are constantly measured, probed, and challenged. The difference being, of course, that the success or failure of these tests are not broadcast to the rest of the world, including the terrorists. We believed these "private tests" were tantamount to a new organization breaking the glass on a fire alarm to see how long it took for the local fire department to respond.

As for the nation's infrastructure itself, the possibilities were endless. The Associated Press listed the number of U.S. targets that terrorists could consider: 600,000 bridges, 2,800 power plants (104 of them nuclear), 190,000 miles of natural gas pipelines, 95,000 miles of coastline, and 463 skyscrapers. The AP report pointed out that our 285 million people were spread out over 3,717,792 square

miles and *The Washington Post* reminded me there was also a national water supply to guard. Everyone was seeing a mushroom
cloud. As *USA Today* put it, "Not since the darkest days of the Cold
War have we worried so much about random, and mass, destruction."

The intense anthrax investigation had gone nowhere. Although
a "person of interest" had been identified by the FBI, mistakenly as
it turned out, no strong case was able to be made against anyone.
Related issues arose. One of them was whether we had the capacity
to address bioterrorism in the form of smallpox. We learned that
the government had 15.4 million doses of a smallpox vaccine,
which, apportioned among the total population of the United States,
would mean that one person out of eighteen could be inoculated.
Who would that person be? How would we tell the other seventeen
they were not worthy? Could we get, or should we have, enough
vaccine to inoculate the whole population? And how could we familiarize the nation's doctors, who, after all, did not ordinarily
come into contact with a disease that had its last U.S. epidemic in
the 1830s?

At this point there was only one company that produced a
vaccine—a firm in the Midwest that had serious financial problems. Nonetheless, at the time it looked to be the only company that
had the capability to give us what we needed. Aside from the shortage, we had no smallpox surveillance system and no vaccine distribution system in place. Even when we determined that it should be
the health care community—EMTs, doctors, nurses—who should
be inoculated first, we met with resistance, and the effort to get
first responders to be vaccinated was a failure. Our case wasn't
strong and persuasive enough. It was known that the vaccine
could cause severe side effects, and medical professionals were
wary of submitting to inoculation when, at the time, all we could
do is name smallpox as a potential threat. We had no specific information that it might be an immediate threat. We were taking, it
seemed to us, a reasonable precaution, but for a large percentage of
the population which might have to deal with that threat, it wasn't
worth the risk. This, then, was a microcosm of our continuing

problem of too early, too late, too much, or too little, and of managing risk. Which measures constituted reasonable preparation, and which were premature, too expensive, or unnecessarily panic inducing to the general public? Just because some threat "could potentially happen," did it mean that we had to address that possibility to the nth degree? Over many months, such questions were always a factor in our initial efforts to create a nationwide network of public partners in the effort to keep the country safe.

Prior to September 11, for perhaps a decade or so, we had ignored our public health system. During the anthrax crisis, and the more public discussion of bioterrorism generally, this failure became quite clear. We began to realize we really didn't have an effective national disease detection system. And, on the treatment side, over the decades the number of pharmaceutical companies in this business—producers of vaccines and antidotes—had been substantially reduced. There were several reasons—cost of research, time to market, and, perhaps at the top of the list, exposure to litigation.

Amid all of these threats, real and imagined, we continued to build our staff in the White House. I'd had considerable experience in my public service career, particularly as governor. In Pennsylvania, we recruited dozens to serve in our administration. That task was so much simpler. There were real offices with clearly defined duties, decent technological infrastructure, and long established roles and responsibilities to be executed. Prospective employees knew what they were in for. At the White House Office of Homeland Security (OHS), on the other hand, we were writing our job descriptions (for which we did not have the staff) while furnishing our offices (for which space we had to fight).

Susan K. Neely had every reason not to consider applying for director of communications, a job I saw as critical to our core mission. Neely had considerable experience which, by then, qualified her for higher paying and less demanding tasks. In fact, she had just that sort of job when we had our first conversation. She had spent fourteen years in the private sector after serving as a senior advisor to Iowa governor Terry E. Branstad and on the staff of two

members of congress. Her private sector experience included creating what became known as the "Harry and Louise" television
spots—humorous and effective—that had helped to defeat President Clinton's attempt to nationalize health care. She was a senior
vice president at the Health Insurance Association of America and,
as she put it, earning "adult wages."

More than that, as I learned during our first few minutes together, she had just adopted little Ben, a one-year-old boy who had
been in an orphanage in Cambodia, and hadn't been in the best of
health. She had not planned for Ben and her four-year-old daughter, Eve, to grow up in a situation in which their mother might have
to reintroduce herself on Sunday afternoons, or whenever she
could escape the demands of the office for the comforts of home.

In this we had much in common. I told her that both of my
children were adopted, and we knew the intricacies, including when
it makes the most sense to tell a child about his or her origins. In
our case we began to use the word "adopted" long before the kids
knew what it meant, so that when the time came to tell them, it
wouldn't be as much of shock. I believe it is important to reassure
them they weren't rejected by their birth mother. Instead, they
were put in a better place. "By law and by love" they were now our
children. We also discussed the frustration of not having the time,
because of the extraordinary pressures of our jobs, to lead a conventional family life.

On the other hand, as Neely later confided, "I would take this
job for all the right reasons. It is about future generations. While
Ben would have been a reason to stay where I was in the work-
place, he would also be the reason to go to OHS. I thought of the
trip from Phnom Penh to the United States, carrying him to his
new home. The minute we passed through border security this in-
fant of a different race from an impoverished land became, by law, a
U.S. citizen, and I thought what a great country this is."

She felt that for Ben and Eve to grow up in a free society there
was a price to pay, and she decided that, as much as this new job
would require great sacrifice, it could also yield great rewards. We
were now at war, and the work she would be doing would be on

behalf of her children's future and that of millions of others. (In this view Neely was typical of my colleagues through the years at the White House and later at the Department of Homeland Security.)

Even so, we did not have, at that point, a job description for her position. What I knew for certain was there had never been an entity in Washington, D.C., that had thought it necessary to do what we needed to do at the new OHS: Create a culture of sharing information in a city of rampant secrecy.

For as long as Washington, D.C., has been the nation's capital, a certain attitude has prevailed of "need to know." That is, you, as an ordinary citizen or a local official, don't *need* to know, and so *shouldn't* know, unless you're part of the inner circle and have the proper security clearance. There are legitimate reasons for secrecy, of course. The FBI and CIA, for example, would compromise many of their investigations if they revealed key details to the public. Even so, those agencies and every other one carry that policy to unnecessary and even dangerous extremes for reasons other than necessity—a circumstance that, we would all learn, impedes the real work of government in regard to homeland security. That culture was incompatible with the mission of the office and ultimately the new department. We wanted to change a "need to know" culture to a "need to share" culture.

Al Qaeda as the newest enemy of the United States posed an entirely new threat. Yet the administration seemed content to use the same approach upon which it had historically relied to deal with the enemies of old. The silly, prolonged debate with the White House over the design of the new department's seal was as absurd as it was revealing.

Believe it or not, the White House thought the eagle in our emblem should hold arrows in both talons. It suggested to us that they believed that the key to victory over the terrorists was strictly through aggression, forward-leaning military and counterterrosim action. We thought differently. There was far more to defeating the enemy than traditional military action.

Nonetheless, it seemed to us that treating the new enemy like traditional ones, communicating with the public would follow the historic model as well. Limit public messaging to a discussion of the actions taken, not an explanation as to why they were needed.

I remember our disbelief when we were criticized for not holding frequent press conferences, as Secretary of Defense Donald Rumsfeld did. He relished the interaction with the press as he discussed combat operations, casualties, numbers killed and captured, conversations with theater commanders, videos from smart weapons, and stories written by embedded journalists.

Our frame of reference was completely different and so was our public messaging. The old paradigm, the paternalistic approach of explaining actions taken, would not meet our needs. The battlefield about which we had to report was the United States. Governors, mayors, first responders, and others were on the front lines back home. Their communities and fellow citizens deserved more information about the conduct of our business and the rest of the administration as it affected them.

The new enemy and new battlefield and new "soldiers" and potential victims required us to develop new communication tools and two-way dialogue. Only disclosure and transparency would generate the confidence and trust needed by our government as it waged its war domestically. Now that the enemy had invaded our world, Americans had a role to play, and to do so effectively, they needed to know more, not less.

Neely's job would have the title director of communications, but it would be hugely different from others who held that title or the traditional position of "press secretary." We would, of course, try to explain our actions in the most favorable light. But our responsibility, we believed, involved transparency and information sharing at a level previously unknown in Washington.

We hoped to turn American citizens into partners of OHS, fully informed and prepared for anything. There would be, in our department, nothing more important than public messaging. And for that to be the case, the communications expert could not be a fifth wheel, someone hired merely to explain. This communications position was essential to the core mission, to everything we were about to do. The person who held it could be relied on at the conference table to help formulate policies that would earn the trust of the public, and once that trust was established, never lose it.

Neely and I agreed that we needed to create a government office with a public information policy that would be groundbreaking. We would find a way to interpret frightening reports in a way that would motivate a sense of readiness and security without sounding like a horror movie. We would attempt to share as much information as possible, certainly more than government agencies were used to doing. The goal was unprecedented, and the task would prove much more difficult than we realized. Nobody to that point had talked about specific threats to subways, stadiums, or skyscrapers. Just the opposite was true: The doctrine was to tell American citizens nothing specific, because if we reveal anything detailed, we would fuel fears that cripple freedom of movement and commerce. We would learn that informed Americans made decisions that contradicted this fear. This policy did not mean, however, there was a shortage of public information.

Just by reading the newspapers and watching reports on television, we knew that, at this point, ordinary citizens were being bombarded from a variety of sources about the anthrax attack. Most of the information was not specific and simply added to the fear and confusion. Sally Quinn wrote in a *Washington Post* column in early October 2001 that citizens were confused about the issues of stockpiling protective gear and antibiotics, and "if all this concern is ridiculous, we need somebody to say it and explain why, presumably Tom Ridge."

One of our key tasks would be to offer particulars and do it in such a way that they would contribute to a better understanding of what potential threats there might be and, we hoped, to an ever increasing confidence in the government's efforts to thwart them.

But that task was complicated by the fact that the national anxiety level remained at a painfully high level, and that we began to implement policies that appeared to threaten personal freedoms and appeared even to be racist—including the Justice Department's aggressive campaign to investigate Arab males between the ages of eighteen and thirty-five simply because they "fit the pro-file."

Our task, in short, would be almost undoable.

My recruiting pitch to Susan Neely went something like this: "Your opportunity to serve your country, Susan, comes with the following benefits: the chance to work twice as hard as you've been working for less than half the wages, with little time for your family, and be on call 24/7 as if you were a pediatrician, to deal with some of the most difficult and deadly subjects you can imagine. And when we must go to the public you will have to deliver unpleasant and potentially horrifying information. There won't be many occasions to tell a funny story. Even when you talk about positive things, it will always be in a negative context. So do you want this job?" Fortunately, in spite of all these benefits, she did.

After Neely had been vetted by Andy Card and Karen Hughes—who were impressed with her passion to do what needed to be done—and had passed her background, fingerprint, and drug tests, she walked into the maelstrom that was the anthrax investigation—just in time to see how unglamorous her job was going to be. The white powder threat had closed down deliveries to the White House. As Neely prepared for her first press briefing, not able to find Post-its or a stapler, she scrounged for some paper clips and thought, well, for fighting a war, we're a bit underequipped, even at headquarters. She found that the new "war correspondents" felt underequipped, too; they knew as little about what we were doing as we did.

Reporters who cover Washington are, for the most part, senior journalists who have developed specialties over the years. Whether they specialize in military affairs or transportation or health care issues or Congress, they become experts in this work and enjoy a certain stature within their area. They know the specific histories and the forces at work on their beat. As annoying as reporters can be at certain times, they are also useful in getting the word out in a reliable way. Now, however, many of them were being asked to report on unfamiliar subjects at a time when the stakes were higher than ever, so we were all learning together.

Some mornings I saw several broadcast journalists at "Pebble Beach." This was obviously not the glamorous golf course in Southern California, but the area adjacent to the West Wing parking lot, where the networks keep their cameras set up on a permanent basis, part of the infrastructure developed for covering the White House. Some days I ran the gauntlet starting at 7:00 A.M., with interviews on ABC, NBC, CBS, FOX, CNN. The nation was hungry for news of developments and for reassurance.

Susan Neely and I knew instinctively that the general public was the first of our two major information constituencies. The second comprised key officials in state and local governments. The latter, I was convinced, should get from us as much specific information as we could provide, regardless of whether or not it could be actioned upon at the time. We had to put an end to the "inside the beltway" mentality. We were all in this together.

Martin O'Malley, mayor of Baltimore, now governor of Maryland complained to the media that it had taken a month for the FBI to put detailed information about people on its post-September 11 watch list into the national crime database, a resource that local and state police officers use when making arrests or even when detaining drivers for traffic violations. O'Malley's constant whine during this time—that the federal government never does anything right—was a source of irritation, but his complaint on information sharing I must grudgingly admit was essentially correct.

Even when information became available, it could serve to compound the frustration, especially when there were conflicting messages from federal agencies. In December 2001, *The New York Times* reported that Al Berndt, the assistant director of the Nebraska Emergency Management Agency, said that in late October, four agencies—the Federal Emergency Management Agency, the Department of Justice, the Defense Department, and the Nuclear Regulatory Commission—issued contradictory information about two power plants.

In response, the plants called the capital at Lincoln, Nebraska, and requested National Guard troops to protect them. "The information they were telling us differed from what the Department of

Defense had told us moments before," Mr. Berndt said. "It didn't translate into what we were supposed to do."

Before I arrived in Washington, Attorney General Ashcroft warned Boston mayor Thomas M. Menino of a potential terrorist attack in September, but he did not disclose the location of the target. Local authorities determined that the threat was based on old intelligence, but the call was leaked to the press and an unnecessary amount of public concern ensued.

Those incidents proved typical and telling. Local and state officials were asked to respond by (and to) any number of federal agencies to potential threats. They were asked to do this despite inadequate information, inadequate staffing, inadequate training, and, significantly, no means to procure financial help from the federal government.

Now, we were asking cities and states to be our front lines in a "new war," but we were not equipping or funding them properly. Mayors were asking for money for command and control centers, disaster coordinators, protective gear, and training. They were also seeking funds for first responders and security at airports, railways, roads, bridges, and seaports. There were now twenty-six state homeland security advisors—a remarkable statistic so shortly after 9/11—all of them assigned ill-defined responsibilities, and lacked financial support while relying on a primitive communications network between public agencies. The task of trying to gather accurate information to deliver to a nervous public was daunting, and there was an obvious need for coordination and direction from the federal government. In short, from OHS and me.

We clearly needed emergency funding and a much smarter approach to disseminating information. We needed to become masters, if that was possible, in determining what the real threats were. Though we were intelligence users, not generators, we had to quickly develop an expertise in intelligence interpretation.

Even though I wanted to establish a culture of sharing information, I knew that subtle distinctions had to be made, that each threat had to be addressed individually. If the public had been listening in on the morning briefings, without the appropriate context, there would have been mass hysteria. The reports regularly included specific threats and targets. There were dozens of threats every single day, and weighing them was a terribly difficult job. When we faced the "traditional" enemy—as in the world wars, in Korea, even in Vietnam—the spy business was much more straightforward. It relied on human intelligence, electronics, and satellites. If you saw troop movements or shipments of supplies, you could reasonably predict the enemy's intention. If a submarine was no longer in harbor, you asked, "Where is it?" Satellites focused on the Ho Chi Minh Trail in Cambodia and Laos could occasionally reveal supply and troop movements.

This new war is much harder. We are woefully deficient in human intelligence. We have not pivoted from the cold war to the new war. We don't have anybody cozying up to bin Laden. There aren't ship or troop movements to track by satellite. Determining what's actionable is a tough job. We now rely on interrogations, electronic intercepts, and, on rare occasions, human intelligence. Satellite photos won't show terrorists or their assets. It's a whole different game of intelligence gathering. There are no more double agents, and there is no such thing as infiltrating Al Qaeda—we did not know how to break into this crowd.

There are basic rules and inquiries that guide the intelligence community, but it is still an art, not a science. We had to determine which plots were credible. Had we previously received reliable information from the source? Was it corroborated by another reliable source? Does the capacity exist to leverage such an attack? How vulnerable is the target? And on and on.

Once those questions were answered, we had to determine whether the information should be distributed, and to whom, and whether it was actionable. There were so many dimensions to consider, and so many ways to be wrong.

On October 31, 2001, the threat matrix addressed possible targets on the West Coast. Las Vegas was on the list. This was not surprising. To the extremists, the city has served as the metaphor for America's sins of excess and hedonism. Hollywood, too, earned that same taint, with its commercially rewarding reliance on sex and violence. You could easily imagine the mind of a suicide bomber, who might anticipate the immortality that would come with blowing a Hollywood studio to bits.

Certain intelligence reports mentioned iconic structures. Among them was the Golden Gate Bridge, a marvel of engineering that is much more than a mere roadway between San Francisco and Marin County. It is a man-made monument. There was a potential threat to the bridge, that it might be bombed during a rush hour in early November 2001. That was not especially plausible. It ranked with other "noise" we received over those weeks and months.

I was determined to share as much information as possible with state and local officials. While there were many occasions we fought or disagreed with the FBI, Director Robert Mueller was receptive to creating a communications protocol between the FBI and our shop. He is an articulate and skilled lawyer, a Vietnam veteran, and a dedicated and unflappable public servant. This new arrangement would allow us to issue joint security bulletins to key state and local officials. The FBI had a well-earned reputation for a "need to know" culture, but I found that its new director was eager to open communication channels it would have never considered before 9/11. I have often wondered how long it will take his point of view to trickle down to the local agents in charge.

Together, we passed along to western state governors and authorities the possible plot against unnamed suspension bridges, along with other emerging threats in West Coast states. We sent out a bulletin primarily for informational purpose. The idea was simply to inform the appropriate state and local officials, sharing what we had learned, to foster a working relationship in the event that future information made action necessary. If we had been convinced of such a threat, we would surely have issued a specific warning. This one didn't rise to that level. Nevertheless, unlike the governors of other states, California Governor Gray Davis decided to share the advisory with his constituents although the original information sent to him neither named specific bridges nor asked for additional security measures.

Davis called a press conference and warned there was "credible evidence" that terrorists were plotting rush-hour attacks in the next seven days on one or more of California's most prominent bridges, including the Golden Gate and Bay Bridges. He told the people of California that he had authorized the National Guard and the Highway Patrol to provide additional security. "The best preparation is to let terrorists know we know what they're up to. We're ready. It's not going to succeed." All of this was unnecessary and unwise and added to a growing sense of vulnerability. Others viewed the actions to be more about politics than security.

Davis may, of course, have had the best intentions. But our advisory was not communicated as an imminent threat, and it soon became clear to the media that this was the case. As *The New York Times* reported on November 3, 2001, "Mr. Davis's decision to disclose it served as a source of irritation, if not anger, among some state and federal law enforcement officials." The FBI, for its part, had said its advisory was "uncorroborated" and had asked that it not be aired publicly. None of the governors had been asked to do anything.

Davis was pummeled in political circles for unnecessarily scaring Californians. The head of the Republican caucus in the state assembly, David Cox, said, "If [the threat] couldn't be corroborated, then in fact it's a publicity stunt that is disingenuous with the public." Others worried aloud that the public would become desensitized to actual threats. We all had a lesson in the complexities of the issue.

Governor Davis called me as this was happening and asked if we could hold a joint press conference by telephone so I could explain that what he did was sensible under the circumstances.

I declined. I thought it would set a bad precedent for me to rationalize a state official's actions, whatever the motives. Instead, I offered to answer a reporter's questions about what happened. It wasn't what Davis had in mind, but I think it helped explain why he had made the decision he did. Governor Davis, being in "unchartered waters," did what he thought was best. As a former governor, I thought he deserved the benefit of the doubt.

Davis wasn't the only one whose actions or comments drew ridicule. That particular commodity was introduced early in my tenure and it hung around, as it turned out, for almost all of it.

The first incident was the Duct Tape Debacle.

Among the questions I was most often asked were: "What can we do?" and "How can we help?" In our judgment we didn't have to reinvent the wheel to give Americans the most appropriate answer. We decided to extend and intensify the public campaign the Red Cross had been promoting for many years—to encourage people to be prepared for an emergency by having valuable, even lifesaving supplies at home.

Our "Ready Campaign," as developed and marketed with the help of the Ad Council, the Sloan Foundation, and the Red Cross, urged people to be prepared with many of the items traditionally recommended by the Red Cross and FEMA in anticipation of natural disasters. We suggested three days' worth of food and water, a battery-operated radio, medical and emergency supplies, and home protection materials intended to seal off threats from atmospheric poisons. These materials included plastic sheeting and duct tape, to be stored in a "safe room." The White House suggested the campaign would have little value or merit, but grudgingly let us proceed. (In later years it was gratifying to see the widespread embrace of the initiative, including TV commercials featuring the first lady encouraging preparedness for emergencies.)

The campaign had some unanticipated results: One was that there was a general run on duct tape and plastic sheeting at hardware and home supply stores. Some homeowners went to great lengths. Paul West, of Winsted, Connecticut, wrapped his entire house in plastic. He explained to a reporter that it was an old house, built in the 1800s, and had no modern insulation. So the wrapping, aside from providing peace of mind against a terrorist attack, also saved money on heating bills. (When oil rose to $147 per barrel in the summer of 2008, Mr. West was probably the envy of his neighborhood.)

Finally, duct tape became a metaphor and punch line for late-night comedians. Duct tape in an age of potential nuclear holocaust?

Duct tape as a symbol of the Bush administration's nickel-and-diming of homeland security? Duct tape as Tom Ridge taking a great threat and reducing it to a home do-it-yourself project?

Saturday Night Live had some fun at our expense, as did Jay Leno. At first, I felt like anyone who is barraged with jokes and ridicule. But at least our Ready Campaign generated a lot of free, high-priced visibility—even if it wasn't exactly what we had in mind. I had to remind myself of that when David Letterman offered his version of a public service announcement: "In case of a terrorist attack, bottled water and duct tape are not going to do a damn thing. So do what Homeland Security Secretary Tom Ridge does: Get really drunk, and pick up a hooker."

I've always believed that humor is an effective means of communicating difficult subjects. But there is a difference between humor and ridicule and, at times, the line was crossed. Admittedly, I still crack a smile reading some of those lines.

We had our own comedy act in the Bush administration. On three or four occasions before we adopted a formal process to review intelligence and issue alerts, Ashcroft, Mueller, and I hosted press conferences, each time with warnings to the public about new intelligence, each time with the empty feeling that we weren't presenting any specific information that people could act on, each time leaving the podium thinking, "What the hell did I just say?"

We weren't exactly the Three Stooges, but we might have passed for the Three Amigos without the fancy embroidery.

As we learned in those early months the intersection between entertainment, information, terrorism, and tragedy could never be precisely defined or anticipated.

Talk show host Don Imus provided us an opportunity to discuss these matters one morning. So, to spread the word about preparedness and security, I appeared on his popular show.

On November 12, following a somber Veterans Day, I called Mr. Imus from my White House office at 9:15 A.M. We had just begun to banter when he informed me of the sketchy details of the fate of American Airlines Flight 587 out of JFK, which had crashed in a Queens neighborhood shortly after takeoff.

In the era of instant communications, this was another example that the world of information gathering has changed dramatically. The federal government often learns of certain situations at the same time as a television viewer, radio listener, or Web surfer would.

It also provided an odd commentary on the state of the American psyche at that moment. As Imus was providing the details, a member of my staff knocked on my door to do the same. Imus and I never finished, as I left to go to the Situation Room. There, with other officials, we thought first that this might be the result of another terrorist plot. The evidence quickly indicated otherwise. The death of all the passengers and crew and five people on the ground was the result, we learned, of a dreadful, but simple mechanical failure and not the work of Osama bin Laden.

This was the state of our nation: Two hundred sixty-five people had died, and collectively we breathed a national sigh of relief because turbulence and a failure of the rudder controls, not a terrorist plot, had killed them.

5

THE COLORS OF FEAR
(AND LAUGHTER)

Tom Ridge announced a new color-coded alarm system. . . .
Green means everything's okay. Red means we're in extreme
danger. And champagne-fuchsia means we're being attacked
by Martha Stewart.

—CONAN O'BRIEN

On December 3, 2001, Lieutenant Colonel John Fenzel sat along the wall in the White House press briefing room. Fenzel, a White House Fellow, had been detailed to Vice President Cheney's office. When September 11, 2001, occurred, he was serving as staff director of the Homeland Security Task Force chaired by the vice president. After 9/11 he and others migrated to the Office of Homeland Security.

Though it was not a perfect vantage point, Fenzel could nevertheless see the frustration etched on my face. Dressed in civilian clothes, the U.S. Army Special Forces officer watched as I warned the room's occupants and the nation—in typically vague fashion— that another dramatic attack on the country might be just around the corner.

It might be connected, I told the media, to the final days of the Islamic holy month of Ramadan, or to some other religious observance, including any of the religious or secular days celebrated in America. It could arrive in any form. "The threats we are picking up are very generic," I said. "They warn of more attacks but are not specific about where or what type. . . . The sources are more credible and, let me just say, the decibel level is high." As I was delivering this litany of nonnews I saw looks of bewilderment on the faces of the reporters. I thought, "If they're confused, imagine how ordinary citizens feel." They must be asking themselves, "What's he really saying?" And, "Is this the best our government can provide?"

Those were the right questions. We felt from the outset that government had a responsibility to offer more than a generic threat warning. America was a theater of the war against extremists. Our citizens were all potential targets, although as polling suggested, some regions had much higher anxiety levels than others. Citizens along the northeast corridor and in several major urban areas around the country seemed to score higher on the dread index.

What terrorists hope to create is the psychological impact of an attack or the threat of an attack—anxiety, depression, or fear. On this day, and on many others, I recalled the words of President Franklin D. Roosevelt (later etched into the American psyche by Norman Rockwell) when he addressed Congress in 1941. He talked about a "world founded upon four essential human freedoms": freedom of speech and expression, freedom of worship, freedom from want, and freedom from fear.

Every one of these has many forms. I believe the greatest fear in dealing with this new enemy is the fear of the unknown. An informed public is an engaged public and a good investment in the security of the community and country. And informing the public required a new way of thinking and communicating and, I believed, now was the time to take up the task. Traditional Washington did not share this point of view.

It was a time when people were paying attention not just to what was going on in their community or state. Suddenly, nearly everybody was tuned in to what was happening in foreign nations. Newspapers, which had dropped or greatly diminished their coverage of international news—in part because it saved money to do so and in part because most readers lacked interest—were consumed overnight with stories about Al Qaeda and related subjects.

During that first week of December, newspapers carried reports of three Palestinian suicide bombings inside Israel and retaliatory Israeli air strikes. They published Associated Press and Reuters dispatches about the fighting in Afghanistan as it intensified and U.S. warplanes bombed caves and bunkers where bin Laden was believed to be hiding. Across continental America it was dawning on everyone that the great oceans that had protected us—kept us remote from events thousands of miles away—had become mere moats.

The FBI and the Justice Department continued to issue general alerts that were of the same character: no real information for the public or public officials to act on. Newspaper editorial pages were uniformly expressing exasperation, almost as if they were reading my mind. Sally Quinn, writing for *The Washington Post,* seemed to speak for many when she said, "Heeding a series of warnings about 'credible threats' that the Administration has issued . . . I tried to find out what the average citizen should do to prepare. And in the process I found, like Alice after she passed through the looking-glass, a lot of jabberwocky."

After my media briefing, as we walked from the press room past the Oval Office to my office, I told Lieutenant Colonel Fenzel who had been detailed to the Office of Homeland Security, "There has to be a better way to communicate through the Department of Defense, the nature and severity of the threat."

When we sat down to discuss how this could be accomplished, Fenzel said, "We'll create a system for you. And we'll have something after Christmas."

I looked him over, this husky and confident soldier, and knew he would deliver. I had no idea what that plan would be, but the good soldier that he was, he knew his duty well.

Fenzel had served in Operations Desert Shield and Desert Storm in Iraq, and had commanded a Special Forces A-Team, a unit of twelve men who had trained, equipped, and advised a Kuwaiti battalion and accompanied it during the liberation of Kuwait in 1991. Over the years, he had commanded three Special Forces companies, leading the initial army deployments into Pakistan and the Balkans.

In Bosnia, Fenzel had led the special operations teams in the U.S. and British sectors, working with the United Nations to get indictments and convictions of those responsible for war crimes in Srebrenica. And he was the only active-duty military officer to testify at The Hague in support of the International Criminal Tribunal, which was investigating crimes against humanity in the former Yugoslavia. In addition, he provided his experience on special task forces, and for about two weeks prior to 9/11 had been working with Steve Abbot, my deputy, and others on a task force whose job it was to try to anticipate how terrorists might attack the United States. The group was well aware of the dangers presented by the Taliban and Al Qaeda, but also focused on Hamas, Hezbollah, and other terrorist organizations around the world.

Though Fenzel had been focusing on such threats, he was as surprised as anyone when the attack on 9/11 came in the form of civilian passenger jets. There had been no "chatter" about that possibility.

When the attacks on 9/11 occurred, Fenzel was in the White House. He walked to a nearby office and watched the television screen as the second plane hit the World Trade Center. Someone asked him, "What's going on?" He said that without a doubt this was a "coordinated terrorist attack." A few minutes later, word came in that the Pentagon had been hit as well.

Except for a handful of people asked to stay behind, the White House was evacuated. Fenzel remembers walking out with the crowd—"It was orderly but swift," he recalls—and looking up at the sky, imagining yet another plane headed directly for the White House. He looked toward the Pentagon, several miles away, and saw smoke billowing.

After Fenzel volunteered to lead the effort to create a threat warning system, he pleaded his case for additional support within the Office of Homeland Security to the director of the White House Fellows program. He was successful, and later described White House Fellow Major Roberta "Bobbi" Shea as a godsend. As the two of them began their work on an alert system, I was trying to earn my stripes with other federal agencies and, in the process, to put out what seemed to be an unending number of bureaucratic fires.

For example, a natural and responsible reaction to 9/11 was to intensify security at airports and nuclear power plants by calling up National Guard members.

No one disagreed with that plan—clearly, emergency measures had to be taken—but who would pay for them? Governors complained that their limited budgets had no provisions to cover the costs. A huge proportion of the new security measures was labor intensive. Governors expected OHS to pay. They were under the impression that I had money to distribute. I had none. This was just one more illustration of the challenges we had as an office of influence rather than a center of authority.

It seemed only natural to us that financial responsibility for calling up the National Guard would have fallen on the Pentagon. But I had to do battle there to sell the notion. In fact, we discovered a statute that allowed for reimbursement to governors.

Donald Rumsfeld, though, was seldom available, and entirely occupied with war planning. We were now engaged in Afghanistan big-time, and the secretary of defense was surrounded by his military advisors. Rumsfeld was a genuine celebrity who was entertaining and provocative and operated by his own rules. He wasn't a participant in our morning meetings, and I was never invited to the National Security Council, where he occupied a primary seat.

So, almost out of necessity, our discussions were hallway encounters. And he was not the sort of fellow with whom I could make small talk. In response to my informal National Guard entreaties, he always nodded, but never agreed to anything. While I couldn't expect him to pull out a budget sheet and go over the line items, I could easily imagine him saying, "I've got troops in the field, plans to make that are going to consume enormous resources. Can't the governors absorb the cost themselves?" This point of view, by the way, had considerable support in the White House. The response illustrated the wider problem we were facing, not only in the hallways of power, but everywhere else. No one disagreed that the government had to respond to the threat. But at the same time no one wanted to pay for the response.

In this case, I knew the best way to proceed was for me to work with Tom White, the secretary of the army, who had direct budget control over the National Guard. I needed to try to build support within the Department of Defense (DOD).

White, unlike Rumsfeld, was available and somewhat sympathetic. I asked military colleagues at OHS to contact their peers in the Pentagon to explain the problem. There was fear, certainly, at the DOD that paying for the deployment of National Guard troops in a domestic environment would set a costly precedent. I had empathy, but it was short-lived, because these weren't normal circumstances. And, understanding that, the Pentagon eventually agreed to reimburse the states.

In the meantime, we were trying to anticipate future needs, and to that end we worked with established federal agencies to beef up their own budgets for the following year so that they would reflect the additional costs that homeland security would require. For that work I relied heavily on a man named Richard A. Falkenrath, a member of the NSC staff who possessed some unique credentials. He was a rare public official who years before had foreseen the global threat of terrorism.

One of these days, *The New Yorker* magazine will profile Richard Falkenrath, who had been serving as that city's top counterterrorism official (head of an operation having 350 police officers), yet its readers won't easily believe the arc of his career and achievements. Falkenrath's childhood, for example, was spent in the northern woods of California in the most basic of circumstances—no indoor plumbing and otherwise very poor circumstances. He went to Occidental College, graduating summa cum laude and earned a Ph.D. from King's College in London, where he studied central European wars. After he returned to the United States, Falkenrath became a fellow at the John F. Kennedy School of Government at Harvard. He later wrote three books, including *America's Achilles' Heel,* which argued that our obsession with traditional state-sponsored dangers, such as missiles and invading armies, was outdated, and that we needed to pay much more attention to the threat of terrorism, a view that was not widely shared among contemporaries.

It was that very book that brought him to the attention of

White House officials. He began working with the NSC in January 2001 and, in the wake of 9/11, he found himself advising both the president and me.

By necessity, because there was no one else, he was thrust into the budgeting process, in which we were very far behind. Here it was, October 2001, and the budget for the next fiscal year was already in its final stages.

The schedule of the Office of Management and Budget (OMB) runs this way: from January through March, it issues its marching orders. In June and July, agencies submit requests. By August and September, the OMB does its "passback," its first reaction to requests. By October, the agency has largely resolved issues and is entertaining appeals.

The Office of Homeland Security hadn't even started, and yet there was a great deal at stake in getting our operations funded, both from a functional and public relations standpoint. We had to secure the resources to do our job, while demonstrating to the public that the administration was committed to this effort. One of our suggestions was to create a mini federal agency, because we were becoming ever more concerned that the size of our mission did not in any way connect with our authority to do the job.

Falkenrath wrote a prescient and detailed memo making an airtight case for the consolidation of the Immigration and Naturalizaton Service, the Coast Guard, and Customs Service into one agency. He had long been concerned by unprotected borders. In *America's Achilles' Heel,* he wrote:

> The failure of the U.S. to put drug smugglers out of business is a good measure of the difficulty of reliable border control. If the risks of detection at the border appear too high, an attacker can manage a weapon or its components into any of a large number of uncontrolled harbors by boat. . . . The chance of being caught would be small.

It also made sense to us that grants to local first responders should be included in the FEMA budget, not from the Department of Justice, which had traditionally provided them.

And there were other provisions that, I am convinced, when staffers around Washington got a hint of them and brought them to the attention of their bosses, they girded up to protect their turf.

Efforts to consolidate agencies, which could better secure our borders and control the flow of goods and services, had been discussed as far back as the Nixon administration. By my count, there had been nineteen different government studies over the previous thirty years, and nothing had been done in response to them. This would have been no surprise to anyone who has worked in Washington for any length of time. Studies don't normally result in action. Unfortunately, in Washington, it takes a disaster to produce action.

Steve Abbot and Falkenrath designed a full-fledged proposal, the twentieth attempt to do something. They proposed using the 2003 budget to merge the separate appropriation accounts of the Coast Guard, the Border Patrol, the enforcement functions of the Immigration and Naturalization Service, and the food inspection responsibilities of the Department of Agriculture into one account for a new agency within the executive branch. The need for this modest step was confirmed by personal experience. I remember the many occasions I returned to the United States from overseas. There were several people from different agencies and, naturally, different uniforms, overseeing my inbound entrance—Customs, INS, Agriculture. Having one face at the border seemed to make perfect sense to me. A Federal Border Administration, a modest unification compared to the department, was a significant part of the proposal we submitted well into the budget process for 2003.

Falkenrath and I did some quick calculations and went to meet with Mitch Daniels, head of the OMB (and later governor of Indiana) anticipating tough negotiations on the consolidation of the agencies and new money. Daniels had one of the hardest jobs in Washington—constantly turning down requests for money—and he was so good at it that we often referred to him, respectfully, as Dr. No. Indeed, it looked at first as if we would fail because he had already identified areas in the existing budgets of federal agencies that were earmarked for counterterrorism efforts, and we weren't the counterterrorism agency.

To avoid the embarrassment of negotiating for pennies, we focused on a few big, and obvious, areas. During 9/11, America came
to know that it wasn't federal government employees who become
instant heroes. It was the first responders—the police, the firemen,
and the emergency medical personnel. The first responders needed
a new level—a quantum leap—of support and training. All of the
9/11 terrorists had come legally through our borders. It was obvious that we needed a great deal more attention to our immigration
processes and to the creation of a new and airtight security at the
nation's airports. In the wake of the anthrax attacks, selling the
need to develop a national defense against bioterrorism and to up-
date our antiquated federal public health system, was not hard.
Nor was acquiring money for the defense of New York City, for
new, reliable, and instant ways for first responders to communicate, or for the Coast Guard to take on new responsibilities.

After we made our pitch, Daniels said, "OK. How much do you
need?" I took a deep breath. I knew this was no time for timidity.
We needed a lot of money. We had to fund huge new programs and
add many dollars to existing ones. On the other hand, I had been
a governor and I understood the standard budgetary ploy of asking
for 30 percent more than you needed, knowing it was going to be
cut. It was in no one's interest to ask for extravagant sums that
could not be utilized effectively. Richard and I had made some pre-
liminary calculations and asked for $20 billion. Mitch didn't bat an
eye. "That sounds okay," he said.

This negotiation was the first element in a chain of events that
I think ultimately led to the creation of the Department of Homeland Security. Having influenced the budget process and directed
the flow of new dollars, I was clearly walking a narrow line between
the legislative and executive branches of government. Ultimately, the
executive proposes, the Congress disposes, and those who advocate are called to the Hill to justify their requests.

Our influence on new spending became a point of contention
with Congress. Committees on the Hill called upon me to testify,
and I would have been happy to go. It was important to develop
relationships with lawmakers to create a base of support and an

atmosphere of cooperation that could accommodate dramatic changes in how the United States would protect itself. But that kind of partnership seemed out of bounds.

As Andy Card pointed out, "You're working for one person and one person only." Indeed, the president prohibited my testimony, holding to the tenet that Oval Office advisors are not subject to congressional subpoena power under the theory of executive privilege and that if I were to go to the Hill it would set a bad precedent. At a news conference, President Bush said, "He's a part of my staff, and that's part of the prerogative of the executive branch of government, and we hold that very dear." This only made members of Congress more determined to find a way. Senator Tom Daschle, at the time the Senate majority leader, called the situation "untenable and inexcusable." Harsh words, certainly, but I did not take them personally. I was caught in a highly visible pickle.

I tried to get in to see Senator Robert C. Byrd, chairman of the Senate Appropriations Committee, on several occasions, figuring that informal briefings might satisfy Congress's need to know. When I finally arranged a meeting, he was, as always, both gracious and persistent. He was one of the most courtly gentlemen in Washington—unfailingly polite and civil in tone. It is a lost art in this town, disagreeing without being disagreeable, and challenging without being confrontational. He was even cordial when he asked me, "What's happening to the money?" By that, he meant the billions that we had secured for the budget.

Then this proud historian of the Senate pulled out a well-thumbed pocket edition of the Constitution. The Constitution is the rule book. Referring to it, Senator Byrd said, "This says Congress has the power of the purse." He wasn't interested, he said, in private briefings. He wanted public testimony. He said, "I am unaware of any instance in which a private briefing has been used as a substitute for responding to a Senate Appropriations Committee request for testimony concerning a funding need."

Senator Byrd's approach with me was clever, cordial, and always gracious. Much later, when I was secretary of homeland security, he ended a session of public testimony by thanking me for my time and offered the view that "next time you appear before this Committee, Mr. Secretary, I hope you'll bring an entirely different set of answers."

There was one person happier than I when the testimony impasse was resolved, Wendy Grubbs. As a member of the White House legislative team she had to use all her legal, business, and Senate staff experience to help me navigate successfully all the private meetings required by Congress.

As I will discuss later, I appeared before Congress too often, and with one exception, the exchanges were civil. On this day, my son Tommy was performing clerical chores in the Old Executive Office Building under the watchful and caring eye of a lifelong friend, Barbara Chaffee. She had been an integral part of my governor's team and had volunteered to lead our efforts in the White House to reach out to the private sector.

I learned that Tommy observed during this contentious grilling, "My dad doesn't like that question!" Since he could hardly have been versed as an eighth-grader on homeland security issues, Chaffee inquired how he could draw that conclusion. My son admitted it was easy. "I have seen that look before," he said.

What could be done with OHS to satisfy the needs of Congress and the needs of the country? To me, it was becoming more and more obvious: a cabinet-level Department had to be established. As Jane Harmon, a House member from California, said, "We have to give Tom Ridge a real job. Never has a person been given so much responsibility with so little authority.'"

After Falkenrath and I worked on the budget proposal, I called a meeting in the Roosevelt Room of high-ranking members of the administration to discuss a proposal to establish a Federal Border Administration. Featuring a portrait of Teddy Roosevelt receiving the Nobel Peace Prize for 1910, the room occupies the original site of the presidential office before the West Wing was built. This windowless space effectively served as my conference room. It was where the president and I occasionally met on homeland security matters. And in this case, the president's highest-ranking staff members were invited, among them Deputy Secretary of Defense Paul

Wolfowitz, Tommy Thompson, John Ashcroft, Robert Mueller, and Treasury Secretary Paul O'Neill. Falkenrath accompanied me. The purpose of the meeting was to try to develop a consensus to lay the groundwork for the concept of a major reorganization.

I spoke first. I mentioned the need for, if nothing else, a better way to track who was coming into and leaving the country and said that our present federal structure left enormous gaps in that regard. I said that, as a start, a few resources could be shifted to plug those gaps, but even this modest measure was roundly criticized. "We don't think it's necessary" seemed to be the consensus. And when Secretary of State Colin Powell voiced his strong objection to this plan, all of the air seemed to go out of the room. What was really needed, these officials argued, was better communication and collaboration. But, of course, from what I had experienced in my first few months in the office, communication and collaboration were in short supply.

The only official who supported the idea of reorganization was O'Neill. He generally thought that much of government was still organized along nineteenth- and twentieth-century lines and needed to be modernized. He recalled that a similar effort had been considered in the Nixon administration and failed. O'Neill was prepared to support any reorganization that had the potential of making government more effective and accountable. The others, however, prevailed with their argument that the president was happy with the way things were, and *they certainly were.* Several months later, the same people gathered in the same room to discuss the same issue. There was one additional participant—President Bush. He announced we were going to create a border-centric agency and that the enabling legislation would be submitted to Congress. I must admit that I still smile when I think of the positive and encouraging response he received. But that would come much later.

I reported to the president, who had become more sympathetic to the problem, that my sales pitch had fallen on deaf ears. And I told him that I would try to make my case to Congress.

After the Roosevelt Room session, we were disappointed and discouraged. Falkenrath and Abbot slumped in their chairs. Falkenrath lamented that if we couldn't persuade the others to adopt a plan that made all the sense in the world, what could we do? I pointed out that this was just the first volley, and we'd be back at them soon.

Every time I am at some political low point, I recall my first race for governor in 1994 against four opponents. Because I was known, at first, only to my congressional constituents in the state's northwest corner, I had the devil of a time creating a statewide campaign. At one point, polls showed I had statewide support from only 11 percent of the voters. In fact, the front-runner in the race sent me a birthday cake with 11 candles on it, just to rub it in. A writer for a Philadelphia newspaper called me "the Congressman no one ever heard of from the city no one has ever been to." I went on to win that race by 200,000 votes.

Tenacity, confidence, and resolve—these qualities abounded within our group. As the group in the Roosevelt Room would learn months later, this was just a bump in the road.

For the time being it was my responsibility to play down publicly the notion of a new cabinet agency, arguing that proximity to the Oval Office was all the influence and power needed. This was in concert with the president's stated and private views. But as time went on, I could see the limits of that strategy, and so did others. After I handed out a document listing every government department, agency, bureau, and office that had some role in securing the homeland, more and more people agreed that something had to be done.

We gave a flowchart to reporters of all the agencies that supposedly had some relation to what we were doing at OHS. There were over a hundred organizations. The chart could be seen as a plan that was working because OHS seemed prominent in every department's missions. Yet the organization was, as *The New York Times* described it, "a morass of lines and boxes so Byzantine and complex that some lawmakers mutter they have not seen anything like it since schematics of the abortive Clinton health care plan." The White House saw the flowchart as a tactic to maintain the status quo, showing how difficult and complicated it would be if lawmakers were foolish enough to establish a full Department of Homeland Security. Some people thought, however, that it was a subtle cry for help. These people were perceptive.

Senator Joe Lieberman weighed in. "To me I thought it was an argument for my bill," said the Democrat from Connecticut, who had introduced legislation to create a Department of National Homeland Security and give me the same status as the defense secretary. The senator had also heard me compare my new duty as being equivalent to "building the transcontinental railroad, fighting World War II, or putting a man on the moon."

Senator Bob Graham, a Democrat who was chairman of the Senate Intelligence Committee, said, "My own feeling is that for Governor Ridge or any other human being to be able to effectively direct all of the boxes on that piece of paper will require more authority than the President can give him in an Executive Order."

A *New York Times* editorial praised the president's efforts generally in his counterterrorism plan but argued that there was a need for greater "coherence" in the management of homeland issues and "not just a discussion of them." It called for the president to give OHS greater powers to provide more funding to help hospitals, health departments, and public safety agencies cope with new responsibilities. The editorial was a response to a front-page report that detailed the resistance to OHS. It said, "The law enforcement agencies he is supposed to coordinate remain fiercely protective of their own power and independence. Mr. Ridge does not have direct authority over any of the agencies, even as spending for domestic security surges. And while officials from several of the agencies said they appreciate Mr. Ridge, respect him and get along with him well, some came close to being dismissive of his office's effectiveness and influence over their operations."

On the other hand, a column in *The Wall Street Journal* warned against turning homeland defense into "another bureaucratic bean feast." The author argued that, "Rather than give government new responsibilities, it would seem to be appropriate for Mr. Bush and Mr. Ridge to try to improve the performance of existing federal security agencies in the jobs they already have." Well, good luck with that, I thought. With what leverage?

During all of this, I met periodically with Lieutenant Colonel Fenzel, who was determined to develop an effective national warning system. In his research, he found several systems, none of which were suitable for our needs. The Pentagon had long established its own warning codes, but those applied primarily to military situations well beyond our borders. This was also true of measures already in place at the State Department. When he looked to other countries, Fenzel found that only Israel had a well-defined warning system for its citizens and public agencies. It seemed quite natural for us to look to that country because the Israelis, in preservation of their democracy and security, had been dealing with terrorism for more than a half century.

Israel had lived under siege since its founding in 1948 and faced persistent threats from hostile neighbors. Its citizens are well schooled. I'll never forget the impressions left on my first visit there in 1985. In America, you don't see defense forces on your streets. But there you see soldiers on the corners and in the marketplace. It's not offensive or threatening, merely reassuring in a tiny, geographically vulnerable country where security is not taken for granted. (On a helicopter ride, I could look out of the windows and see both the eastern and western borders.) We, of course, don't have that problem in this country, and we are not likely to invite, as a regular sight, soldiers to stand guard on street corners. And we can't reach all of our territory with large sirens and speakers.

Another model for us seemed to be Great Britain. Like Israel, it had a far more aggressive surveillance capability than we did, though Brits still do things consistent with their culture and their laws. They have always known how to bounce back. All you need to do is listen on the Internet to the reports during the London blitz by Edward R. Murrow to be reminded how harrowing the Nazi bombardment was during World War II. But the blitz unified Great Britain, made the Britons determined to succeed. In later decades, when the country had to endure the terrorism of the Irish Republican Army they did it in their own way, and no country does it better. They mourn, deal with the horror and the consequences, and then get back to work. Though we did a good job after 9/11 getting Wall Street up and running, I felt we still had a lot to learn from Britain and Israel.

The United States has rarely been under siege in that way. There were folks, of course, of my parents' generation who lived along our coastlines and became part of an informal reconnaissance network, watching out primarily for German U-boats. But we had never suffered mass civilian casualties in war the way so many other countries had. Now, with the threat clearly with us, how could we quickly communicate its nature in a way that would be instantly understood?

Fenzel talked to dozens of people around the country—even to the Disney folks in Burbank. They were concerned, of course, about terrorists striking their theme parks, and similar fears were expressed by executives from any number of companies who saw themselves as vulnerable.

As we worked on the alert system, emergencies—real and otherwise—became part of the everyday chatter. Whenever we thought we had a handle on things, we had to remind ourselves that the only thing that we could count on was surprise. And yet, as we had shown before, the upstart OHS had more talent to deal with its expanding role than generally recognized.

It was Mike Byrne, a former New York City firefighter who had lost many friends and comrades at the Twin Towers and moved from his job at the Federal Emergency Management Agency to become our senior director of infrastructure management at OHS, who brought the color code idea to John Fenzel. Byrne was a first responder by trade, and, as such, he argued on behalf of a system that could be easily understood. Fenzel embraced the idea, though both agreed at the time that Jay Leno and that crowd might have a field day with it.

Of course, colors as alert symbols had been used before, but almost always in secret ways, not in ways to inform the public at large. For example, before World War II, the navy worked on War Plan Orange for many years. Orange, in those days, was the code for war with Japan.

Indeed, color usage was not merely historical. When other agencies got wind of what we had in mind, some worried that it would interfere with programs already in place and cause confusion.

Early on, we had our own confusions. There were questions about how many colors should be used. What would each distinctly signify, along with the desired response to it? At one point, one of the threat levels was white. That had a short shelf life. Deputy Chief of Staff Josh Bolten objected. He argued that it wouldn't show up clearly on television. As one White House staff member observed, "Don't you know that white means surrender? You can't do that."

Even so, we were confident of the concept we had developed, in that now we could speak clearly and simultaneously to our two major constituencies, the general public and people responsible for public safety.

We introduced the Homeland Security Advisory System (HSAS), later called the "terror alert system" to the nation in March 2002. We settled on five levels represented by five colors: green (low risk), blue (general risk), yellow (significant risk), orange (high risk), and red (severe risk). In each case, specific measures were to be taken at airports and other public facilities. But of course we couldn't agree on where we were, colorwise, on the day we introduced the system. Ashcroft had vigorously campaigned to open with orange, arguing that we were under siege. Since he would be responsible for setting the threat conditions, his humorous conclusion that, if adopted, it was tantamount to having an attorney general "term limit bill," brought smiles and levity to our discussion.

As always, Ashcroft was compelling and articulate, but this is the only time I can remember that he lost an argument with the White House. Others argued for blue, which was of course the second lowest. I felt yellow (significant risk) best reflected the nature of the threat at the time. The group couldn't come to a consensus. The president was fully engaged during the discussion. He voiced concern that it wouldn't be effective long-term if we were on high alert constantly. He concluded that the level we should initially use might condition people that we would be dealing with this enemy for a long time. I remember him wondering when the country might get to one of the lowest levels. He was the "decider" and he decided. Yellow it was.

In announcing the system at a press conference on March 12, 2002, I said that the nation "currently stands in the yellow condition, in elevated risk. Chances are we will not be able to lower the condition to green until . . . the terror networks of global reach have been defeated and dismantled. And we are far from being able to predict that day."

Some people praised the new system as a simple way to get the message across or as an extremely important first step. But some experts cautioned the blanket alerts might do little to help citizens prepare and might actually increase panic. We quickly heard criticism along the lines of "What good is it going to do?" and "If you've got anything specific to tell us, just tell us. Forget the damned color code." Initially, the system was designed to alert two important constituencies. The first was to tell the public that a consensus existed within the president's Homeland Security Council about the level of threat. This meant that several cabinet members and their intelligence units had agreed that the threat was at a particular level. The second constituency was the security professionals in the public and private sector. The color indicated that a very specific set of prearranged security measures were to be used.

For example, a high-risk condition (orange) would, in addition to other protective measures, alert the federal government to cancel public events and prepare to execute contingency plans, including moving key personnel to an alternate site. A severe condition (red) would have the federal government pre-position and mobilize specially trained teams and resources and close both public and government facilities. Each color, much like a traffic signal, required certain action to be taken by both the public and private sectors. When implemented, the federal government's prescribed conduct was mandated. The goal was to have the rest of the country build alternate levels of action and conduct that would be taken at every level of risk. Government and business know what is required of them at each and every threat level. There may come a time when the threat is so specific as to time, place, and type that the public will "need to know" exactly the precautions they should take. On those occasions, we must tell them. Some governors have evacuated thousands from paths of hurricanes. Pray we would have such notice prior to a potential attack to direct specific security measures.

No broad system could eliminate the need for direct communication, a lesson that became clear in early 2002. Some intelligence reports included a threat that terrorists were planning to smuggle a ten-kiloton nuclear weapon into New York City. At the time, the information wasn't shared with the mayor or any other public officials. The intelligence was determined to be a false lead, but word leaked out about the episode. *Time* magazine offered a full report to its readers. State and local officials were rightly exercised about being left in the dark. I called Governor George Pataki and Mayor Michael Bloomberg and told them they would be apprised of any future credible threat. But I reached Bloomberg while he was in the middle of a dinner party with his five borough presidents, a fact I didn't know at the time—so this situation pointed out the delicacy of our task. That is, in my view the *Time* magazine report was overstated. The threat—when ranked with other "noise" we'd been hearing—had not ranked very high in terms of credibility. And yet I could very well understand why the mayor of New York City would be upset by not being in the loop. He, in turn, asked his five borough presidents, a question: If he got news like this from OHS, should he pass it along to them? They, of course, said yes. Absolutely. But where would it stop, and who would call the *Daily News* or Channel 4 with the tip, and how panicked would New York City become? Or, worse, how quickly would New Yorkers become hardened to such reports and decide to simply ignore them and leave themselves vulnerable should a credible threat arise.

There were many other issues, as this was part of the new frontier of homeland security. Everything was a work in progress. In normal circumstance, an organization is able to devise and test systems well before they are made public. Corporations do this, and so do other institutions, including government entities. We didn't have that luxury. And so, as in all cases with our programs, we were retrofitting the airplane in midflight.

To add to the frenzy, federal agencies were still issuing their own public warnings, creating confusion among first responders and the public at large. Reports in the media were often filled with misinformation, but we couldn't blame television, National Public Radio, or the Associated Press for that. The misinformation was the natural result of a system that still needed a great deal of refining.

Part of the problem was the level of specificity that we could offer with each warning. There was a natural conflict in Washington between the view that intelligence should be tightly held, so as not to compromise the counterterrorism effort, and informing the public to the fullest extent possible. I have always been of the opinion that information is overclassified. One can justify the process with the claim that it is done to protect sources and methods. I think it is frequently done simply to avoid sharing. I believe that information that was closely held could be formatted in a way to protect the source and to satisfy the requirement to share. Members of the public could easily see the manifestations of the counterterrorism efforts, such as the barriers constructed around many buildings, or the extra measures of security at airports that resulted in long lines. Even so, law enforcement and intelligence officials are naturally protective of their information, and in some cases they can articulate a strong reason for that policy.

What we developed over time was something of a reasonable compromise. While we often couldn't cite certain specifics about intelligence, we could point out the reasons we felt it was credible; that is, the information was corroborated, or came from sources that had been reliable in the past. As time passed, we gained our footing. But, as usual, what we were doing was fodder for criticism, and for satire.

On *Saturday Night Live,* a skit featured an actor portraying me and saying: "You have probably wondered just what this agency has been up to and what, if anything, we are doing to prevent terrorist attacks within our borders. Tonight, I am proud to unveil my agency's new weapon in the war on terror: the homeland security advisory system. It's a simple, five-tiered system which uses color codes to indicate varying levels of terrorist threat. The lowest level is condition off-white, followed by cream, putty, bone and finally, natural. It is essential that every American learn to recognize and distinguish these colors. Failure to do so could cost you your life. For those who may have questions, an excellent guide can be found on page 74 of the newest J. Crew catalog."

Jay Leno, not to be outdone, said, "This color coding thing is so confusing. Yesterday the alert went from blue to pink; now half the country thinks we're pregnant."

I wound up on the show a few times and knew that, to communicate, I had to get into the act. I took my sense of humor with me. One night Leno proposed a hypothetical: "I'm sitting at home in my underpants watching the game and, oops, we're in orange, what do I do now?" I tried not to miss a beat in my reply: "Change your shorts."

In those days you didn't have to be a professional comedian to weigh in. Representative Jane Harmon of California, said, "Who does Tom Ridge think he is, an interior decorator?" I called her later and inquired if she wanted me to paint her office. She declined with a laugh and words of encouragement.

Some of the commentary on the issue was serious. *Washington Post* columnist Richard Cohen wrote: "Soon the time will come when we pay no heed to any alerts, regardless of color, and walk into situations we could have avoided. It's also likely that the police will themselves tire of the constant warnings and relax their vigil. As for the government, it will appear more and more inept, issuing warnings just so that if anything happens, it can always say afterward that we were warned. Here's our warning: It won't work."

Criticism of the overall effort to protect the country came from other quarters. In May 2002 *USA Today* published an editorial that argued "urgency has been lacking at many of the federal agencies with a critical role in protecting the country against future attacks," and "the agencies remain mired in mindless bureaucratic inertia and turf wars, or adrift with unfocused goals."

In response, I wrote an op-ed piece for *USA Today* that said that Americans were safer and better prepared than on 9/11 because the government was doing more than was apparent to the eye. Some of the improvements included deploying thousands more border and airport inspectors; stockpiling millions of doses of vaccines; freezing $100 million in terrorist assets; implementing more secure standards for food inspection, ventilation systems, and water treatment plants; increasing intelligence information sharing, reforming the INS; and building stronger partnerships across the country. I wrote that we were "working with leaders from all 50 states to help each develop one seamless antiterrorism plan" and "partnering with the private sector to map the nation's critical infrastructure and identify risks." I wrote this not only to persuade the public but also Congress, which—like those administration officials in the Roosevelt Room who balked at my idea for a new agency—were mired in traditional thinking at a time of unprecedented and highly innovative threats. It was a situation that would continue to the end of my tenure, and well beyond.

6

THE POLITICS OF TERRORISM, PART 1

> Politicians and governments worldwide have expanded the war against terrorism by redesignating their own enemies as terrorists. This has been easy because Washington's definition is elastic and arbitrary. Terrorism is what bad people do.
>
> —WILLIAM PFAFF,
> *International Herald-Tribune*, January 10, 2002

On the evening of September 11, 2001, members of Congress gathered on the steps of the Capitol in, as one network anchor described it, "a remarkable tableau of unity." Tom Daschle, Senate majority leader, stood before the microphones and said, "We will speak with one voice." Dennis Hastert, Speaker of the House, said, "Senators and House members, Democrats and Republicans, will stand shoulder-to-shoulder . . . to make sure that those who brought forth this evil will pay the price."

When it was over, members of Congress began to disperse. But then a few of them began singing, and a spontaneous chorus arose. Suddenly America's most prominent lawmakers from both parties offered an impromptu rendition of Irving Berlin's unofficial anthem, "God Bless America." Those who were there—I was in Pennsylvania at the time—will never forget the sight and sound of it. The rest of us can get a pretty good idea of its effect because it was recorded on video and can be viewed on YouTube.

At the time, and for months afterward, there were signs—physical and emotional—of unity all around America. As a nation, we held in awe the men and women who attempted rescues at the Twin Towers, rushed to help their comrades at the Pentagon, and prevented United 93 from reaching the hijackers' destination. Under the most adverse conditions, ordinary people reacted heroically. Afterward, there were dramatic contributions to the common cause in support of those affected by the attacks. Restaurant owners cooked for firemen and policemen, without charge, and citizens donated sums large and small to relief efforts. American flags sold at such an unprecedented rate that, for a time, there was a nationwide shortage. Flag pins and decals contributed to the patriotic fervor.

The unity extended, uncharacteristically, to Congress which in short order and with but one dissenting vote passed the USA Patriot Act. The name of the act itself seemed to be a preemptive effort to mitigate potential criticism. The USA Patriot Act is an acronym derived from the title: Uniting and Strengthening America by Providing Appropriate Tools Required to Intercept and Obstruct Terrorism. The bill was introduced on October 23, 2001, and three days later, with only Senator Russ Feingold (Democrat of Wisconsin) voting nay, it was sent to the president for his signature.

As the newly appointed official in charge of homeland security, two weeks into the job and besieged by the anthrax threat and much else, I knew the law enforcement community needed more tools to do its job. I supported the Patriot Act. Its most important language tore down the legal wall that had prevented the intelligence and law enforcement communities from talking to one another. Creating an environment in which they actually did so was the next step. (An even larger challenge remains: enhancing their willingness to share information with state and local governments.)

The Patriot Act was in many ways a natural response to 9/11 and contained some enlightened provisions. For example, it condemned discrimination against Arab Americans and provided mechanisms for addressing any such episodes. In addition, there seemed to be enough uncertainty about the effectiveness and constitutionality of some of its provisions that Congress limited their duration so that the provisions could be reviewed at a later date. It was the right approach for Congress to move cautiously and carefully down this path.

Yet the Patriot Act was not and is not without controversy and concern. It authorized indefinite detentions of immigrants, and widened the investigative authority of law enforcement. The president had directed that the FBI would be the preeminent counterterrorism agency within the United States government. The president was determined to identify and defeat the terrorists. The tools within this legislation enabled the Justice Department and the FBI to do exactly that.

The FBI was now empowered to gather foreign intelligence information from both U.S. and non-U.S. citizens, to obtain sneak-and-peak search warrants (the recipient is not notified until after the search), roving wiretaps, and national security letters (NSLs). Many of these measures were ultimately challenged, and either through legislative modification or judicial rulings, were modified or struck down.

The NSLs seemed to generate the greatest public outcry. Just the notion that the FBI, without a warrant, could identify the literature private citizens were reading frightened many. The concern over the potential abuse of these new investigative powers undoubtedly echoed the anxiety felt during Joe McCarthy's time. Thoughtful people with an appreciation of history recalled the cultural, legal, and political impact of those tumultuous years. Uncorroborated accusations, blacklists, formal government inquiry into the loyalty of citizens or what they were reading—all were manifestations of an abuse of legislative authority. It was understandable that some citizens worried about the potential violation of civil liberties and would be concerned about the potential abuse of executive authority. Professional librarians reacted with outrage, arguing it was nobody's business whether patrons are reading Danielle Steele or a manual on how to build a nuclear bomb. The reality was that the FBI wasn't at all interested in what Joan Q. Citizen was taking out on a three-week loan. It did want to know what was on the reading list of suspected terrorists.

I often heard objections to the expanded federal power firsthand. In the effort to get the word out about homeland security, we took part in a number of public forums around the country coordinated by the Council for Excellence in Government, a highly respected Washington-based nonpartisan nonprofit. At every forum, during question-and-answer sessions, comments came from the audience about the Patriot Act. The fear that it was trampling rights guaranteed by the U.S. Constitution was raised at every meeting. My usual approach was to wait—to allow full venting on the subject. And then I would ask the audience member, "Which of your rights is being trampled?" Most people couldn't come up with an answer. The few who did feared the FBI knocking at the door and asking, "Why did you borrow books on explosives and Osama bin Laden?"

One of the unique and least appreciated safeguards of our democracy is the constant internal review of programs and procedures. The Patriot Act required certain preconditions be met before a national security letter could be issued. The General Accounting Office determined in an investigation that the FBI, though it has internal checks to prevent abuse, used NSLs in scores of cases where it shouldn't have. Director Robert Mueller took immediate steps to correct the problem.

The key here, as in other categories covered by the Patriot Act, was public trust, and fine lines between privacy and security in a democracy under threat of attack. There is a natural, healthy, and predictable reluctance of average citizens to give their government indiscriminate law-enforcement powers without some preclearance or overview. We should be distrustful of government's reach when it comes to civil liberties and privacy. For two hundred years Americans have died on battlefields around the world in the defense of freedom. Although presidents Abraham Lincoln (suspension of habeas corpus) and Franklin D. Roosevelt (detention of citizens of Japanese descent), under the guise of emergency powers, used their executive authority to institute practices clearly unconstitutional, precedent does not immunize such actions from scrutiny and criticism.

Any new authority conferred on our intelligence and law enforcement communities to combat extremists will and should be subject to intense public and private scrutiny. We should expect no less. As we consider the means that we have—military, political, economic, legal—to combat this new enemy, the public's engagement should be encouraged, not condemned. We must never forget that, in America, disagreement is not disloyalty and unity does not require unanimity. That is another cherished freedom, the freedom of speech.

We understood that the extremist attacks and the new reality they created would require new offensive and defensive measures to protect the country. We knew we would be compelled to adopt new security measures, practices, and programs to meet our responsibility to secure America. Within the department, an informal three-part test emerged to assess each and every one of them. A passing grade required a perfect score. Two out of three wasn't good enough.

Will the new measure make us safer?

Will it be consistent with the Constitution and the rule of law?

Will it have good or bad economic consequences for our country?

And while we would be subject to scrutiny and criticism regardless of the perfect score, knowing that the measure had passed this test provided a comfort level about doing the right thing. However, we were accountable publicly for all security measures regardless of origin.

After revelations of domestic spying by the intelligence and law enforcement communities, Congress, in 1978, passed legislation that created a special court whose proceedings and rulings are secret, but to which applications must be made to authorize electronic or physical searches to obtain foreign intelligence information. The Foreign Intelligence Surveillance Act (FISA) became another political lightning rod and focal point for debating constitutional protections and responsibilities. It prescribed procedures for physical and electronic surveillance as it related to "foreign powers" and "agents of foreign powers" (a definition that included foreign citizens). It was the basic framework for the intelligence community to gather information about people threatening to harm the United States. The Patriot Act took into account that the 9/11 terrorists were neither foreign powers nor agents of foreign powers, that is, they were not state sponsored. The act therefore expanded the definition of surveillance targets.

The technological means of gathering such information in 1978 had been rendered obsolete with the passage of time and the dramatic changes within the telecommunications industry, including electronic intercepts. The first cell phones had only been in the hands of the public for limited testing for one year. It wasn't wiretapping as the public imagined it or Congress had intended in 1978. The way the media covered the story, you would have thought that Robert Mueller and Tom Ridge were listening intently on earphones, drinking cold coffee, as the tapes rolled inside a commercial van marked Ridge Catering parked outside the apartment of a suspect.

The 1978 legislation was static, but the new surveillance technology was dynamic. And the enemy was unlike any the country had previously encountered. The president argued that the oath of office in which he swore to "preserve, protect, and defend the Constitution" was an acceptance of the responsibility to provide for the common defense. That was the only authority needed to deploy technology allowing for more sophisticated intrusions, making use of satellites and supercomputers and digital methods of discovering key words or numbers that might lead investigators to a target.

In time, it became clear that the President had authorized the National Security Agency to exercise its authority without applying for the requisite warrants. The administration had argued that the FISA law could reasonably be interpreted to allow for these expanded powers because the nature of the threat to America had changed, and there was a need to respond much more quickly than ordinary court procedures allowed. The administration may have had a strong point here, but in carrying out its own legal interpretation and keeping it a secret, the long-term effect presented an appearance of employing unauthorized power.

So it should not have surprised anyone that once the practice became known, citizens and public figures of all political persuasions voiced strong objections and concerns. And yet, astonishingly, some reacted in what I believe to be an even more troublesome fashion. I had several people admit to me they had no objection to the government listening to their conversations. They weren't doing anything wrong, and if the government listening in kept them safe, they were willing to accept the practice.

Do you remember the scene in the Batman movie *The Dark Knight,* where Morgan Freeman voices strong objection to eavesdropping on all of Gotham City in order to find and capture the Joker? He agrees to oversee the effort and vows to resign when he's finished. In Gotham, the end justifies the means. Not in the United States. The price is too high.

The Fourth Amendment to the Constitution is unambiguous:

> The right of the people to be secure in their persons, houses, papers, and effects, against unreasonable searches and seizures, shall not be violated, and no Warrants shall issue, but upon probable cause, supported by Oath or affirmation, and particularly describing the place to be searched, and the persons or things to be seized.

Under no circumstances can we voluntarily surrender a constitutionally protected right. Thomas Jefferson and our Constitution describe these rights as "inalienable." And as previously mentioned, Benjamin Franklin cautioned: "They who give up essential liberty to obtain a little temporary safety, deserve neither liberty nor safety."

After I left the administration, the White House inquired if I could publicly support the President's use of FISA. I said I could and would but felt it was imperative the White House work with Congress to amend the FISA statute to comport with the new electronic means of surveillance and the original congressional intent. At that point they lost interest in having this discussion. I never got a call to defend their use of FISA.

Congress had every right to conclude the executive branch was evading the law. At the heart of the objection was its concern that the program exceeded legislative intent and constitutional authority. The administration's philosophy—if you're not with us, you're against us—sent a message beyond the original intention of the Patriot Act, which was to demonstrate resolve and unity in the face of an external threat. That's what was needed, and that's what occurred. But as time went on, critics claimed that a major motivation behind many administration initiatives was not so much concluding the war on terror as gaining political advantage. Republicans took full advantage of the fact that their party was clearly the strongest on national defense and security issues. Not only that, but any softness on the issue—for example, standing up for personal rights—was not only unwise but unpatriotic. The president didn't help matters when he argued that if lawmakers were against this new electronic program they were also opposed to catching terrorists.

Neither did the media with few exceptions go out of its way to present nuance nor explain complexity. Cable television talk shows took extreme sides—shouting matches yielded high ratings but very little thoughtful discourse. Various publications resorted to hyperbole and oversimplification. One argued that opponents of going to war in Iraq were part of the "axis of appeasement," comparing them to Neville Chamberlain at Munich.

The darkest possibilities of the politics of terrorism became obvious in the summer and fall of 2002 as the midterm elections approached. Members of my own political party carried out a campaign of shameless character assassination.

A heated campaign for U.S. Senate developed in Georgia between the incumbent, Max Cleland, a Democrat, and challenger Saxby Chambliss, a Republican, who was at the time serving in the House of Representatives.

Cleland was a war hero. At Khe Sanh, where a key battle was fought during the Vietnam War, he was severely injured by a grenade and lost three limbs. Nevertheless, in the years afterward, his physical handicap was no impediment to public service. But in the wake of 9/11, Cleland's votes against creating the Department of

Homeland Security came back to haunt him. He specifically objected to measures that would give the secretary greater flexibility to hire and fire workers than existing civil service principles allowed.

Chambliss's campaign, then, used this as evidence that Cleland was unpatriotic, and way too soft on national defense. In a campaign commercial, Osama bin Laden's photo was shown followed by a portrait of Cleland—implying that the two were somehow in cahoots, or at least of like minds. Cleland described this tactic as "like a mackerel—it shines and stinks at the same time." It stuck with voters, and Cleland, though having been heavily favored early on, went down to defeat.

It was an early and brutal example of playing the patriotism card, and set a new standard for low. But the tactic worked, and the GOP picked up a Senate seat. But in the end it was very much a pyrrhic victory. The accusation that we were playing politics was something we dealt with often, and the Georgia campaign gave those accusations a basis in fact.

As the threat warning system was introduced and became part of the daily crawl of the round-the-clock news networks, we knew at OHS, and later at DHS, that we could easily be accused of playing politics by raising the threat level.

Many observers, including those in the media and most Democrats, believed that the Republican Party had used terrorism to leverage political support. After all, Karl Rove and the reelection team decided to ride counterterrorism and national security to victory in the 2004 reelection campaign. Opponents charged that the president benefited politically whenever he turned the nation's attention to national security. Indeed, that phenomenon was quantified by a Cornell University study that tracked 131 Gallup polls between 2001 and 2004 and found that the president's approval rating increased by nearly three percentage points each time the government issued a terror alert. That may not sound like much, but as someone who won his first election by 729 votes, I know that a small percentage could provide a huge competitive advantage and be the difference between winning and losing in a tight race.

For our part, I was convinced that if we were ever found to be playing politics in homeland security, we would lose the trust of the public and undermine our reason for being. I had been happy to join the list of cabinet officers—including the attorney general, the secretary of defense, and secretary of state—who are not traditionally invited to party nominating conventions. This practice was intended to keep those critical posts apart from the political fray, as they should be.

In spite of allegations of playing politics, as time went on, our office was more often than not the most reluctant to raise the threat level. Despite perception to the contrary, the White House couldn't, as a matter of course, call us up and say, "Go to orange, Tom." First, we would never have done so regardless of where the order originated. There would have been mass resignations, and no change in the threat level.

Let me make it very clear. I was never directed to do so no matter how many analysts, pundits, or critics say so. Secondly, the threat advisory system approved in 2002 created a system that included cabinet members whose consensus drove the recommendation. No one, not even the president, can unilaterally alter the threat level.

The politics of terrorism played out in other ways as well. We wanted to learn more about the kind of pathogens that terrorists might use, but our early efforts to carve funds out of the budgets of the Centers for Disease Control and the National Institutes of Health were frustrated. The CDC and NIH were getting billions every year for research and development, so we proposed setting aside a small percentage of those dollars to develop countermeasures to respond to potential biological attacks. Those who argue that the federal government is more reactive than proactive can surely point to what happened here as classic. Nobody was against the idea of trying to outwit terrorists, of course; it was merely a question of what agency was going to pay for it. Both the CDC and the NIH and their patrons on the Hill objected to setting aside any of *their* money for this purpose. Ultimately, we sought and were awarded a separate appropriation. Everybody wanted to take credit for keeping the country safe, but actually sacrificing something, financial and otherwise, to do that was another matter.

Actually, one of the most vivid examples of politicizing homeland security occurred after I left office. Even now, people assume that as the official responsible for the security of the United States against terrorist attacks, I would have been fervently opposed to Arab management of port facilities located in the United States. This circumstance nearly occurred early in 2006. But this presumption only serves to illustrate that protecting the homeland requires thinking that may seem counterintuitive. In fact, when we turned thumbs down on Dubai Ports World purchasing port facilities in the United States, we sent the wrong signal to an ally and to the global economic community.

The matter of maritime security has been of concern since 9/11. Commentators and editorial writers were not shy about pointing out the holes in security. The Council on Foreign Relations released a persuasive report in the fall of 2002 that concluded, "A year after 9/11, America remains dangerously unprepared to prevent and respond to a catastrophic terrorist attack on U.S. soil." This view was not that of professional skeptics. Among the panel members were two former secretaries of state (George Shultz and Warren Christopher), two retired chairmen of the Joint Chiefs of Staff (Admiral William J. Crowe and General John W. Vessey), and a former FBI director (William F. Webster). They took specific notice of the maritime world.

America's seaports were highly vulnerable. The efforts to improve airport and air cargo security after the 9/11 attacks overshadowed the potential for attacks through shipping containers, boats, and container trucks.

The report pointed out that 95 percent of the trade from outside North America to the United States moves by sea, but vulnerability studies for the nation's fifty largest ports were still years from being completed. A catastrophic attack at one of those ports, the report predicted, could shut down American trade and cripple a large portion of the nation's economy. It concluded, "If an explosive device were loaded in a container and set off in a port, it would almost automatically raise concern about the integrity of the 21,000 containers that arrive in U.S. ports each day. A three to four week closure of U.S. ports would bring the global container industry to its knees." Indeed, in the Port of New York and New Jersey alone 11,000 vessels carrying three million shipping containers, 560,000 automobiles, and nearly 30 billion gallons of oil and petroleum products move in and out annually.

The council recommended developing global standards for security at loading centers for containers and other measures (instead of waiting until they arrive in port). And it managed to focus the nation's attention for a while on an issue that had once been ignored.

Moreover, as those who worked on the report and those of us in the OHS well knew, it wasn't simply a matter of the contents of unloaded containers sitting dockside. We knew that it was entirely possible that terrorists who wanted to use the shipping lanes to deliver weapons of mass destruction didn't need to come ashore and offload. The detonation of a nuclear device as the vessel approached a major harbor would result in the devastation the terrorists sought.

But what to do? After all, in the course of ordinary commerce— keeping the flow of goods, the market for employment, and the overall economy healthy—requires robust port operations. We needed a process in place that was generally reliable and efficient, using the proven technology, and a team of inspectors that was well trained and dedicated to the task.

We quickly devised a risk management system of container inspection that, as a strategy, pushes the perimeter of defense as far from our own ports as possible. It had the additional advantage of demonstrating that homeland security requires a foreign policy that embraces not only traditional allies but those nations with which we have had difficult relationships. Any soldier will tell you that as part of combat strategy, the defensive perimeter should be pushed as far out as possible.

Our plan, named the Container Security Initiative and developed by Robert Bonner, the head of Customs, former commissioner of the Drug Enforcement Agency, and former federal judge, was to put in place an inspection system in the largest fifty-eight ports that regularly ship to the United States, including those in Singapore, Yokohama, Hong Kong, Rotterdam, Hamburg, and, yes, Dubai. Those ports could become transfer stations for goods from Pakistan, Afghanistan, Iran, and many other exporting countries that are known to harbor terrorists but who also engage in legitimate business practices crucial to their economies and our own. It was important and delicate business that required buy-in from our foreign partners while at the same time developing as everywhere else in our work, a risk management approach to enhancing security.

It is impossible to examine fully the contents of every container. To do so would greatly impede the flow of goods; in short, it would cripple international shipping and economic chaos would follow, which was one of the effects we were trying to avoid. Shipping is one of those areas where the technology of detection will continue to play a most significant role in limiting the threat. Congress has mandated that all cargo containers be screened, and I believe that in a few years we will have the capability to inspect all containers and to detect nuclear and radiological material without impeding the flow of goods through ports.

One of the first countries to accept our earliest inspection abroad was Dubai. Indeed, it was the very first Arab country to do so, and it even agreed to absorb the cost of these inspections.

Several of our traditional trade partners in Europe did not agree to this program as quickly as Dubai did. To those who are still stuck in Eurocentric thinking, this refusal is probably shocking. Indeed, in these days of delicate political, trade, and energy issues, we learn more and more about the often subtle and sometimes clear opportunities we have with partners we once could never have imagined.

Dubai is one of those potential partners. A country of less than two million people, and one of the seven emirates in the United

Arab Emirates, it had emerged as a world business hub. The transaction that caused the political stir arose when its state-owned
company Dubai Ports World agreed to pay $6.8 billion for Penin-
sular and Oriental Steam Navigation Company, a British outfit
that, through a subsidiary, P&O Ports North America, operated
shipping terminals in a few American seaports. Among other projects, the company ran the New York City Passenger Ship Terminal,
owned a 50 percent interest in the Port Newark Container Terminal,
and had an interest in a port with which I am very familiar, Philadelphia.

The news of the Dubai Ports World deal was enough to cause
an uproar in 2006, a congressional election year. Two years earlier,
President Bush had won reelection narrowly and since that time
the war in Iraq and related issues (Abu Ghraib, Guantánamo, etc.),
as well as the tragically bungled federal response to Hurricane Katrina, had greatly diminished his job approval ratings, and had
made fellow Republicans feel vulnerable. One tactic that was still
working for Republicans was seizing on defense and security issues in a way that Democrats hadn't. Republican Representative
Peter King of New York became one of the early critics of the Dubai
Ports deal. "This can't be treated in a pre-9/11 way," he told the
media. "There was a tone deafness here that indicates they didn't
show the level of concern that it warranted."

But it was the Democrats who aggressively seized the moment
and correctly anticipated the country's uninformed view of the
deal. I remember seeing Charles Schumer, New York's senior senator, conducting an interview on this potential purchase. A smart
and agile partisan, Schumer saw a rare political opportunity: a way
to position Democrats to the right of Republicans on port security.
And he didn't miss the chance. They say that in Washington the
most dangerous territory is between a United States senator and a
television camera. Schumer used his few minutes on network television to cast aspersions on the deal, on the Bush Administration,
and on Arabs in general.

He said that he was concerned that the company could be infiltrated by terrorists with designs on exploiting the vulnerability

of American ports. He noted that the September 11 attacks were financed in part by money that had passed through banks in the United Arab Emirates.

While that may have been true, it was also true that we had no evidence that the government of the country or Dubai Ports World had anything to do with planning or carrying out the attack. It was true that Ziad Jarrah, the man who flew United Flight 93 into the Pennsylvania countryside, passed through Dubai in early January 2001 on the way to other Middle East destinations. But there was never any indication that officials in Dubai knew anything about the terrorist plans.

The issue here is that, in an atmosphere of intense politics, Schumer's protest struck a sensitive nerve and ultimately killed the deal. Schumer had beaten the administration at its own game of using national security as a political weapon. The companies involved in the transaction and their political advisers must have had a political tin ear not to understand that this would become a hot topic.

The administration spent no time informing the Congress that the terminals being purchased by Dubai Ports were not—as many members of the House and Senate believed—currently owned by a company in Houston; they were owned by a company in the United Kingdom. By the time the facts became known to the Congress, the deal was dead. At the time there was great concern about maritime security generally, but this deal could have been consummated if the parties had taken the time to engage lawmakers in a more strategic and thoughtful way.

After all, the maritime industry is a global enterprise. Many of our port terminals and practically the entire international shipping fleet are operated by foreign entities. Owners and managers do not set security requirements. They are obliged to follow those set by the U.S. Coast Guard and related agencies. American longshoremen would continue to load and unload the cargo, not foreigners. The campaign against Dubai Ports World was a clear case of political gamesmanship. And if you disagree, you should know that during subsequent negotiations between the Bush administration and the United Arab Emirates on a deal that would allow nuclear fuel and components to be sent to the UAE, Schumer never uttered a word of protest. Shouldn't the fact that the UAE trades with Iran be a source of concern?

This successful political ploy ignored the reality that America's future security and prosperity is now and forevermore tied to the rest of the world. We become more dependent and interdependent every day. Foreign investment and ownership in the global economy is inevitable and essential. Spending by foreign investors in the United States increased 67 percent in 2007, reaching more than $275 billion. It followed an increase of 81 percent in 2006. Manufacturing led the way, with foreign investments in transportation, finance, and real estate also being significant. In the current economic downturn, no country is capable of escaping from this recession while the rest of the world continues to suffer from it.

We were not made more secure by blocking the Dubai transaction. We sent a signal to the rest of the world to proceed with caution as they considered investing in the United States. Surely that signal has become several degrees colder with the Wall Street debacle of 2008. Our security and economic interests were not advanced by rejecting this transaction. These worlds are truly bound together, unless undone by the politics of terrorism.

7

BEHIND THE SCENES

Politics and poker . . .
Neither game's for children, either game is rough, . . .

—JERRY BOCK AND SHELDON HARNICK'S'
Fiorello!

In February 1993 two unrelated events occurred that, in hindsight, signaled where my passion for America would lead me.

The first event affected only me and my family. I had been elected six times to the House of Representatives, and I enjoyed my job. I considered it a great privilege to be a member of Congress, but I had my own term limit in the back of my mind. As I increasingly understood, a representative's ability to affect public policy is limited. In Congress, you're one of 535. Each member is independently elected. Each has a constituency to be served. Securing agreement on legislation is difficult.

I decided I would run for governor. A dozen years inside the Beltway were enough for me. So I set my sights on Harrisburg and the governor's office, because, in my view, it was a better fit for me and the programs I wanted to promote. But I knew I had to announce early—nearly two years before the 1994 election—in order to have any chance. My name was probably known to 95 percent of the people who lived in my northwestern Pennsylvania district and maybe 10 percent statewide. That would have to grow.

I knew well that the reality of running a campaign is very different from the fantasy. A couple of years earlier, I had considered becoming the Republican candidate for governor, and had actually gained some support. In the end, however, the Republican Party bosses were looking only for somebody who was credible—a long shot to run against a popular incumbent, Democrat Bob Casey. There was no sentiment that the Republican candidate could actually win. I was not interested in being a credible candidate; I wanted to win. So there was no point in keeping my hat in the ring. But I felt that I'd have a legitimate shot in the 1994 election if I could get the word out early and build support around the state. In those days, the issues on my agenda were the traditional concerns of state government—the economy, the environment, education, and the like. Terrorism was not in my legislative or political lexicon.

Less than a month after my announcement the second event so important to my future took place. Of course I did not see the connection at the time. A terrorist attack on the World Trade Center should have awakened me—all of us—to what was coming but it did not. In the hours before the attack on February 26, 1993, the perpetrators, members of a radical Islamic sect, sent a letter to New York media outlets outlining three demands: an end to U.S. aid to Israel, an end to U.S. diplomatic relations with Israel, and a pledge by the United States to end interference "with any of the Middle East countries' interior affairs." The letter went on to admit that the World Trade Center bombing was an act of terrorism, but that this was justified because "the terrorism that Israel practices (which America supports) must be faced with a similar one."

At 12:19 P.M. on that winter day a car bomb exploded in the garage of the North Tower. Made of urea nitrate and hydrogen gas, it packed an enormous punch. The device was intended to bring down the building and at the same time destroy the South Tower. The buildings did not fall, but the terrorists did manage to kill six people and injure more than a thousand. Afterward, one of the plotters, clearly disappointed with the results, sent another letter. "We promise you that next time it will be very precise and the

World Trade Center will continue to be one [of] our targets unless our demands have been met."

For a while, America was shocked by what had happened, but quickly it went back to business as usual. Even I, a public official charged with the duty of protecting constituents, considered the World Trade Center bombing to be an aberration—the expression of the aspirations of a zealot—one of those oddities that required no sweeping change in our planning or defense strategies.

When a little more than two years later the obviously deranged Timothy McVeigh exploded a truck loaded with explosives in front of the Alfred P. Murrah Federal Building in Oklahoma City and killed 168 people, including nearly two dozen children, the country had the same reaction. This was horrific, but it wasn't a phenomenon that, on a day-to-day basis, we had to worry about. Life's ill fortunes are numerous enough. Don't take on any extra anxiety by harboring fears of terrorism.

The views of some were changed by what happened in Tokyo that same season. Members of the Aum Shinrikyo cult (also known as the Supreme Truth Sect) placed packages containing a chemical mixture on the floors of five trains in the Tokyo subway system. Each bag was then punctured with sharply honed umbrella tips, and the material inside spilled onto the floor of the subway cars as the trains neared the center of Tokyo. The liquid, sarin, a vaporous nerve agent developed by the Nazis in the 1930s, spread through the trains. It is five hundred times more toxic than cyanide gas, and on that day it injured nearly six thousand subway riders and killed twelve of them.

By then, I had been installed in Harrisburg. In an uphill battle I won the nomination and then the general election. Even so, the legislative agendas at the capital did not include terrorism.

This is not to say there weren't those in positions of authority who predicted such acts. In the years after the Tokyo bombing— and as attacks on U.S. embassies increased, even as acts of terrorism proliferated around the globe—Congress examined our capacities as a nation to defend ourselves against such attacks. The U.S. Commission on National Security/21st Century chaired by former U.S. senators Gary Hart, Democrat of Colorado, and Warren Rudman, Republican of New Hampshire, was an independent panel created by Congress in 1998. It released its initial report, *Roadmap for National Security*, on February 1, 2001. The U.S. Congressional Advisory Panel to Assess Domestic Response Capabilities for Terrorism Including Weapons of Mass Destruction, chaired by former Virginia governor Jim Gilmore and known as the Gilmore Commission, functioned from 1999 to 2003 and released several reports to both the Clinton and Bush administrations. Both Commissions issued reports on behalf of Congress warning that the nature of threats to America was changing. In the first paragraph of its conclusions, released in 1998, Hart-Rudman was eerily prescient:

> The combination of unconventional weapons proliferation with the persistence of international terrorism will end the relative invulnerability of the U.S. homeland to catastrophic attack. A direct attack on American citizens on American soil is likely in the next quarter century. The risk is not only death and destruction but a demoralization that could undermine U.S. global leadership. In the face of this threat, the U.S. has no coherent or integrated governmental structures.

The report called for what became, in effect, the Department of Homeland Security, although it was not as sweeping in its recommendations, and did not anticipate such a large reorganization.

What happened, specifically, as a result of Hart-Rudman, was what happens to so many federal reports that consume forests, time, resources, and shelf space but catch the attention of almost no one. When it was made public, the country was focused on the impeachment proceedings against President Bill Clinton. A stain on a dress, a wagging finger at the camera, the meaning of "is," and behavior in the White House were the matters at the center of public discourse. The 1998 congressional campaigns seldom if ever mentioned terrorism as an issue.

Even an ominous event on our northwestern border in December 1999 failed to alert lawmakers and the public to the inevitable. Days before the Millennium New Year's Eve, Customs inspector Diana Dean stopped a driver coming into the United States from Canada. His was the last car, a Chrysler 300, to come off the last ferry from British Columbia that day in Port Angeles, Washington. She noticed the driver's suspicious behavior, beads of perspiration on a cold evening, and unusual answers to her questions. Acting on her instincts and training, she asked the driver to step out of his car and open his trunk. When she and her coworkers opened the spare tire compartment they discovered what proved to be the makings of an explosive device. The driver was apprehended as he tried to flee. He was later convicted in the case known as the Millennium Bomber. Dean's action saved perhaps hundreds of lives.

There were some in the government who clearly focused on the emerging threat, and tried to warn the White House and Congress, but their entreaties were not heard. The Clinton administration didn't make counterterrorism a major priority, and when George W. Bush took office in 2001, it was, and would remain over the next eight months, a secondary matter.

The attack on the World Trade Center in September 2001 was a clarion call for President Bush and his closest advisors. There was an obvious need for high-profile change, and by appointing me to the new post of assistant to the president for homeland security, the president took the first major public step in response to 9/11 as he made combating Islamic terrorism his highest priority.

Skeptics argued that OHS would be nothing but window dressing. After all, in my job in the White House, I had no real budgetary control, no legions of workers, no authority to make anything happen unilaterally. The strong and widely shared sense of urgency about our security supported the proposition that the new position within the White House could get the job done. It quickly became clear, however, that though our mission was critical, our resources were nonexistent. The momentum was building for a border-centric agency. Despite the resistence I'd experienced from cabinet members in earlier meetings, a new department became the goal—details to be determined.

We could see that from the competing agendas of deputies who attended regular meetings of the new Homeland Security Council (HSC). The idea at the deputies meetings was to narrow the issues so they would be ready for discussion by the cabinet members of the HSC. Either Richard Falkenrath or my deputy, Admiral Steve Abbot, presided. They reported to me the difficulty they encountered getting things done. The meetings were unwieldy and too often unproductive. Everybody wanted an equal voice. Everybody wanted veto power. Everybody was suspicious, and rightly so, that precious resources from their departments would be siphoned away by the White House. These participants weren't in a position to speak for their cabinet secretaries who, after all, woke up each morning thinking primarily about their respective responsibilities, not homeland security. It became clear to us that we needed to pull together a core group of government agencies that could focus upon and rally around homeland security as its primary mission.

While I don't believe the president had such an organization in mind when he created the White House office, it was clear from day one that the president sought to take back the power of the executive branch that, in his view, had been improperly ceded to Congress over the years. To do that, he needed a strong cabinet around him, and to support that cabinet, it was politically necessary to keep things as they were, at least until the president himself— not Congress or the media—decided there was a need for a change. Even so, he had no higher priority after 9/11 than taking the measures necessary to defend the country from terrorists, and this might well require sweeping changes.

Against this backdrop were several political realities. First, Congress was increasingly upset over its lack of oversight over the direction of billions of dollars—though not in my budget—over which I had influence. Accordingly, a *New York Times* editorial said: "Tom Ridge . . . is in the news a lot. This month, he was in Mexico to negotiate a new border agreement. The other day he was unveiling a new color-coded warning system on threats to public safety. He holds news conferences about the administration's plans to defend the nation against terrorism."

The litany of events was followed with a criticism of my failure to appear before Congress and a demand that the Bush administration "unmuzzle me."

As a compromise, in July 2002 the White House sent OBM director Mitch Daniels to testify before Congress. It did not go well. Members of Congress became frustrated with Daniels's answers, particularly regarding my unavailability to testify. One member of the Appropriations Committee, David Obey, Democrat of Wisconsin, warned Daniels, "No information, no money." He said the administration as a whole had a "severe attitude problem." Afterward, Senator Byrd, usually very tactful, referred to Daniels, a former pharmaceutical company executive senior staffer in the Senate and new governor of Indiana, as "Little Caesar." Clearly, relations between Congress and the administration were deteriorating. Simultaneously, in certain ways after 9/11, the shortcomings of homeland security–related agencies gained visibility.

The INS, almost on cue, provided the primary example. That agency, which was then under the Department of Justice, had long been criticized as ineffective, a charitable description. Part of the problem was inevitable: Our national policy on immigration was (and remains) confusing and full of contradictions, assuming you agree America even has an immigration policy (which I don't). It also suffered from the lack of up-to-date technology and inadequate funding. In the midst of this confusion, in March 2002, the INS did the unthinkable—providing a clear and timely signal that some dramatic correction had to be made.

One of the important tasks the agency performed was the issuance of visas to foreign students, an average of 600,000 each year. By its own estimation, the capacity of the INS to keep track of those who entered the country on such visas was antiquated, and the results inaccurate, or worse. The agency's incompetence was demonstrated when two visas were sent to a flight training school in Florida six months *after* 9/11. They were for Mohammed Atta and Marwan al-Shehhi, two of the dead hijackers.

The event was so shocking that Congress immediately held an investigative hearing. Commissioner James W. Zigler acknowledged the embarrassment to the agency but described the error as a case of bad timing. Lost in the testimony—because the news of issuing the visas had been so shocking—was the fact that at the time Atta and al-Shehhi applied for their student visas, there was no information at the State Department or anywhere else that they were potential terrorists. Though the act itself—the issuing of these visas—caught the public's eye, and rightly so, there was a deeper problem.

Under intense questioning by members of Congress, Zigler said, "My goal—and I think I can safely say that the administration's goal at this point—is to at least start the process of unraveling the service and the enforcement side of this agency, because regardless of what happens it is clear . . . that the service and the enforcement side of this agency needs to be unraveled, and there needs to be a change of command. And to the extent that we can start doing that, it will facilitate almost anything that the mind can imagine in terms of reform." In short INS became the whipping boy for a fragmented system that had fallen tragically short of protecting us.

At the Office of Homeland Security, our ability to deal with this and other crises was limited, and everyone knew it. There was universal agreement that OHS was an office that often had to rely on smoke and mirrors to undertake some of the most daunting tasks in the federal government.

By this point, however, we had begun to make some inroads, and quietly exert some influence inside the establishment. A case in point was the impact of OHS in what became known as the case of the Lackawanna Six, and specifically the expertise and persistence of a single individual.

Colonel Joe Rozek served over twenty-nine years in the U.S. Army, most of it in the Special Forces (Green Berets). Before we began working together, he had a senior position at the Defense Department and served as the subject matter expert for combating terrorism on the vice president's National Domestic Preparedness Review Group. In his capacity as my de facto intelligence officer in OHS, surrounded by a staff of one, he tracked daily reports from the intelligence community, including the Drug Enforcement Agency. He had a unique perspective with regard to the new threat America was facing. He frequently observed that not all criminals are terrorists, but all terrorists are criminals. His army experience taught him that outfits such as Hamas, and, as he would subsequently conclude, Al Qaeda, would raise money through various unsavory means, including drug running. While extremists themselves may not take drugs, they understand the revenue-generating capacity of the marketplace.

He outlined for me his rationale to examine reported activity in northwestern New York. He was aware that several individuals with Yemeni backgrounds had been apprehended attempting to take large sums of money out of the country to the Middle East. He noted that the reports from the Buffalo, New York, region of several drug-related arrests involved Yemenis. He tried to persuade the FBI to view this activity as being potentially terrorist related. His argument failed, at the outset. His FBI counterparts considered it strictly a criminal matter not related to terrorism. He persisted. After a couple of more meetings, he broke through the conventional approach.

In time, members of the group pleaded guilty to charges of providing material support to Al Qaeda and were sentenced to terms ranging from eight to ten years in federal prison. The FBI took credit for the bust. But even they understood the contributions of Joe Rozek and OHS.

The president was aware that our effort to build the Federal Border Administration through the 2003 budget had been rejected. Neither his cabinet nor Congress was supportive. But with the Gilmore Commission, Hart-Rudman reports, the Lieberman legislation, and the controversy over whether I should testify before Congress, the White House turned toward a political inevitability. It would be better for the administration to be the architect of the new department rather than allowing Congress to take the lead. So, with the president's tacit approval, we held a series of meetings over several weeks in secure areas of the White House. In order to maintain secrecy and to streamline the process the small group included only some of the most trusted policy and legal minds in the White House. The purpose, process, and participants were known to but a handful of us. We all knew the realities of the Washington fishbowl. You can trust the cabinet not to leak the fact that we might have a stealth bomber flying over Iraq, but if you're threatening to take away authority, finances, or personnel from a department and it's discovered, *The Washington Post* will learn about it in a matter of minutes.

A variety of ideas were discussed over that time, everything from less ambitious plans—a "drug czar" minimal structure—to a new cabinet department. As time went on, a consensus emerged. Protecting the country from attack had become the highest priority of the federal government. None of the key decisions that emerged from the group—including the plan to create a new federal department—were leaked.

The ultimate decisions are reflected in the organization of the department. In spite of some internal support to include the FBI, the White House, I think appropriately, said absolutely not. Some thought FEMA should be independent, but the team decided to include it. If a response and recovery unit was not part of the department, you would need to create one. We didn't need two, so it became literally an "all-hazards" FEMA.

Indeed, when the announcement of the plan was delivered on June 6, 2002, at a meeting of the HSC, many key members of the administration expressed frustration that they'd been left in the dark. As Richard Falkenrath recalls, "You never saw so many jaws hit the table, especially those of White House senior officials who are accustomed to being in the loop."

Donald Rumsfeld was told just before addressing the Naval Academy graduating class. Andy Card informed other cabinet members on the day before the news became public. John Ashcroft said if he had known about the plans he would have fought them. Even so, he later acknowledged that he was thrilled to transfer the INS to me. Tommy Thompson was upset about some of the changes, and lobbied successfully to keep certain agencies in Health and Human Services.

On the evening of June 7, President Bush announced in a televised address that he would propose to Congress the creation of a new cabinet position, the most dramatic reorganization of the federal government since 1947, when, in the Truman administration, the National Defense Act took the Air Force out from under army supervision, combined the War and Navy Departments into the Department of Defense, and created the Central Intelligence Agency and National Security Council. The president said, "I do not believe that anyone could have prevented the horror of September 11, yet we now know that thousands of trained killers are plotting to attack us, and this terrible knowledge requires us to act differently."

The new Department of Homeland Security would be composed of nearly 180,000 federal employees, drawn from parts or all of twenty-two units of government, including the Coast Guard, the Secret Service, elements of the Department of Justice, INS, security guards at airports, and Customs. The department would have an initial budget of $37.5 billion. Even so, it was less than the budget of the Department of Education and less than a tenth of what the Department of Defense spends in a year. Though it would be responsible for the security of the homeland, it would not have any control over the CIA or FBI, which would continue as independent agencies and would, according to the plan, be required to provide appropriate intelligence to DHS. We would be a consumer of intelligence, not a generator of it. But the hope was that the new department would provide a fresh eye, one that would review intelligence reports from a different prospective, and plug an existing gap.

Public reaction was, as expected, mixed. An op-ed piece in *The New York Times* by Amy E. Smithson, director of the Chemical and Biological Nonproliferation Project at the Henry L. Stimson Center, contended there "are cheaper and quicker ways to coordinate counterterrorism efforts, without a massive executive branch makeover. . . . A prudent Congress would first try interim steps." Later, an editorial in the paper predicted that I would face "a gargantuan task in making sure the creation of the Department of Homeland Security is something more than the Washington equivalent of rearranging the deck chairs on the *Titanic*."

Though supporting the idea in an editorial, *The Wall Street Journal* reported that "privately many Cabinet officials and agency heads are gnashing their teeth as they see important parts of their budgets and power slip away." In *The Washington Post,* columnist Mary McGrory was critical of the department's scope, calling it "a new federal bureaucracy the size of Texas." The Brookings Institution said that the DHS proposal "merges too many different activities into a single department" and should be significantly scaled back. Even an updated version of Hart-Rudman, which had supported the creation of a department, suggested that the task of protecting the nation was so complicated and expensive that the government's multibillion-dollar efforts would barely dent the problem.

There were other issues to address as well, including labor agreements. For a while, we had to address union complaints that DHS would disregard certain workers' rights that had been negotiated in previous agreements. Federal union leaders said the proposal would diminish the rights of federal employees to form and join unions. This particular assertion troubled me. I had carried a union card, Laborers Local 603, in Erie, Pennsylvania, all through college and the first year of law school. I was never considered, in my public service career, to be antiunion. Indeed, I still fumed at the thought that my father, a nonunion salesman, after putting in nearly thirty years with Armour and Co., was given only two weeks' termination notice and no severance pay. I am aware of the painful and personal impact of companies and institutions that devalue workers.

The legislation to establish the department was, by Washington standards, quickly enacted, but not without rancor. One of the provisions under the microscope was the attempt to limit the legal exposure of companies working on security technology. And there was much wrangling on the issue of labor rights, specifically civil service protections. I argued that to address its mission—one of the most challenging in the federal government—it would need as much flexibility as possible. I told a meeting of business leaders, "The status quo is not enough. We need to get people where they are needed and when they are needed." On its face, these words were taken as a threat to union rights. There was also a fear expressed among Democrats that certain employees would be laid off because they didn't agree with the administration's political leanings. Such a charge was overstated. Union employees had little reason to worry. Their contract protections were strong. As a former union member, these men and women had my respect and support as long as they performed.

I suspect political support is an inquiry that all administrations, Republican or Democratic, make. It's my view that your political affiliation or personal contribution to a candidate of the other party should never be a bar to appointed public service. My approach as governor was generally apolitical. I believe some of my cabinet members in Harrisburg were Democrats. I never inquired. They believed in our mission, enthusiastically supported our agenda, had the experience and ability to perform at the highest level, and were exceptionally loyal to me and supportive of each other. That standard worked extremely well in Pennsylvania.

As the political wrangling proceeded, the media kept an eye on questions of real security. Todd S. Purdum wrote a front-page article in *The New York Times* that began:

> Cockpit doors are stronger, but not all cargo is screened for bombs. The directors of the Federal Bureau of Investigation and the Central Intelligence Agency now jointly brief the President on terrorist threats, but there are still critical gaps in intelligence gathering and analysis. The Super Bowl has become a superfortress, but the local cineplex remains a soft target. The government issues a rolling rainbow of threat alerts, but Congress and the White House are still battling over the creation of an agency to coordinate security. One year after the worst terrorist attacks on United States soil, Americans are safer but still far from safe.

To add to this, pressure was coming from official sources. Former senators Gary Hart and Warren B. Rudman, in an addendum to their report entitled *America Still Unprepared, America Still in Danger,* expressed their frustration that the administration had not yet adopted the sweeping measures necessary to protect the country from terrorism. They accused Washington of taking "symbolic" action while allowing meaningful legislation—such as creation of an effective Department of Homeland Security—to languish in an atmosphere of political bickering. Rudman said, "It's time for action, and if you don't take it, there will be hell to pay."

The political rancor intensified. Senator Phil Gramm, Republican of Texas, said: "It's not that the Democrat leadership loves national security less, it's that they love their political security more. And they are so tied to these public employee labor unions that they're not willing to cross them on issues that have to do with the life and safety of the American people."

Even as this went on, and as issues were resolved in reasonable enough fashion to pass the Homeland Security bill, rumors spread about alternative choices for the first secretary. Richard Armitage's name was prominent. He was the widely regarded deputy secretary of state. Meanwhile, I just did my job, and didn't worry about that. The first inquiry that I had about my willingness to take this job was from Card and Cheney. I said to them, without expressing why, that I needed a couple of days to think about it. My concern was that although OHS had been embraced publicly, we had had to fight for everything. The same could happen with DHS.

On November 19, 2002, the Senate finally approved the bill establishing the new department by a vote of 90 to 9, but not before more compromises were made. A week later, President Bush signed it and announced that I was his choice to lead the new department. The struggle for personnel and space had been a needless distraction and disappointment and I had had enough experience with turf disputes to anticipate a whole lot more. Yet we had developed a national strategy for homeland security, an intellectual blueprint to build a twenty-first-century cabinet agency. If the president was prepared to let me start construction, the only answer was yes.

Even longtime supporters of the effort knew this would be no cakewalk. In referring to the task ahead, Joe Lieberman said, "He has a monumental task in front of him. It's like asking Noah to build the ark after the rain has started to fall."

I was sworn in as a new cabinet member on January 28, 2003, but the doors to our new department, at the Nebraska Avenue

Complex (NAC), didn't open until March 1. I had people scattered all over downtown Washington, an incredible maze of complexity. Since those early days, I've described DHS as a huge holding company that includes a couple of mergers, acquisitions, divestitures, and startups, all going on at the same time. A private sector plan of this magnitude would probably be given nearly a year to work on transition and regulatory requirements. We had barely weeks to merge a variety of agencies—all of them having their unique institutional qualities and ways of doing things—into one body, and, at the same time, meet the mission of protecting citizens from external and internal threats to their safety. All who joined in this task—either because their jobs were shifted to us or because they volunteered—quickly understood and accepted the idea that evenings and weekends were no longer their own, and that we had an almost impossible job to do. Failure was not an option. We had to be right in our work 100 percent of the time; a terrorist had to succeed only once. As the British scholar Paul Wilkinson said, "Fighting terrorism is like being a goalkeeper. You can make a hundred brilliant saves but the only shot that people remember is the one that gets past you."

We addressed the issues of homeland security from a spartan headquarters. The NAC was hardly the ideal location for housing the merger. It happened to be the only site available. It is five miles, and a great deal of traffic, from the White House. It is an understatement to observe that the building needed a lot of work to make it suitable as a headquarters for the new agency. It is a building with many nooks and crannies, with rooms and offices that cascade down hidden stairwells. This was once the home of Mount Vernon Seminary, a school for girls, from 1917 to 1942, before the navy took it over. And yet the complex of buildings had, at least in one sense, housed an appropriate precursor for DHS. In the efforts to break Japanese and German codes during World War II, more than a thousand government cryptologists had worked there.

Once we were installed in this old complex, bringing only a few of the key leaders of the new agency together, we still had to overcome huge deficiencies. The State Department, Department of

Justice, and other agencies had up-to-date technology and labored in facilities tailored, at large expense, for their missions; our facilities were ragtag at best.

While the headquarters' accommodations were less than optimum, the deficiencies didn't diminish anyone's commitment to the mission. An omen of how complicated and demanding that mission would be surfaced on Friday, February 28, 2003, just three days before the department opened its doors at the NAC. Colonel Bill Parrish, my acting operations officer, attended a meeting called by the NSC. It had begun contingency planning around potential military action in Iraq. Verbal warfare with Iraq had been raging for months. The administration had clearly indicated it was prepared to use force. Additional troops had been moved to the Persian Gulf.

Parrish was told of the need to develop a domestic defensive plan in anticipation that, once an attack began, terrorist cells in the United States sympathetic to Saddam Hussein or affiliated with Al Qaeda would attack infrastructure or population centers. It was our responsibility to operationalize a protective umbrella around the country. The NSC even recommended a name for our security plan, "The Perfect Storm." Parrish thought that was strange. *The Perfect Storm* tells the story of a fishing boat captain who ignores weather reports and in failing to give due consideration to the forces of nature condemns himself and his crew to death. We would certainly find a more appropriate name, but the immediate task was to develop a comprehensive plan to "button up the country."

So our first and immediate task, aside from showing everyone where the washrooms were, was to figure out how to secure the public's safety and to get the word out. It would have been easier if we'd had paper for our copy machines.

8

"BUTTONING UP"
AMERICA

Every war when it comes, or before it comes, is represented not as a war but as an act of self-defense against a homicidal maniac.

—GEORGE ORWELL

B ill Parrish arrived at a meeting of the White House Homeland Security Council with a bold and innovative plan. By the time he left the Situation Room that day in early March 2003, he was livid, still disbelieving that he had heard what he had heard.

If there was anybody who logically could be given a heavy responsibility at DHS on the eve of the Iraq war, it was Parrish. When asked to button up the United States—that is, to secure the nation from any hostile response to the invasion—he didn't ask, "How do you 'button up' a country of 300 million people in 3,537,441 square miles?" I can't recall how he responded. I suspect it was simply "Yes, sir!"

Parish was a retired marine colonel who had commanded the U.S. Marine Corps Security Forces. He had been involved in multiple security operations to reinforce U.S. embassies during heightened threat conditions and to provide security to naval ships and other government installations around the world. While accustomed to working in hostile and threatening environments, he was unprepared for an encounter later in his career while continuing his service at the department.

He was, then, a natural choice to fill in for my one-man intelligence "group," Joe Rozek, who was recovering from surgery. It was left to Parrish and his small team to create over a period of a few days an ambitious and practical way of defending the country should terrorists strike on our soil in response to "Shock and Awe." This term would be used later to describe the initial military campaign against Iraq that began on March 21, 2003. "Shock and Awe" is technically known as rapid dominance, a military doctrine based upon the use of overwhelming military capabilities against an enemy to alter their view of the battlefield and undermine their will to fight. It was a concept first introduced in a report to the National Defense University in 1996.

Parrish was the one who changed the name of the NSC plan from the Perfect Storm to Operation Liberty Shield. But much more than that, he had expressed a vision and the particulars of what had to be done. He is one of those rare people in Washington who can call on a wide network of acquaintances to come together for the common good, and he certainly did it here. The extent of his plan looked to me like threat level Orange on steroids. Among the measures it called for were greatly increased security at borders and ports; heightened infrastructure protection focusing on dams, bridges, and power plants; cyberspace patrols; restricting flights over nuclear facilities and certain cities; intensified public health protection; and a readiness campaign involving not only state and local officials but also the private sector, giving businesses a chance to become partners of government in security. A key aspect of this—a provision entirely ignored two years later, after Hurricane Katrina struck—was a detailed and ambitious plan for responding to *any* disaster. For one thing, it specifically staffed all recovery teams and described how these teams would operate in tandem with agencies at the federal, state, and local levels.

There would be, of course, a price for this. We were told to plan Liberty Shield "unconstrained by cost." However, the bean counters at the Office of Management and Budget didn't like that idea and kept demanding we give them a dollar amount. I understood the view. Fiscal responsibility is much of what drew me to the Republican Party in the first place, and as governor I had always subscribed to the policy of making every public dollar count. But we were in uncharted territory here, and we had to come up with our own fiscal route to safety. If *Homeland Security for Dummies* had a chapter that provided a fiscal equation to calculate the precise amount, I would have referred to it. A formula would have made it easier to justify our plans to the bean counters than "We just don't know."

Not having any historical data to go by, or any real sense of what it would take, we nevertheless provided a rough estimate of $10 billion. This, as far as we could determine, might cover costs to federal agencies as well as reimbursements to states and local government. Bill Parrish and I, along with former General Bruce Lawlor, my first chief of staff, who brought a relentless work ethic and organizational, operational, and consequence management experience to these critical early months in the new department, went to the White House for a meeting with Andy Card, Karl Rove, representatives of OMB, and a few others. When I argued for the money, the others in attendance said it was "too much." The push-back was focused on the reimbursement of state and local agencies. I said, "We can't ask or expect governors to be able to pay for what we are asking that they do under Liberty Shield, which is, after all, a federal operation." In the end OMB agreed to $6.8 billion.

This issue remained a constant source of tension between the Department and the White House. I viewed the states as our partners in the national effort to combat terrorism, for it was the federal government that asked them to take on new responsibilities in this new era. My bias obviously was showing. I had served as governor of Pennsylvania for six years, nine months and five days, and I had no doubt that the federal government should assume a substantial part of the additional costs. Federal money should not be used to hire more police or firemen. That is, and always should be, a responsibility of state and local governments. Other costs related to the deployment of state and local personnel for security purposes, as well as for their training and the equipment essential to dealing with the new threat environment, I felt Washington should bear.

Aside from setting the funding, the plan had a few other requirements. Parrish and I presumed, for example, that we could count on a buy-in from a variety of federal agencies. Indeed, this was an early opportunity for all cabinet officers to show the full extent of the teamwork necessary to secure the homeland at a time when nearly everyone was certain Al Qaeda would follow up 9/11 with another spectacular demonstration of inhumanity.

Many members of the cabinet were still far from convinced this was the right thing to do. Grudging acceptance is far different from enthusiastic embrace, and it had its practical costs.

There was not a unanimous stony glare. Some agencies joined our efforts with minimal fuss, but others only after it became clear there was no other choice. Some agencies had security as part of their core missions and had no enthusiasm for the new departments. In each institution, tradition is ingrained, and habits are not easily changed. There was a lot of educating to do quickly in a time of very high tensions. Agency cultures cannot change overnight without consequences, but most attendees understood the stakes and didn't want to be seen as impediments to public safety.

Parrish and I hoped the Pentagon would provide us with trained planners to help us anticipate and respond to internal threats. In the context of all that DOD spends in the course of a year, ours was pocket change, though we knew from our earlier attempts to persuade the department to pay for National Guard deployments that the strings to this enormous purse were tightly held.

With the planning completed, Parrish, accompanied by the first deputy secretary of the department, Gordon England, arranged to present Liberty Shield to the deputies meeting. It was standard procedure to brief the second in command of the relevant agencies and to work out operational details or resolve any differences before taking the matter before the secretaries.

England, a retired Lockheed Martin executive, had been the secretary of the navy before being asked by the White House to move to the department. I always admired his commitment to President Bush and the country. He, like so many others, could have been living a very comfortable, stress-free life, but the call to serve was stronger. Several months later, Rumsfeld pulled him back to the Pentagon to serve as his deputy.

At this meeting the Department of Defense representative announced that his department would not be a part of Liberty Shield. No surprise here; at least DOD was consistent. After he spoke, there was a brief silence in the room. After a moment, the meeting moved on to other issues. But Bill Parrish wouldn't let it go. "Did everyone hear that?" he said. The man who otherwise never seems to be rattled was clearly upset. DOD would provide support, but not at the direction or under the auspices of the fledgling department. Parrish asked, "Does everyone understand that?" To Parrish, and to others involved, it didn't appear to be a matter of finance. Everybody who has ever read a newspaper knows that the Pentagon often demonstrates its remarkable talent for spending money without there being a direct relationship between dollars and value.

The costs related to the kind of support we were seeking from DOD were numbers in the margins of a single hardware acquisition. When it spends, though, Department of Defense does so always with an eye on offense, not defense. "Lean forward" was a favorite saying of Donald Rumsfeld. It was probably a case of authority, of who's in charge. Whatever the reason, we were incredulous. Parrish and I had naïvely thought we were all on the same team, fighting the same fight. In the aftermath of 9/11, the Pentagon had responded with fighter jets to protect the airspace over American cities. But it became clear early on that the Pentagon was reluctant to use its resources within our borders. Ultimately they would again, but they weren't happy about it. The response at the deputies meeting was indicative of what, on many levels, lay ahead, in terms of turf warfare.

(Months later, a Pentagon official visited Parrish with the plea, "Don't shoot the messenger." The Defense Department wanted DHS to reimburse it for the services of intelligence analysts who had been working with us on Liberty Shield. Parrish cleverly responded that he would tally the number of Coast Guard cutters supporting military operations and send the Pentagon a bill for them. "When everything is added up, you'll end up owing us money," he responded. The Pentagon absorbed the cost.)

After the formal HSC meeting ended, a few people remained to begin to develop more comprehensive plans. Representatives from DOD stayed, too, but were told, "Thanks for coming, but there's no reason for you to stay."

Details were hashed out. And when final plans were made, our public affairs office cranked out what some remember as the press release from hell. In fact, it remained a classified document in the days before the Iraq invasion, while it went up and down the line. The White House, of course, weighed in. By the time it got back in the hands of Jeff Karonis, the DHS official who wrote it, it was decorated with an array of insertions, deletions, and arrows. Some who read it thought it revealed too much, that it would provide information that terrorists could use in order to avoid being caught. Others argued for more emphasis on certain features reflecting their own areas of responsibility. As Karonis likes to point out, everybody in Washington is an expert at three things: sports, terrorism issues, and how to do public affairs. In the end, the release did its job, getting the word out to public officials and citizens alike about an unprecedented effort to unify response to a threat.

What Parrish and the department were able to do was nothing short of miraculous. Within the first week of its operation, the department was able to develop a strategic plan and quickly operationalize it. In the process, the rest of the federal government learned that we were empowered to assign roles and responsibilities in the face of threats and had the primary responsibility for coordinating them. We all understood that while we passed this first critical test, our long-term credibility and acceptance as a full partner would only come with relentless effort and consistent quality performance. The foundation had been laid with the success of Liberty Shield.

As it turned out, the response in the United States to the

invasion of Iraq was not violent. Whether the measures initiated by DHS or Justice or the FBI or anyone else were the reason for that we'll never know. That's how it was at the department. Successes were often measured only by life going on as usual. That result doesn't make headlines, but to the men and women who worked long hours behind the scenes it was satisfying.

There was, and remains, a great deal of controversy over the reasons for the invasion of Iraq, and how the war was subsequently conducted. There was, to be sure, criticism of Operation Liberty Shield, particularly from human rights groups objecting to events that occurred that were not a specific part of our plan.

The Justice Department and the FBI, emboldened by the up-graded federal effort to intensify security, made it much harder for foreign nationals to claim political asylum. Many of those arriving from any of the countries thought to be harboring terrorists or suspected of abetting them were detained, and many were sent back. Eleanor Acer, of the Human Rights First Asylum Program, said, "Operation Liberty Shield is targeting the very people who have stood up to, and in some cases been persecuted and tortured by, the same regimes that the U.S. has singled out for condemnation. We have heard the President justify the war against Iraq as a war of liberation, directed not at the Iraqi people but at their leaders. But 'Operation Liberty Shield' will target individuals for detention based solely upon their nationality, including Iraqis. By treating asylum seekers in such a manner, we will certainly not be shielding liberty, but making a mockery of it."

Such criticism was not unexpected, but it was misdirected at us. We were learning as we went along about the challenges of dealing with those who were not soldiers of a sovereign country but captives of a hijacked theology.

When we "stood up" the department (to "stand up" an organization is a term civilian agencies have borrowed from the military, meaning "opened for business.") and combined multiple agencies with different traditional missions, uniforms, pay scales, histories, and cultures, we privately adopted an internal slogan that spoke to unity of effort. "Same Team. Same Fight." It is axiomatic that, regardless of a cabinet member's position on an issue, once the administration has made its decision and set the course, the same sense of unity is expected.

Regardless of the department that took action to reduce the threat of attack, public inquiry about my views was frequent. The fact that neither the department nor I was involved in the decision making was immaterial. Guantánamo and all those attendant issues were of great and continuing interest.

I had absolutely no reservations about the creation of the camp at Gitmo. These were not POWs in the traditional sense. Those apprehended were not soldiers of a sovereign nation. They were zealots who embraced a theology, not a country.

Several months after the opening of the prison I met with a friend over dinner, an army general, who had been involved in many of the interrogations. "Some of those bastards," he said, "should remain on that rock forever." Others, he disclosed, were in the wrong place at the wrong time. We are still wrestling with how to distinguish who is and who is not a terrorist. We still argue about the type of due process, if any, and promise to close the prison without any clear plan of how we will deal with those we do identify as terrorists.

Security trumped all other considerations immediately after 9/11 and during the first several months of our engagement in Iraq. Identifying males within a certain age group from Muslim countries for additional interrogation and or apprehension was racial profiling that many found unacceptable. Nobody particularly relished the idea of detaining people seeking asylum simply based on their country of origin. It conjured up the same idea that is or should be morally repugnant to all, the international version of the highway crime of DWB, Driving While Black. In time, the president through Attorney General Ashcroft set up specific guidelines to deal with profiling under these circumstances. The face of terrorists changed, so the initial "profile" proved inadequate, too limiting, and just plain wrong. Gender, economic circumstance, education, and age were now variables, not markers. The only constraints were the intellectual or spiritual embrace of a notion that killing innocents to advance an extremist cause was justified.

But the broader concern about human rights was, is, and will always be subject to vigorous and appropriate debate and concern. There is a dimension to this part of the picture that reflects a value system America holds dear, though we sometimes ignore it. It is not enough that in the ordinary course of business we passionately protect human rights. It is in the midst of extraordinary times that America will be judged. Even in the midst of war and the great stresses and fears that it brings with it, we should not undermine our core values. And it is not in our interest to withdraw from the rest of the world under the color of self-protection.

In protecting America, we always worried about terrorists slipping through the net. But our approach to the treatment of those labeled "unlawful enemy combatants," as opposed to traditional "prisoners of war," began to concern me when it became clear no plan existed other than indefinite if not permanent imprisonment. The administration argued that because these people are not state-sponsored, they are not entitled to the usual protections of the Geneva Convention, and have no rights to our time-honored (and constitutionally guaranteed) principle of habeas corpus. The White House had been staunchly opposed to giving detainees access to civilian courts, later arguing that military tribunals sufficed. Constitutional lawyers argued—and the Supreme Court agreed—that such a position was impermissible and that habeas corpus extends to those captured in a time of war even if they don't fit into traditional categories.

President Barack Obama will close the detention facility at Guantánamo Bay and remove the "unlawful enemy combatants" status from those detained. Both changes will accelerate resolution of the basic questions that remain: What is the adjudication process and what is the standard against which their actions will be measured to justify release?

Interior Minister Otto Schily of Germany, a true friend of America, held a position in the German government that enabled him to interact with Attorney General Ashcroft and myself. In Germany the job of interior minister is not at all like our secretary of the interior, who is overseer of land use—conservation, national parks, and off-shore oil leases and the like. Schily's office is responsible for German federal policing, national security, and immigration. His support of America begins with American GIs befriending him, his family, and others during the closing stages of World War II.

One evening in Berlin our private conversation turned to the issue of Guantánamo. As a lawyer by profession Schily asserted that there are many reasons to admire America, but for him, the fundamental reasons were our constitutional government, the rule of law, and due process. America celebrates these values and often lectures the world on them. He then asked whether we planned on keeping the detainees there forever in violation of our own legal principles. He admitted that neither the Uniform Code of Military Justice nor the civilian or criminal justice system might be in order, but some form of recognizable "due process" was. His argument, his plea, was for America to be true to itself.

The very name of our department might indicate to some that we would favor as a matter of course any measure that would, on its face, enhance the public safety, but that is not the case. The lessons of history are clear enough on this score. If you accept that the growth of Al Qaeda came in part from the martyrdom that resulted from the torture and periods of indefinite incarcerations of political opponents of Middle East leaders, it is not a big leap to worry that many of today's prisoners will follow a similar path. That is not justification to hold all of them permanently.

And so leading DHS was always a balancing act—within our own government and with allies abroad. We had to keep good relations with others as we addressed our own internal shortcomings. The 9/11 attack had been perpetrated by foreign nationals who had slipped through our outdated and ineffective screening system. A second could be perpetrated the same way. We had to somehow fix the system that allowed nineteen of the twenty men who conspired in the 9/11 attacks to pass through our gates with legitimate visas, wearing casual business clothes, and giving no hint that they were ready to sacrifice their own lives in the commission of a heinous act that would kill thousands. We needed to learn lessons from the case of the twentieth hijacker.

On August 4, 2001, an immigrations inspector, Jose Melendez-Perez, had found Mohammed al-Kahtani's story odd. Arriving in Orlando on a Virgin Atlantic flight from Heathrow, al-Kahtani carried $2,800 in cash and no return ticket or credit cards. As al-Kahtani spoke only Arabic, Melendez-Perez called in a translator. When questioned about his intentions, al-Kahtani said that he was going to Disney World, though he said he had no hotel reservations. When Melendez-Perez grilled the visitor on how he would get around in the United States without knowing how to speak English, al-Kahtani answered that a friend would drive him. When the inspector asked where the friend was, al-Kahtani answered that he was meeting him at the airport. Melendez-Perez asked for the friend's name, and then noticed how nervous the man became. Al-Kahtani was denied entry. As he was sent back on a plane to London, he said, in Arabic, "I'll be back." He was captured four months later in Afghanistan by forces fighting against the Taliban and was sent to Guantánamo. The FBI traced him through a cell phone to Mohammed Atta, one of the hijackers. Atta was allegedly to meet al-Kahtani in Orlando once he cleared customs.

We will never know if he would have been the fifth hijacker of United Flight 93. Melendez-Perez's vigilance may have denied the group its full complement. Would one more terrorist have made a difference and enabled the flight to strike either the White House or Congress? We'll never know. That is the nature of our mission.

Operation Liberty Shield ended quietly two months after it began. It had been labor intensive and costly. We hadn't seen any spike in the intelligence. There was no noise, no banter, either domestically or internationally, that indicated the Iraq invasion had been used as a catalyst for an attack inside our borders. So, without fanfare, most of the provisions of Liberty Shield were set aside. A few practices, however, such as intense scrutiny at airports, became part of our standard operating procedures.

There was a fear among many that the politics of terrorism would extend to a Big Brother society, citizens spying on citizens.

Nobody in our shop was interested at all in turning George Or-well's oppressive vision into reality. In my view, we had the perfect right in a time of war to introduce measures of inconvenience. It's annoying to have to take off your shoes at the airport and to wait in long lines. But our measures were far less restrictive than those implemented in earlier times of crisis in America. Historians will point out that John Adams, one of our greatest patriots and a fighter for personal freedom, championed the Alien and Sedition Acts, which trampled the First Amendment during an undeclared naval war with France. Abraham Lincoln, when the Union was at risk, temporarily suspended the right to habeas corpus. Franklin D. Roosevelt approved the arrest and relocation of more than a hun-dred thousand American citizens and lawful residents of Japanese descent during World War II. Our ideas were much more benign. We knew, in time, that Americans would adjust to them and pro-duce picture IDs when buying Amtrak tickets and understand the need. But I would trade inconvenience for loss of freedom any day, and I believe most Americans would as well.

On the domestic front, we didn't want neighbors to spy on each other, or patriots to turn into vigilantes. It wasn't our inten-tion to fill citizens with unnecessary worry or to increase the phar-maceutical industry's profits from the sale of antianxiety drugs. We simply wanted people to become more aware of what was happen-ing around them, to be on the lookout for anything that didn't look right. We are a society that takes many things for granted. We were saying, in effect, "Pay attention." It was our hope, of course, that things that didn't look right were nevertheless benign in terms of public safety. In a war zone, soldiers are taught to look for ordinary things in unusual places.

During Operation Liberty Shield, we got a call from the police chief in a small New Jersey town that had oil storage facilities. He reported that there were a couple of men "hanging around" the tanks, and that they had been questioned. One was a student from Egypt whose visa had expired, and one was an American citizen who had moved to Yemen. When we got that information, the Coast Guard looked into the scheduled port deliveries in the area, including those vessels carrying oil. One of ships coming in was captained by an Iraqi citizen and its crew members were Pakistanis. That in itself was not unusual. That's the way oil and other vital imports are delivered. But it was only natural—and sensible—to wonder if that ship had any connection with the two young men who'd been questioned. Did the men's cell phones, for example, indicate they had made contact with the ship? Our quick investigation revealed that there was no connection, and no cause for alarm. But the event itself reassured us because it showed that all involved in homeland security—a much broader cast than the federal government—were thinking outside the box and taking our common welfare seriously. They had seen an ordinary thing—two men walking around—in an unusual circumstance, near an oil tank farm.

We began to feel that communication with the public at large and public entities was improving, and it was. But at the same time—particularly when we were frustrated by the lack of cooperation of some other federal agencies—we could have been better at communicating to our peers in Washington. For example, we learned from intelligence reports that there might be a plot to attack U.S. embassies in Islamabad, the capital of Pakistan, and in other capitals, using small aircraft. We put out an advisory to the embassies, noting that it was possible that people were trying to rent small planes and load them with heavy equipment. What we hadn't done was notify the State Department of this advisory. It hadn't yet notified its own officials of the threat, so State was unintentionally scooped by us. We had moved quickly to share information and ignored protocol. It would not be the last time.

I was often asked, and am still asked, whether invading Iraq has made us safer or more vulnerable as a nation. Everyone has an opinion on this matter, but I saw it from a viewpoint that was different than any other official or citizen.

DHS was never involved in any of the decisions leading up to the invasion of Iraq. Iraq, for us, was an inevitability to be reckoned with, for we would likely become more susceptible to attack, not less, at least in the short run. That is not to say that in private moments, moments when I had a chance to catch my breath and to consider what was about to happen, that I didn't form an opinion. I had seen no intelligence that contradicted what Secretary of State Colin Powell had presented to the United Nations, where he made a strong case that Saddam Hussein harbored weapons of mass destruction in secret locations. As I quickly learned in the business of counterterrorism, what you worry about most is what you don't know. And I had strong reservations, in any case, about the power of the United Nations to solve the issue on it own.

Early on in my political life, I was a strong supporter of the United Nations. It had always seemed to me that having some kind of international forum at which representatives from countries around the world can interact and collectively take action to prevent human rights abuses or avoid war or address poverty was an inspired idea. What a wonderful gift to humanity to achieve that kind of outcome. But with notable exceptions, such as UNICEF and its response to national disasters, the organization hasn't served the purposes its founders intended. The mantra is always "Take it to the U.N." In the case of Iraq, what was the magic number of sanctions that the international body could impose on Saddam before taking more drastic action? Twelve, twenty, fifty? Like many Americans, I had grown impatient with the posturing and impotence the United Nations displayed. After all, Saddam had used poison gas against his own people, and thousands of Kurds had died as a result. The United Nations could not prevent such a disaster, nor could it adequately respond to it. The gassing of the Kurds was prima facie evidence that Saddam possessed weapons of mass destruction, at least he had in 1988.

Most of our key intelligence agencies maintained that he still had them. It has been alleged that the Bush administration cherry-picked the intelligence in order to go to war. Although this was not in my lane, I find the suggestion contemptible and unworthy of comment, particularly in light of the fact that President Clinton's intelligence community thought it, and so did Prime Minister Blair's, and those of other leaders including, by the way, the French. I was prepared to give the president the benefit of the doubt on the wisdom of invading Iraq. Privately, I had my doubts about both the target and the tactics.

Freeing Iraq of a dictatorial government—and doing so with no American and few Iraqi casualties—was an ambitious goal, in a region where, except for Israel, democracy remains an elusive goal. I knew that Iraq was not at that point any kind of Al Qaeda stronghold. I also knew that the job in Afghanistan, the source of the 9/11 attack, had not been completed. Moreover, as a Vietnam veteran, I was not at all impressed with the Defense Department's public relations message. Yes, Shock and Awe lit up the Baghdad sky and did tremendous damage to the country's infrastructure, and no doubt it caused great casualties among Saddam's inner circle. But I learned in Southeast Asia and afterward that technology—we Americans do love our toys—has its limits. It's very clean when you can fight a war from the sky. But you can't topple a regime with high-tech weapons from aloft. Boots on the ground are needed to take and hold territory. And as anyone who has been in the military knows, you have to have a reasonable definition of victory and a strategy for ending combat operations. In Iraq there was no real understanding of what constituted military victory. Even so, I wasn't asked for my opinion. Nor did I express my reservations about invading Iraq to the president or anyone else in the White House. I wasn't asked and didn't volunteer. Even so, I thought, "We'd better find WMDs," and "We don't have enough troops to do the job." After all, General Norman Schwarzkopf had nearly three times the forces at his disposal twelve years earlier when he'd kicked Iraq out of Kuwait.

The public policy was something like "It's better to fight the terrorists there than here." This view made several assumptions, including the idea that the terrorists in question—people who were blowing up police stations and mosques in Iraq—were the people who, if they hadn't been occupied by that, would be otherwise engaged in terrorist activities in America.

Al Qaeda had no defined presence in Iraq at the time. As the years went on, it did have influence there, and that, combined with other outside forces, including support from Iran and Syria, made our mission in Iraq much more difficult than originally imagined and expressed by administration officials.

I have no doubt that in a way Iraq was a magnet for terrorists. There have been statements, written and oral, where Al Qaeda has declared it as a strategic battleground. Recruiting to fight America extended throughout the entire region. Many of the participants in the attacks and suicide bombings were not people who were in Baghdad or other key Iraq cities at the time of "Shock and Awe" and the occupation that followed. In 2006, the National Intelligence Estimate attributed a direct role to the Iraq war in fueling radicalism in the Middle East and elsewhere. The report included input from sixteen intelligence agencies and concluded that the Iraq war made the overall terrorism problem worse. It pointed out that the treatment of prisoners at Abu Ghraib and Guantánamo fueled anti-American feeling. Our enemies will forever exploit those rare occasions when America's actions are inconsistent with our traditional, respected value system. At a minimum they provided more grist for their propaganda mill. At worst, they were recruiting posters for terrorists-in-waiting.

Has the invasion and occupation of Iraq made us safer at home? Can the hundreds of billions of dollars and the loss of thousands of lives be justified in terms of protecting America?

I never participated in any of the National Security Meetings prior to invading Iraq. That is not a complaint. It's just a fact. I knew little more than what Secretary of State Colin Powell shared with the world in his speech to the United Nations. Powell's statement coupled with my cynicism about the United Nations and its ability to offer little more than meaningless, unenforceable resolutions led to my conclusion that preemptive action was warranted.

Admittedly, the relationship between the Saddam regime, Al Qaeda, and 9/11 was tenuous, if at all. If our intelligence community had hard evidence of such a linkage, it would have been wise to share it, not only with me, but with the rest of the world.

My public support was tempered by my private concern about troop levels. I never believed we started with the right number. It took very little reading of history, particularly from the British perspective, to understand that only a tyrannical and repressive regime could silence the centuries-old ethnic and religious fault lines within Iraq.

The war in Iraq did not make our job any more difficult than it already was. At the outset we scrambled to pull together the national security plan we dubbed Liberty Shield. Our sense of urgency and commitment had to remain at the highest level as we worked to get more timely information, connect with governors and mayors, build border agreements, meet congressional deadlines—for these and every other effort we had undertaken. Building the department while fighting a war was just a part of our work environment. Did the war make us less safe at the time? I don't think so, but it did make us more vigilant.

Our unwillingness or inability to build a broader international coalition to support us in Iraq and some of the tactics we used to prosecute the war created a serious but not irreparable image problem throughout the world. There is no doubt that the invasion, these practices, and our prolonged presence were used by the radicals as a recruiting tool for combatants in Iraq and sympathizers elsewhere.

But here is the irony. We ultimately inserted more troops. In response to an expanded, violent Al Qaeda presence, Sunni and Shia forces united in opposition to that presence. Provincial elections were held with over a 50 percent turnout in January 2009. Iraqi police and military assumed much of the country's security and law enforcement responsibilities. On January 1, 2009, the security responsibility for the Green Zone in Baghdad was turned over by the Americans to the Iraqi military. On the same day, the British turned their responsibility for the country's second largest city, Basra, over to the government as well. The judicial system took hold. The transition to a form of self-government has, of this writing, gained momentum.

The question still remains, "Are we safer because of the invasion?" In May 2004, Charlie Rose—longtime host of an influential PBS current affairs interview show—questioned me about the war and the outcome I foresaw. My response provides the context for my answer to this question several years later.

"I think in time it [a self-governing Iraq] will occur. I don't think we should expect an immediate transition to a government that looks like ours, to a value system that necessarily reflects ours—there are unique cultural differences, historical differences, religious differences . . . but I think that even around those differences—the one centerpiece that is not different is the notion in the heart of all human beings to be free . . . and to determine their own future, their own fate."

If a Muslim country previously subjugated by a despot can, by the intervention of "the infidel Americans," be free to establish a legitimate form of self-government that offers a better life for its citizens, then we will be safer. In the battle for the hearts and minds of over a billion Muslims, we will have won a significant victory.

If you're looking for a direct connection between our Iraq policy, the recruitment of terrorists, and the threat to the homeland, you might consider the life and death of Raed Mansour al-Banna, a young lawyer from Jordan.

In June 2003, al-Banna arrived in Chicago on KLM Flight 611, direct from Amsterdam. Preflight intelligence had indicated al-Banna was a passenger that U.S. Customs and Border Protection needed to interview. At the time, CBP had no firm evidence that al-Banna was a terrorist, but there was enough information to be suspicious and to subject him to a rigorous interview. In fact, he had been in the United States before, arriving in 2001, settling in Los Angeles, and working at an unlawyerly vocation: He became a pedicab driver at LA–Ontario International Airport, bicycling passengers between parking lots and the main terminal. A former friend of al-Banna's described him as "a cool guy to hang out with for a long time," and as "a hedonist" who loved motorcycles, women, and partying. "His purpose in life was to have a good time"—in short, somebody who didn't stand out in LA.

When he returned from the Middle East in the summer of 2003, he told customs officials his intention was to visit an uncle in Oak Lawn, a suburb of Chicago. According to the officials, al-Banna was calm and polite, and his documents were in order. He possessed a legitimate B1/B2 tourist visa to enroll in English classes. When he told the customs officer that he had supported himself in the United States earlier by holding various odd jobs, he opened himself to further investigation because regulations prohibit work without a green card. As Rob Bonner, the Customs commissioner at the time, recalls, "We didn't know if al-Banna had entered the U.S. to carry out a specific terrorist attack, but we also didn't believe him." Al-Banna was photographed that day wearing a big smile and a baseball cap worn backward. He was also fingerprinted, and as he was considered a potential terrorist, officials assigned him to an escort officer and put him on the next plane back to Amsterdam.

A year and a half later, at 8:30 A.M. on March 28, 2005, a suicide bomber drove a sedan full of explosives into a crowded bazaar outside a health clinic in Hilla, sixty miles south of Baghdad. The explosion killed 166 men, women, and children, and wounded scores more. The bomb was so powerful it set fire to a row of shops across the street. In all, it was the single deadliest attack on civilians during the Iraq war.

Investigators examined the vehicle that had been used to deliver the explosives. An Iraqi fireman found the driver's hand—without the driver attached—chained to the steering wheel. The fingerprints taken from that hand matched the fingerprints taken at O'Hare Airport. They belonged to Raed Mansour al-Banna.

9

MATTHEW BRODERICK'S DAY OFF

Politicians may flirt with reviving the draft, but they are too late; it's already happened. Some citizens willingly enlisted, some were conscripted, some gathered on Saturday to conscientiously object—but when Homeland Security chief Tom Ridge put the country on heightened alert, he began our basic training. Watch for men with nicks on their faces; they may be freshly shaved jihadists. Report suspicious bags. The soda bottle in the subway could be cyanide. France says it wants more weapons inspectors? We now have millions of them.

—*Time*, February 24, 2003

There are at least two talented Matthew Brodericks in American culture. One of them played Ferris Bueller in a movie and starred on Broadway in *The Producers*. The other is a producer of an entirely different mold whom I came to know in the early days of DHS.

His story, like those of many whose work is largely unknown to the public, was at the heart of our efforts at DHS. The political bullet this retired marine brigadier general voluntarily took for others in the Bush administration in the wake of Hurricane Katrina (more about that later) tells you everything you need to know about people who consider duty more significant than reward and recognition.

As a young officer in the Vietnam War, Broderick, like many of his counterparts, undertook many difficult and dangerous assignments. It was his marine command that guarded the U.S. Embassy as, under fire, the last desperate helicopters lifted off the roofs of the compound carrying Vietnamese women and children to safety.

He was part of another withdrawal under fire in Somalia many years later. He concluded his career as the operations officer for the entire Corps.

Broderick came to us after his retirement from the military and after stints with the Institute of Defense Analysis and in the private sector and seemed the ideal candidate to run our operations center. The hiring process, though, was awkward and typical of how things were often done in those early days of DHS. Bruce Lawlor asked him to come for an interview, and when he did, it all went very well. Lawlor was impressed by Broderick's experience, attitude, and ability. A few days later, Broderick received a letter from our Human Resources Department pointing out that by going for the interview without the arrangement being made by Human Resources he had violated the process. The sense of the absurd was heightened when, in a subsequent interview, he was asked by Human Resources if he had voted for George W. Bush in the 2000 election. This, he learned, was often asked. When Broderick answered that he hadn't voted for candidate Bush, jaws dropped. The interviewer called in other people from the office and they all stared at him incredulously, as if he had purple hair. One of the officials asked him, "How can I send you down for the White House interview if we tell them this?" Broderick explained two things. He didn't want to become a political appointee; he preferred to become part of the Senior Executive Service (SES), which were part of an apolitical workforce. And second, he revealed the reason that he, a self-proclaimed Republican, didn't vote for candidate Bush, was because he was traveling on business to the West Coast on the day of the election and couldn't get to the polls. Even so, he didn't like the idea of being asked about his vote, and neither did I. How a person votes has little to do with their qualifications to fill a critical job and is a private matter. But of course in that regard I may have been in the minority.

If Broderick wondered about the wisdom of joining us based on the hiring procedure, his concern was only heightened by the working conditions. As a marine, his exploits took him to distant places and hostile environments, but he was also accustomed to having up-to-date technology available, even in remote locations and under tents. That wouldn't be the case in his new office in a building that might be called, in Dickensian fashion, "The Old Curiosity Shop."

"I thought the Marine Corps was humble until I arrived at the NAC," he recalls. He expected to see individual consoles, enormous movie screens, satellite communications, a variety of private spaces available to gather during crises, where decisions could be made. In short, the facilities that almost every other federal agency had in spades. Instead, he saw every available square inch filled with sweating humanity in a building with no air-conditioning. Tables had been pushed together, and people worked very close to each other in twelve-hour shifts. He noticed that DHS was relying on television sets, to bring us news from CNN, and on laptops. "I was in total shock," he said, but obviously not at all "awed" by what we had to work with.

Dozens of interviews were held at the NAC. It could have been an acronym for "no amenities campus." "Spartan" would have been a step up. If OSHA standards had been applied to the facility, the government would have either shut us down or reduced our complement substantially. Many who were interviewed toured the site. Those who agreed to serve knew that their counterparts in every other agency worked in more desirable conditions. To them, however, mission was the only concern.

Broderick's space and equipment challenges were illustrative of those confronting just about everyone at the NAC. Ironically, several component units, such as Customs and Secret Service, had modern, comfortable headquarters, often with eating and workout facilities. In spite of his political misstep, we were given permission to hire Broderick. His office—as director of the operations center, he was responsible for coordinating critical information with federal, state, and local agencies—was in the only place he could fit: a janitor's closet. He pulled the mops and pans out of it and shoved a desk to the back of the deep but narrow space. His three managers also had to work in the closet. If a movie were made of the early days of DHS—showing key personnel who had the safety of the country on their shoulders working out of a janitor's closet—it would be dismissed as Hollywood gimmickry.

Initially, he didn't have a budget. He recalls, "I noticed that all of the people working there already were using paper and pens, and other equipment. I thought, if there's no budget yet for the ops center, where did that stuff come from? I quickly learned. Secretary Ridge's office was a floor above us and, late at night, after he and others on that floor had gone home, our people went upstairs and 'borrowed' paper, cartridges, and other supplies."

Later, when Broderick saw for the first time DHS's secret remote location—where it could operate if Washington was attacked or became contaminated—he saw further evidence that the new department was the inheritor of equipment that should have been peddled at three cents on the dollar at a tag sale. "That was the site from which we would run the U.S. in a nuclear or biological crisis," he recalls, "and all it had was rotary phones, desk lamps with pull chains, and some old chairs."

In those early days, what Broderick and his team accomplished in a very short time was remarkable. He pulled the ops center together, though the frustrations were often DHS-inflicted. We had managers whose job it was to hold down spending, and they complained that Broderick and his colleagues were just boys looking for toys.

Meanwhile, the White House was calling him directly. That is, junior White House staffers, certain there was a terrorist behind every tree, bombarded him with warnings, insisting that he follow up every "lead." They were worried the president might see something on CNN and ask them for details and they'd have none. Or they just wanted to be able to brag to their colleagues at the local watering hole that they'd given DHS a task. As Broderick recalls in his inimitable style, "The White House wore our asses out."

Oftentimes, normal events in a time of anxiety or fear lead people to draw abnormal conclusions. One day the ops center got an anxious phone call when a hazardous-material truck drove near the West Wing. Some White House staffers had interpreted this to mean that Washington was under a biological or chemical attack.

It did not occur to them that hazardous-material trucks had been driving around the capital city for decades without making headlines; they are needed in the ordinary course of business. Whether it was someone in the White House or a citizen calling the local police chief, they should have known better.

One day in 2003, a grainy photograph found its way into the intelligence stream and for a brief period got everyone's attention. A surveillance camera along the Canadian border caught an individual in a remote area carrying an object on his shoulder.

Our border with our northern neighbor has regular crossings mostly at points along mapped roads. But these are few in number compared with areas having no border control, narrow gaps in rivers, large lakes, and, most significantly, vast woods. There are also hundreds of logging roads and recreational trails and rights of way owned by utility companies; altogether there are thousands of places where people can come across the border without being noticed. Perhaps you saw the movie *Frozen River,* a story of down-on-their-luck people in upstate New York. Because they are in such desperate economic straits, they smuggle aliens across an icy waterway in the trunk of an old sedan, using a Native American reservation as a point of ingress. The movie provides a fairly accurate picture of just how vulnerable the country is to illegal immigration and why the issues of economic security and border security are so closely intertwined.

The open border was another case of risk management. We devised plans to address the issue, knowing we would never be able to entirely secure the border. We relied on two resources. The first was intelligence, and much of that came from our counterparts in Canada, with whom we forged a close relationship. The other was technology, surveillance cameras mounted in remote locations. It was one of those cameras that had detected the man with the large object on his right shoulder.

I saw the photos during one of our morning sessions with the president. One individual. Unclear picture. Remote location. Unidentified object. The only course of action was for DHS and the FBI to intensify their investigation, engage their Canadian counterparts, and visit the site. Our gut feeling was that it was nothing, but it had to be investigated.

The circumstances, indeed, looked strange. Some could interpret the photos as showing an individual transporting a shoulder-fired missile. If, indeed, the object was such a weapon, it could be used on a variety of targets, including infrastructure and commercial aircraft. I believe we were all privately skeptical of such a view, for it seemed unlikely that terrorists would be transporting weapons on foot through rural America one at a time. Still, the photos required an immediate and thorough assessment.

At the heart of this episode, we all knew, was that old question of credibility. The public was going to trust us only if our decisions were responsible. On the one hand, we knew that terrorism is, by definition, a phenomenon that usually provides no specific warning, and so vigilance is a key element in combating it. On the other hand, there were scores of "plots" coming across our desks at any one time, and it was very clear that almost all of them were neither plausible nor likely.

We had photo experts examine the evidence from the north woods. Our intelligence chief, Pat Hughes, went to Canada to work with the Royal Canadian Mounted Police, who over the years proved excellent partners in matters of counterterrorism. The collaboration was effective, the conclusion unanimous. This potential terrorist was actually participating in some form of "paint ball" exercise or game.

In this instance there was great collaboration among our domestic agencies, but that certainly wasn't the case on all occasions. Determining the meaning and credibility of intelligence was often hard enough. There was also a larger related issue: not knowing. And to many within the department, the primary culprits in not sharing information were our counterparts at the FBI, which, Broderick would still argue, "went out of its way to emasculate DHS."

As DHS began gradually to get the kind of equipment it needed, it participated in secret videoconferencing twice each day with counterparts at the Pentagon, the Central Intelligence Agency, the National Security Agency, the State Department, and other agencies.

The CIA proved helpful, and the NSA seemed to have no reluctance about passing along key information. But the FBI was almost never forthcoming. As Broderick says, "One FBI official told me, 'If you need to know it, we're going to tell you, but we can tell you right now, you'll never need to know it.'"

At the very beginning, the FBI's general attitude about information sharing with us was unreasonable and frustrating. The breakthroughs we eventually made were the result of the persistence of many of us in engaging them and challenging them to share. With the help of Bob Mueller, there came a gradual recognition that we were an integral part of the defense team and should (and more important, could) be trusted. I suspect collaboration still remains a work in progress.

Even so, I would occasionally get blindsided at my daily morning meetings with the president. He would ask about something that he'd learned from the FBI and often I hadn't a clue what he was talking about. It is not a good strategy for the secretary of homeland security to say in response, "I am unaware of it, Mr. President." At least, not very often.

One night, out of frustration, I called Matthew Broderick at home. He had gotten there "early"—by 9:00 P.M.—and gone directly to bed. During the first twelve to eighteen months these were fairly common work hours for everyone at the NAC. This, for him, is what passed for a day off. When he answered, he assumed I was calling because of a terrorist threat. I wasn't. I just had to vent about the FBI. It was a constant battle to convince them we weren't the enemy. We had a need to know.

Among our department's most critical missions was the development and refining of a system of communications and response that would be as seamless as possible. From its earliest days the department was focused on building communications with our partners at the federal, state, and local levels. The department is federal, the mission is national. Building relationships with them and their first responders was essential to securing America, so we labored long and hard at it. Simulated disaster scenarios in real time requiring simulated responses demonstrated the need and practiced the integrated effort required at all levels of government. In May 2003 we conducted TOPOFF 2, an exercise that tested the communication, decision-making, and response capabilities of Seattle and Chicago. Public officials, police, firemen, and emergency service and medical personnel were involved. Volunteers posed as victims as ambulances took people to hospitals, citizens congregated for treatment, public officials held hypothetical press conferences, and those running the exercise added complicating factors along the way. Though the context of the exercise was known in advance (radiological and biological attacks), the scale was realistic, the complicating factors reasonable, and the communication and decision-making pressure palpable. As it turned out, this mammoth exercise proved that much work remained to be done.

At Pike Place Market, the "Soul of Seattle" on nine waterfront acres downtown, men behind the fish counters tossed whole salmon to each other, producing gasps in the crowd, as always. Hundreds of shoppers inspected the wide array of produce and dry goods, as if there was nothing awry. But not far away, in an industrial neighborhood of this, the Northwest's largest city, home to Microsoft, in a scenario we had developed in a multistate training exercise dubbed "TOPOFF 2," 150 people lay dead and thousands were injured. A fictional terrorist organization called Glodo, working from a safe house, had detonated a dirty bomb in a vacant lot next to a coffee roasting plant. Plumes of "toxic" smoke filled the air for miles. Firefighters in protective chemical suits milled about the scene of overturned buses and police cars, and fake victims wandered in a daze, car fires smoldered, and a few news helicopters flew overhead. The casualties were taken to a nearby hospital.

Meanwhile, in Chicago, hundreds of residents showed up at hospital emergency rooms complaining of "flu-like" symptoms, the result of a biological attack mimicking a strain of the plague.

That was the script, anyway—Hollywood disaster scenes as written by the new DHS. They were part of the congressionally mandated series of dry runs that had begun several years earlier, and were inherited by us, to test the ability of major cities to respond effectively to terrorist attacks.

This particular two-city exercise, conducted over five days in May 2003, was advertised as the most extensive exercise of response to terrorism ever undertaken. It had a budget of $16 million and was carried out just two months after the formation of our department. The new DHS, among its other duties, had become, in a way, a movie producer. We sought volunteers to become traumatized victims and media reporters looking for the best stories to tell.

During the exercise, key DHS personnel were on site. I observed both from my office and on location. Members of the administration portrayed President Bush and Andy Card. There was, of course, a happy ending. All of the casualties were miraculously freed of injury and illness, and in a short time the cities were back to normal.

Yet, it became clear that there was much work ahead, because we had learned just how ill-prepared we were to respond as a nation, even after the shock of 9/11. In planning these exercises, and trying to avoid another *War of the Worlds* panic like the one that ensued in 1938 after Orson Welles's Halloween radio broadcast, we made sure that officials and residents were aware of our plans. In this, Robert B. Stephan, a retired colonel with extensive special operations experience in the air force who was at this point a special assistant to Broderick, and others played key roles.

The fact that the attacks weren't real eliminated the certain psychological devastation, and the measure of panic, that would have occured during an actual emergency. We knew that would be the case from the beginning. We were aware that critics would complain about the how federal government was spending its money and argue that the administration was once again using fear as a political tactic. Moreover, we always knew there were limitations to what we could learn from something so well rehearsed. But we were convinced that there would be real benefits to these exercises. Preparation is vital, and this would test the ability of responders to work together, among many other things. No matter how well prepared a city can be (and no matter how well rehearsed the exercise), something would go wrong. That was the advantage: We could identify problem areas.

I flew to Chicago to tour emergency operations centers. We watched a triage scenario in a cold May rain. On the flight home, several of us huddled to discuss the training exercise. There was the fundamental and ongoing concern about keeping the public informed and reassured during a crisis. During these exercises we actually replicated TV and newspaper interviews. This was to show that while we were doing triage—deciding what needed to happen and in what order—in the part of the country directly involved, we also had to remember we were communicating to the country at large and to the rest of the world. How do we reassure with any sense of accuracy and authority? Two cities in the exercise had suffered attacks. How best to reassure people in other cities who naturally felt they might be next?

A few months after the Seattle and Chicago training exercises, an unclassified summary of a secret report was made public. It showed that in Seattle there were "critical" problems trying to determine where plumes of radiological contamination from the dirty bomb had spread. In Chicago, the exercise showed the same phenomenon that had been apparent in New York City on 9/11—that local and federal officials lacked "an efficient emergency communications infrastructure." Chicago had relied heavily on regular telephone lines and fax machines—landlines were jammed for many hours and slowed the sharing of vital information. In Chicago there was confusion over the location of stockpiles of medical supplies and antibiotics that could be used to treat the plague and other bioterrorism agents.

As we headed back to D.C., another issue was raised that highlighted the complex decisions that would be required if the terrorists exploded a "dirty bomb." A radiological dispersal device (RDD), the technical name for such a weapon, disperses radiological material through a conventional explosion. It is important to understand that this is something quite different from a nuclear explosion. The damage inflicted depends on several factors, including the amount of explosives and the amount and type of radiological material that is dispersed.

A dirty bomb, though it will cause some deaths in the area of the explosion, is primarily a psychological weapon and a means to contaminate a large area. If the measured level of contamination should turn out to be moderately higher than the existing federal health and environmental standard, but at a risk level that people were prepared to accept, would the government force them to leave? What level of additional health risk would citizens and communities be prepared to accept in order to maintain their communities?

It is clearly not a "getting back to business" scenario. Awaiting the restoration of electricity, the repair of the roof, and the removal of debris, as after a violent storm, after which it is appropriate and safe to return home, is a predictable scenario having readily understood thresholds of safety. Decisions by government officials, scientists, and individual citizens on what level of radiation is acceptable in order for them to resume their lives are not. If decontamination of the affected area could not reduce the danger of cancer death to one in ten-thousand, which means in a city of five hundred thousand an additional fifty deaths would occur, should we or would we abandon the city? And how could the government arrange for a trustworthy response devoid of panic and politics, with a clearly scared (and rightly so) population.

Statistically, this is minimal. But it is not hard to imagine the media frenzy whipping the population into a panic. On sober reflection, why would you want to leave the city that gives you a livelihood and where you know and love the neighborhoods? The idea of risk management is not just a problem for governments and big business. It is a question for everyone. What risks are you willing to take during your life? Do you want or need reassurance from your government or anyone else that you can be protected from harm in any circumstance?

The fact is that despite the best efforts of scientists, Occupational Safety and Health Administration, the Department of Defense, devoted mothers who hover over their children, driver education courses, protective clothing, and every other imaginable safety measure taken, there will always be some injury and death. In a grown-up society, there has to be a realization that anecdotal evidence—that small percentage—may be indicative of harmful trends, but as a society we have to keep our wits about us and make informed decisions about the level of risk we will accept. We make those kinds of decisions daily: What do we believe is the level of risk to our lives and what are we willing to do, if anything, to avoid it?

In the post-9/11 world, we need to be informed and realistic about the level of contamination we will accept. In such an attack, most of the casualties come well after the initial explosion. The difficulty is determining the subsequent level of contamination and its long-term physical and psychological effects on the population. We believed we could address these problems, but we were also left with major policy issues at various levels. The exercises proved we had a lot of work to do.

As for Matthew Broderick, he came away from the exercises with the reaction of one Seattle official ringing in his ears, reminding him of the real obstacles in the matter of national cooperation, and that it wasn't only federal agencies that were finding it difficult to put aside their cultures and traditions. The city official asked him who he was. Thinking she would be impressed, he responded, "I'm the new director of operations for Homeland Security."

She said, "Well, I'm from Seattle, and I've been playing in this exercise and I'm going to give you some advice. Seattle does what Seattle wants. The state of Washington can try to tell us what to do, but we don't listen. And the federal government? I've got news for you. We don't listen to you, either. As far as we're concerned, we'll do the thinking. Your job is to write the checks. That's it."

This was a minority view. I was very proud that from our days in the White House through my tenure as secretary we maintained excellent relationships with state and local officials. It wasn't a matter of courtesy. It was absolutely essential. For the country to reach its highest possible level of security we felt they should be treated as partners.

As we planned and conducted these exercises we were also dealing with many other matters, real and imagined. This was always the case at DHS. We could never go home at night thinking everything was being handled. The best we could do was to think that every-thing that everyone in the Department had tried to do had some measure of usefulness and, because of that, the country was a little safer than it had been the day before. It isn't appropriate, for exam-ple, to arrange an office party to celebrate the fact that the Brooklyn Bridge still connects Manhattan with Brooklyn or that Kansas City hasn't fallen prey to bubonic plague. Our jobs were rare in Ameri-can society: The absence of news was the best news, and even that could never be measured in absolute terms.

Every major event that drew large crowds had a homeland se-curity dimension to it. This applied particularly to big cities, where huge crowds commonly gather. But we were always concerned, too, about terrorism showing up in a variety of forms, not just at an outdoor rock concert in a major city. For those who would wreak havoc, what could be more effective than catching unawares, for example, a crowd swarming around a county fair? Thousands of communities have major athletic and social activities and rely on local resources—police and fire departments—to keep people safe and secure. Any of these could become the target of terrorists dem-onstrating that ordinary life can't go on as usual, anywhere in the nation, without fear.

These dark possibilities, however, had a silver lining because they led to new relationships. The situation required that we work to develop excellent communications. We had to know everything that was going on around the country that could draw a significant crowd. We had to know, too, about any threat to the public welfare that, in previous years, could simply have remained a local phe-nomenon. Whenever anything suspicious occurred in a major met-ropolitan area, officials in other cities wasted no time dialing our office and asking what they should do to avert a disaster.

A few months after we completed the exercises in Seattle and Chicago, it looked to us as if we had a real bioterrorism threat.

We had helped develop BioWatch as an initial response to the anthrax attacks in the wake of 9/11. As the White House described it, this was "the first deployment of early warning sensors to detect biological attack." It operated with a system of filters in over thirty of our largest cities at an initial cost of $60 million. There will be, must be, better detection systems in the future. At the time, this was an effort to put limited technology to its best use. The operation of the system and the route of information gathered from it illustrates why everyone has to get into the act, from local officials to the Environmental Protection Agency to the Centers for Disease Control to the FBI to DHS.

The first incident of a positive BioWatch result was reported on October 9, 2003, in Houston, Texas. The Houston Department of Health and Human Services reported detecting low levels of the bacterium that causes tularemia, which is commonly known as rabbit fever or deerfly fever. Annually, about two hundred cases of the illness are reported, and most occur in the south-central or western United States. The government considers it a primary bioterrorism threat. We knew firsthand of tularemia's possibilities because the U.S. government had developed the bacteria for its own arsenal of biological weapons during the cold war. We also knew that the Soviet Union had done the same thing. Other countries had experimented, too.

Officials estimated that 50 kilograms (about 110 pounds) of the bacteria dumped from an airplane onto a city of 5 million people would infect 250,000 people and kill 19,000. Because the initial symptoms produced from tularemia infection—fever, fatigue, and so on—are difficult to distinguish from influenza and acute pneumonia, it would be difficult immediately to detect that a bioterrorist attack has occurred. The result would be a significant number of deaths because, untreated with antibiotics, tularemia is fatal in up to 15 percent of its victims.

There is a time lapse between manually taking the filters out, taking them to a lab, and getting the results. Technology is under development to provide instantaneous analysis but it is not yet available. Here lies the challenge for citizens and health care professionals as well as an economic opportunity for the entrepreneur or company. The technology of detection is a substantial potential market. Whether the microbes are thrown at us by Mother Nature or terrorists, they need to be identified immediately. Any delay of hours or days has the potential to turn a limited but serious health problem into a substantially larger, potentially uncontainable one.

One of these days continuous monitoring systems will be able to capture and immediately identify hazardous airborne substances. The offices and public spaces of tomorrow will be integral parts of our early warning system.

And for a while in the fall of 2003, the anxiety level was high. Positive results for tularemia were detected on three consecutive days in Houston's air. Even though there was no sense of panic, everyone had to take the situation seriously. A variety of local and federal agencies became quietly involved. Men and women in protective white suits combed the areas where the readings were the highest. Even so, there had been no reports of injury or illness. The director of the Houston Department of Health and Human Services addressed the issue publicly: "We are investigating to determine if the bacteria was always present or newly present and if it represents a health threat to the community." In Washington, we had to assume, until we found otherwise, that this was possibly a terrorist attack. This meant dispatching people to the site, using all newly designed lines of communication, and coordinating efforts with a variety of agencies. Eventually, it was determined that a certain amount of the bacterium Francisella tularensis appears naturally, and this case was not a result of terrorism. Another crisis averted. We went home that night, but never thought "everything's being handled."

10

ANTHRAX AT THE OSCARS

Tom Ridge—what have you done with my panties?

—Letter from an airline passenger who complained of
baggage theft by TSA screeners

Washington, D.C. is a company town, and the company is the federal government. There, in a highly charged atmosphere, all matters are momentous. Those who live and work inside the Beltway actually believe that the programs they develop On High trickle down to Main Street, USA.

At DHS, it was our job was to inform citizens on security issues, provide a sense of safety, and inspire a readiness to partner. Inside the Beltway, it looked as if we were slowly succeeding. But we knew we weren't developing our "brand"—our position in the public mind-set—as efficiently or effectively as possible. There was a need for a reverse flow. We needed to hear directly from members of the public about what they understood, what they feared most. To do that, we had to introduce opinion makers to a new way of thinking. That goal led us down many avenues, including, eventually, the red carpet to Hollywood.

Our first external effort was to join a series of town meetings with the Council for Excellence in Government, an organization that had become a primary resource for federal managers and that had produced a variety of public projects and reports. Through focus groups, a meticulous program of polling, and several public meetings, we felt we had the best chance of learning the attitudes and sensitivities of the general population. At these meetings, we knew we would face questions, and even hostility, about matters beyond our control: Guantánamo, the issue of personal rights, and the Patriot Act. In the public's mind, DHS was at the heart of all matters that had to do with security, so we knew we were in a delicate position.

Still, we were intent on pressing the idea that homeland security is not restricted to the federal government. The Council on Excellence invited an array of local leaders, corporate officers, first responders, and ordinary citizens to each session. Our moderator for most of the town meetings was Frank Sesno, the former Washington reporter for CNN and professor of communications at George Washington University. He was drawn to the work, he confided, because of his view that the news media should do a better job of conveying useful information, ideas, and measures sans political spin. In these forums, we learned, once again, that the view from inside the Beltway is limited. In short, ordinary citizens were trying to figure out how to adjust to this new kind of threat, just as we were, and their interest could inform us.

During World War II, the government engaged in a highly successful public affairs campaign encouraging volunteerism, buying bonds (my mother sang at those rallies in Pittsburgh), and providing instructions in case of an attack. People knew, for example, to create a blackout effect by covering their windows. They knew what they could and couldn't consume; they accepted the rationing of gasoline and certain foods and other goods, sacrificing on behalf of the war effort. For all the dangers apparent from confronting Germany and Japan in the 1940s, there were concrete and easily understood steps to be taken. But in this twenty-first century, for a stateless conflict devoid of time-tested battlefield strategies and highly reliant on surprise, fear, and civilian vulnerability, it was much harder to devise and promote specific programs. There was no modern equivalent of a scrap-iron drive. It was as if this new kind of confrontation also created a new kind of homeland helplessness.

During a town meeting in Fairfax, Virginia, a suburb of Washington, D.C., a woman told us, "I'd love to volunteer to help with homeland security, but I don't have a clue about what's needed, or where to start." In St. Louis, a woman asked, "What can I do personally to break my own denial there's going to be a problem?" A woman from the same neighborhood asked if tap water was a logical target for terrorists. Another asked, "If there is a terrorist attack and we don't have computer access or electricity, how do we talk to each other?" A college student in Miami said, "I don't know exactly who our enemy is anymore." In San Diego, the father of a grade-school student said, "We were told by our son's school that we should come up with a family evacuation plan, but it's hard to come up with that if you don't know what the school's plan is in the event of an emergency." A retiree, aware that during 9/11 New York City firefighters and police had been using different radio frequencies, wanted to know if that problem still existed or whether all first responders were now in synch. Unbelievably, the answer today would be the same. We have not fixed it yet! A businessman in Boston suggested a "*do* call list," a real-time system for citizens to sign up to receive emergency information immediately on their cell phones. "I want my kids to get this. I want my coworkers on it. I want all of us on it." In Houston, a representative of a school system said, "We are not first responders but we deal with the most important thing people have, their children. We need to make sure we are an integral part of the planning process."

As a result of this ambitious public program, and feedback we received in other ways, several conclusions became apparent:

1. **IT'S NOT MY PROBLEM.** There was a near-unanimous assumption that there would be another attack. And yet there was a disconnect between the anxiety citizens felt and the level of their personal preparation in case of a catastrophic strike close to home. A disappointingly small percentage of those who were asked—and these, remember, were people with enough interest in the subject to come to a public program—had stocked cellars with water, batteries, emergency food supplies, first aid kits, and other provisions that would assure them, at least in the

short term, some measure of self-sufficiency. The knee-jerk answer to where people would get most of their information was television, until it occurred to them that very few operate on battery power. Without electric power in the homes of audience members, news anchors could issue all the updates and advice they cared to, but no one would see or hear it. Ironically, in the age of electronics, when the world is available to us at the press of a button, we have suffered from unexpected consequences. Retreating into our homes to enjoy our entertainment toys, we have dismantled the system of mutual community support that sustained us in many other times of crisis.

There is still an attitude that although disaster may happen somewhere in America it won't happen in my backyard. Even if it does, I'll deal with it, though I have assembled no tools nor conducted a single meeting to assure the family's survival.

2. **PRIVACY, PLEASE.** A growing number of citizens became concerned over the years about government intrusion on their privacy. There was increased criticism of the Patriot Act, and the revelations about the administration's expanded definition and use of the FISA provisions. A woman in Houston voiced a concern held by many when she said that efforts to protect the homeland are acceptable as long as they don't impinge on personal freedom. None ever felt that the FBI had eavesdropped on their telephone conversations, yet, with rare exceptions, they hated the idea that the law would allow the government to do so.

3. **CHOOSE YOUR POISON.** It became clear that the public had fairly strong ideas about the form the next terrorist attack would take. Though opinion was divided, a survey revealed that bioterrorism was by far the most prominent fear, followed in order by the use of chemical weapons, suicide bombing, nuclear attack cyber-terrorism, and another airplane hijacking. Several years later, in December 2008, the intelligence community also rated bioterrorism their greatest concern.

4. **CLUB FED.** Our efforts at DHS were focused on the idea of inter-agency cooperation and on a partnership between federal, state, and local officials, a plan that also intended to draw in private entities and ordinary citizens. We could see very well what we were up against—the idea in the public's mind that when disaster occurs it would be the federal government's job to respond and to make it go away.

To a certain degree that's understandable. What mayor has Department of Defense assets at his or her disposal? If, as Tip O'Neill famously pointed out, all politics is local, so is all disaster relief, or almost all. What number do you call when there's a crisis in your neighborhood? Do you call the White House? Some people who attended the public meetings seemed to understand the problem; they urged us to light a fire under local officials, some of whom seemed indifferent to homeland security, or at best, gave it low priority. Indeed, at the national convention of governors in 2004, one of the attendees said he'd been assured by the FBI that his state was not a target of terrorists, so he wasn't especially concerned.

We tried to point out that terrorism is not limited to obvious targets—skyscrapers or airplanes or major bridges—but also included "ordinary" places, shopping malls and sports stadiums, where terrorists could demonstrate to us and to the world that we could take nothing for granted. All of this reminded us just how far we had to go in the process of sharing responsibility.

5. **NEW BUT NOT YET PERFECT.** Immediately after 9/11, Congress had mandated the creation of a massive airport security force and gave the Transportation Security Administration (TSA) the responsibility to do so. That was the positive news. But legislators, as they often are, were unrealistic when it came to practical matters, such as the time it takes. Creating a new workforce of 45,000 trained, competent, and ethical employees would typically take years, not six months. Even so, the hiring practices were extremely thorough under these unprecedented circumstances. Indeed, 99.9 percent of the new TSA employees were

representative of others in our agency—dedicated and honest. But, in the haste to establish a large force, mistakes were inevitable. TSA hired a few people who were capable of giving a bad name to the whole enterprise. These were the people responsible for the myriad of items missing from baggage. Among the items, according to passengers who contacted us: Two "delicious" Cuban cigars and the expensive leather case they were in, "really nice" high-end chocolates, vials of Viagra, new shoes, music CDS, digital cameras, DVD players, Swiss Army knives, a knockoff Rolex (bought for $2), a Louis Vuitton handbag, a $1,600 Armani suit. And a pair of panties—for which I personally (but undeservedly)—took the blame. In time, more than twenty baggage screeners at airports in New York, New Orleans, and Fort Lauderdale were charged with stealing valuables from checked bags. In Philadelphia, another agency screener was charged with stealing $335 from a passenger's carry-on bag at a checkpoint. And in Detroit, four screeners were charged with stealing laptops, digital cameras, and other electronic gear from passengers' bags. Considering the impeccable work that was being done daily by TSA, the screening of 2 million passengers and their luggage daily at over 450 airports, these thefts were almost meaningless—except to the victims—and they were frustrating. Travelers were upset by the lines and inconvenience of getting through airport security, but most of them—especially frequent travelers—understood the need for it and benefited from it.

6. **THE PRICE OF SUCCESS.** In the pursuit of homeland security, the government and all its employees were being penalized for doing their job well.

　　In some of these town meetings we occasionally detected a point of view that suggested that our efforts were a waste of time and money because people's lives had returned to normal. The real threat, some said, was overblown, and was being kept high for political reasons. While we measured operational success internally, the general population was primarily interested in only one metric: Has there been another attack?

7. **AND WHILE YOU'RE AT IT.** Homeland security could be improved by better information sharing, by more effective border security, and by smarter spending of public dollars.

On that last point, public dollars, there was a feeling around the country that though homeland security required a different kind of thinking than was traditional in Washington, when it came to actual dollars we had something of a dilemma on our hands. How do you apportion dollars to address the threats of a war that has untraditional targets in a country as vast as ours? Some basic needs seemed obvious to us and to others. But the range of difficulties and costs went from the easily identifiable to the your-guess-is-as-good-as-mine category.

Harvard University's Belfer Center for Science and International Affairs released a study, "Filling the Gaps in US Homeland Security," on September 1, 2004 that reflected its research on measures needed to protect Americans from terrorism. It identified "key gaps" and priority action needed to fill them. For example, it would take $350 million to provide compatible radios for first responders, and $3.5 billion to vaccinate first responders against the six top bioterrorism threats. It would take several billion for the FBI, CIA, and DHS to develop the technology and programs for complete information sharing about known enemies. And it would take tens of billions (the report wasn't specific on this point) to create financial incentives to lure corporations to help the government secure key facilities like power and chemical plants. Over the years, I had seen sundry reports and analytical pieces all recommending massive investments. With finite resources and the need to set priorities with Congress, it was an annual exercise to determine the right amount for the most critical needs.

In terms of spreading the money around to the country, I held a few strong beliefs. When it came to paying for police and firefighters, it is and will always be a local responsibility. But in the matter of sophisticated equipment and extra measures like emergency training, it is a shared burden. The challenge was always how to distribute money against a backdrop in which the White House didn't want to give it. Even after 9/11, the administration wanted to eliminate the federal program that had existed for decades funding local emergency management officials because it didn't consider it to be a federal responsibility. While the administration's budget eliminated the program, Congress, responsive to its state and local constituencies, was wise to reinstate it.

Most members of Congress never object to the feds spending more money as long it is in their district. In all my years of public service, no one ever walked into either my congressional or governor's office to lobby me for less money than they had received the previous year. Can you imagine that conversation? "Thank you, Governor. We needed last year's appropriation, but believe we can provide the same programs and services with less this year." Never happened!

When it came to first-responder grants, the guidelines we ultimately established took into consideration population density, critical infrastructure, and threat information. It wasn't a perfect science, but we believed it reflected the desire of Congress to target the communities with the greatest need. There had never been a financial plan for protecting the country's infrastructure and population against terrorists. Within the challenge of developing one was the opportunity to further unify our security efforts.

The country at large may assume that federal, state, and local agencies have always worked together. In fact, there has always been widespread suspicion among and between them, fueled by a fierce competition for resources. One of the things we did, and much of it through the work of our coordinators with state and local officials, Josh Filler and Matt Bettanhausen, was to structure the grants to require cooperation of all officials. Information sharing, for example, was part of the buy-in.

Moreover, we had a paradox. On the one hand, we had concentrated on population centers that seemed obvious targets for terrorists. On the other, we knew that we needed participation and a buy-in from communities of all sizes around the country in order to have a seamless response to the threat. While it was obviously true that New York City and Washington, D.C., had been the targets of the 9/11 terrorists, it was the case that some of the planning for the attack took place elsewhere. No state is totally immune from a potential act of terrorism. All states need a minimal level of preparedness to help themselves and render aid to others.

While DHS was addressing the threat of terrorism, we attended to our traditional responsibilities as well. Planning for and responding to natural disasters remained one of the most critical. Channeling federal "all hazard dollars" to the states and cities was necessary, appropriate, and, not surprisingly, controversial.

A two-part plan was developed initially, something akin to the congressional system itself, with its split between the equal Senate (two senators per state) and the unequal House (representatives based on population). That is, about 40 percent of the grants were spread around the country without regard to population size in order to, as pointed out by Josh Filler, who led our state and local operation, "give everyone some skin in the game." The remainder was apportioned according to population density. In addition, the money was tied to certain conditions. Even so, as time passed, there were abuses. The media reported that one community bought leather jackets for its policemen, and that a harbormaster at Martha's Vineyard accepted a grant without having any idea of what to spend it on. Aside from a few examples, most of the media reports were misleading. The spending restrictions actually worked in almost all cases. Some of the questionable expenditures had been made with grants from the Justice Department. Because of the high-profile nature of our work and the tremendous number of public dollars being distributed, the media seemed to run everything through a DHS filter. Regardless of the source, the public had every right to complain about grant abuse in any form.

In time, our own approach to investing in security became less dependent on spreading money around and more on actual need. We worked with the FBI on analyses of the previous years' threats and used the results to determine how much specific cities received. Even so, because our system was based on what seemed to be a paradoxical approach (based both on full participation and on needs), we came in for a great deal of public criticism.

We gave a ton of money to New York City, of course, though no matter what the amount, Mayor Michael Bloomberg argued it wasn't enough and once said DHS grants were "pork barrel of the worst kind." He added, "New York City has already been targeted by terrorists six times since 1993. Yet inexplicably, today New York State ranks forty-ninth among the fifty states in per capita Homeland Security funding." During a televised hearing, he said, "During fiscal year 2004, New York State received $5.47 per capita in Homeland Security grants. Nebraska got $14.33 per capita; North Dakota $30.42; Wyoming $38.31; and American Samoa $101.43." *The Nation* reported on a specific federal funding shortfall: "The Fire Department of New York has only one dedicated hazardous materials unit for the entire city of 8 million people. Meanwhile, the fire department in Zanesville, Ohio (population 25,600) has federally funded thermal-imaging technology to find victims in dense smoke and a test kit for lethal nerve gases. The FDNY is still asking for radios that work in a crisis."

The per capita comparison was misleading. If you look at the numbers, New York and Washington got the bulk of the money. In the second round of grants, we got the FBI to assess the threats and tied grants to them. The political reality is you're not going to get representatives and senators from smaller states to vote in favor of a program that send funds to only a few large states, and nothing to anyone else.

Some cities made good arguments for more money. Population was a key factor in determining grants, but as we found in the case of Las Vegas, census figures were inadequate. Officials argued that the census figures should be increased to account for tourists occupying tens of thousands of high-rise hotel rooms every single day. It was a persuasive case and demonstrated that when it comes to national security, formulas can take you only so far.

Each year we refined the process of grant making, looking to ensure that the targeted dollars were spent to achieve the security outcomes we desired. How do we define success? More equipment, better training, mutual aid agreements? We were developing a plan for regional departmental offices that could help evaluate whether the dollars were going to the right people for the right reasons and being used effectively.

If our efforts to distribute money became something of a complex combination of statistics, need, and practicality, our effort to distribute information became more sophisticated as time went on. As we developed our "brand" we tried to respond to the new twenty-four-hour news cycle by anticipating its needs. We hosted a dinner with major network anchors and personnel at a friend's home in New York City. We convinced them to send producers and staff to a table-top exercise in Washington. Our goal was to familiarize them with DHS and show how the collaborative decision to raise or lower the threat level was made. We knew that if we didn't do this, the round-the-clock news cycle, needing to fill air space, could do it in a way that didn't reflect reality, and would probably make our jobs harder.

We had a similar plan for Hollywood. In our efforts to get the word out—the right word—we knew that we had to have some contact with the entertainment industry. It rivals, certainly, the news media in terms of public influence. This is a reality the federal government adjusted to long ago. If you've seen any film about American wars, and you've stayed until the very end to read the credits, you know that producers as a matter of course thank the Department of Defense or its specific agencies for their help. Indeed, the DOD does help. The Pentagon has a full-time staff in a swanky office on Wilshire Boulevard that consults with movie and television executives and writers who seek guidance on questions of authenticity. The connection between the Pentagon and the entertainment industry is so tight that no one blinks an eye when Cher produces a music video aboard an aircraft carrier. It has become part of our culture.

We knew at DHS that a wave of films and TV series would emerge following 9/11, and that was the case. We had no intention of interfering with the creative aspect of these efforts. We had no desire to be censors, and had no authority for it even if we did. If a writer wanted to create a DHS employee on the take, it wouldn't be our intention to talk them out of it—as much I might have wanted to—but we were concerned as a new department that our mission and regulations were not misrepresented. To put it more positively, we viewed this new subject matter for the industry as an opportunity in the sense that, if we were able to educate producers and writers, we could also educate the public at large. Like the Pentagon, we wanted to be sure that they reflected some sense of reality. If we could, we wanted to help producers and writers demonstrate the complexities of the issues so that Hollywood would—though it would cringe at the thought—become something of a partner with us. After all, it certainly did during World War II.

As we might have anticipated, there wasn't a lot of political support for this idea. The White House balked, saying it wasn't worth the investment, though by Washington standards it was parking meter money. Even so, we did what we could. For help we turned to an actress whose life had taken her down several career paths.

Bobbie Faye Ferguson always had a talent for the stage and camera. After teaching school in Arkansas and Texas, she got into show business. She started with commercials and small parts and ultimately appeared in roles on such TV hits as *Dallas* and *Designing Women*. As fate would have it, she ultimately found her way to Washington.

In time, though, Bobbie Faye wanted to return to the home she owned in California. Her chance came with an offer from DHS to do for us what the platoon of people from DOD does for the Pentagon. It wasn't easy to get this approved. She had worked in the Clinton Administration, but we prevailed.

Her first major assignment, with the help of others in our department, was the creation of a tabletop exercise for producers and other key Hollywood figures. We wanted to create a hypothetical situation involving a realistic, potential terrorist attack that could get their attention. Knowing how difficult it is to get on the calendar of an entertainment exec, she sent out a compelling invitation—to the world premiere of *Pacific Cloud*. This wasn't a movie but a hypothesis: What would happen if the annual Oscar ceremony became the target of a bioterrorism attack?

We were amazed and pleased with the cast of characters this invitation drew to the exercise. A partial listing of who was there: James Cameron, producer of *Titanic*; Bob Shaye, president of New Line Cinema; Michael Apted, president of the Directors Guild of America; Daniel Petrie Jr., president of the Writers Guild of America; Gary

Newman, copresident of 20th Century–Fox and the Fox Entertainment Group; Tom Jacobson, president of Paramount; and representatives of Disney/ABC, NBC, Golden Touch Media, and others of influence.

We met in a conference room at a Hollywood hotel. I'm not a big-time moviegoer, but I was grateful for their participation. I gave an introduction and we distributed to each present a briefing book, just like the ones I regularly get, featuring the threats that have emerged overnight. We also used a PowerPoint presentation that dealt specifically with the prospect of anthrax being used as a weapon at the Kodak Theater during the Oscar ceremonies. Frank Sesno pulled them into the discussion. What should be done? Cancel the show? Hold a press conference to announce the winners? What were the risks of going through with it? How could those in charge be reasonably assured that participants would be safe? What if the threat turned out to be false?

We posed the questions we faced on a daily basis to a group of people who have enormous influence on the populace. None of this seemed far-fetched to the people in the room. All had imagined, in one way or another, their industry as a terrorist target, and as a result we had their attention.

We used the exercise to get across the vital points they needed to know as they developed their own film and television projects. I think they were surprised to see the collaboration and exchanges among the federal, state, and local officials who participated in the exercise. They somehow had in their minds—even knowing of the courageous and often heartbreaking work of the New York City police and firemen on 9/11—that antiterrorism remained an exclusively federal issue. We showed them how interconnected the efforts were. We also showed that the real threats to the United States were much scarier than anything their writers could concoct as fiction.

Our biggest fear had been that very influential people would think there was no threat at all, or would make the scenarios so bizarre that a terrorist threat would be dismissed by their audiences. After the meeting we were confident they had gotten the point. Several in attendance expressed surprise at the complexity of the security infrastructure and thanked us for the insights.

In pretty short order, Bobbie Faye was called on to consult on films that featured agents from Immigration and Customs Enforcement (ICE). The first request came from Donald Sutherland, who had worked with her on *Space Cowboys*. The script for *Human Trafficking* needed work in terms of accurately reflecting what an ICE agent really does. These agents are another group of unheralded public servants who operate effectively and without fanfare within the department. They are entrusted with a wide range of responsibilities, from financial crime investigations to immigration law enforcement. Bobbie Faye explained how a raid is conducted and other key components of the work. As she says, "Actors just can't walk in and become ICE agents. They have to know the training." All the work resulted in a script that was both accurate and hair-raising.

There have been other huge dividends from DHS efforts in Hollywood. Not the least of them is ABC's new reality TV series, *Homeland Security USA*. Based on *Border Security: Australia's Front Line*, the hit show from Down Under, it follows DHS employees as they do their jobs. In one episode, customs finds a human skull shipped through the mail. In another, the Coast Guard chases cocaine smugglers. Others trail the Border Patrol in Texas and customs inspectors in New York. Executive producer Arnold Shapiro's comments when he announced the show were just what I hoped to hear when we began our Hollywood initiative: "We're showing everyday heroes risking their lives to protect us." More than that, these efforts help inform Americans how complex the issues can be in matters of immigration policy.

In the end, for Bobbie Faye, all of the issues with homeland security completed a full family circle. Her son, Jay R., won the role of the FBI supervisor in the hit Showtime series *Sleeper Cell,* which ran for three seasons. It was one potboiler that largely got it right, just as we had hoped. In its first series, it tracked the workings of a small group of Al Qaeda operatives—most of whom appeared to be sturdy American citizens, not obvious Islamic terrorists—intent on setting off a dirty bomb at a packed stadium in Los Angeles. For ordinary viewers, the show kept them on the edge of their seats. For us at DHS, it merely reflected the plotlines we followed every day.

11

INTERNATIONALLY SPEAKING

There were pieces of flesh and ribs all over the road. There were ribs, brains all over. I never saw anything like this. The train was blown apart. I saw a lot of smoke, people running all over, crying.

—LUZ ELENA BUSTOS,
witness to the train bombings in Madrid,
March 11, 2004

As governor, my goal was to make Pennsylvania a leader among states and a competitor among nations. I believed that every program, old and new, should be tested against this standard of comparison and excellence. It was clear to me from my first day in office that my state and its communities, families, and workers needed global connections and relationships. We tripled the number of overseas trade offices. We took small and medium-sized companies on trade missions. They were encouraged to think strategically and to look for more than a single selling opportunity, to build relationships that would endure.

My worldview of the irreversible nature of America's interdependence on the rest of the world for economic and security reasons was confirmed again when I traveled early in my tenure with the U.S. Coast Guard to New Orleans. During an inspection of the port, we were invited to board a bulk cargo ship. I ascended the pilot ladder and boarded the ship registered in Singapore, with an Indian crew, awaiting American grain to transport to Japan.

As I say repeatedly throughout this book, our future security and our ability to prevail over terrorists is also linked to our global relationships. Their support may come in varying degrees or forms, but we must relentlessly pursue it and work as hard as we can to sustain it. America has always enjoyed the complete, unapologetic, and unwavering support of one world leader who survived a terrorist attack.

José María Aznar López is the former prime minister of Spain. He teaches a seminar in European politics at Georgetown University in Washington, D.C. Occasionally we get together for lunch or dinner at Café Milano not far from the Georgetown campus. I'm always struck by his enormous presence for a man who is slight of build. Dressed in his usual blazer, jeans, and open-neck shirt, he nevertheless has an aura of urgency and his first sentence reveals a dazzling intelligence. As I sit across from him and listen to his impeccable and impassioned views, I can easily see why he and former British prime minister Tony Blair alone among European leaders became fervent allies of ours in the Iraq War. He often talks about how interconnected the world has become and, therefore, the need to combat terrorism wherever it exists. His story illustrates several points, among them the realities of living under constant threat and the limits on the power of a democracy to guarantee safety to all its citizens.

Prime Minister Aznar was having breakfast on March 11, 2004, when terror struck Madrid. The morning's newspapers noted that with the election only three days away, Aznar's Popular Party held a four-and-a-half point lead in the polls. Having come to the end of his second four-year term, he had enjoyed widespread support. But there had been growing dissatisfaction with Spain's participation in the Iraq War. Aznar and his party were harshly criticized by the Socialists, and the Iraq policy was not supported by the majority of Spaniards.

At that time, Aznar was also—as always—concerned with what the ETA (short for Euskadi Ta Askatasuna, or Basque Homeland and Freedom) would do. Some would view the ETA as the Spanish equivalent of the Irish Republican Army in Northern Ireland. The ETA supporters had continually made threats in their efforts to secure an independent state for Basques. Aznar himself had been the victim of an attack, having survived a car bombing in 1995 with minor head injuries. ETA, since its founding in 1959, had killed more than eight hundred people, most of them politicians, security officials, and journalists. Aznar had cracked down hard on the separatists. It was a priority of his time in office. His intelligence chiefs had often warned that Madrid could become the target of an ETA attack.

Indeed, Madrid did become a target on the morning of March 11, but the ETA was not responsible. For all of the damage it did over the years, ETA often issued specific warnings beforehand, such as in a shopping center bombing in 1985. Tragically, police said in that case the warning came too late for an adequate response. If ETA had planned to bomb a train, it might have placed a cassette tape that urged passengers, in advance of the explosion, to leave at the next station. No such warnings were offered on March 11.

At 7:37 A.M., which is rush hour in every major city on earth, three devices exploded in a train that was about to enter the Atocha station in Madrid. A few seconds later, four bombs were detonated on another train, which at the time was about five hundred yards from the station. Three miles away, two bombs went off in a train at the El Pozo del Tío Raimundo station, and, minutes later, one more exploded at the suburban Santa Eugenia station. The result of all this was widespread carnage. Office workers, students, immigrants, and others who relied on public transportation to get them to work were killed or maimed. In all, that morning, there were 191 deaths and more than 1,600 injuries. This far exceeded anything ETA had ever done. Its highest body count had been twenty-one shoppers at a Barcelona grocery store in 1987.

At first, Aznar and his government considered ETA the prime and only suspect, in spite of the absence of a warning, which had been its usual practice. But the attack, vast though it was, otherwise fit the profile. Just a few months earlier, on Christmas Eve, when we, in the United States were obsessed with Christmas Orange, the Spanish Civil Guard had stopped an ETA van carrying 1,100 pounds of explosives on its way to the capital; they also arrested two ETA members who had planted backpack bombs on trains. Aznar told the editors of Spanish newspapers, "ETA is behind these attacks." This fervent view, in the hours before the election, turned out to be fatal for his party's candidate.

Police soon located a white van that contained detonators used in the attack. The tape player in the van held a recording of recitations from the Koran. At roughly the same time, investigators concluded that the kind of bombs used in the train attacks did not fit the ETA profile. The case became clearer when a police officer found a sports bag containing a bomb that hadn't exploded. It also contained a mobile phone attached to the detonator. The chip inside the phone held a record of phone calls made—many of them—to a network of young Arab immigrants known to Spanish intelligence.

This led investigators to a small shop in a neighborhood near the Atocha station owned by a Moroccan who had been under surveillance because of his alleged connections with Al Qaeda. The shop owner was arrested, and the police were quickly at odds with the Aznar administration. The next night, millions of Spaniards participated in public demonstrations—angry about the violence, but also concerned that the government, perhaps for political reasons, had accused domestic political terrorists rather than Islamist fundamentalists.

Muslim radicals, after all, had long named Spain a target because of a centuries-old grudge about the lost colonies of Islam. After 9/11, bin Laden called attention to the long struggle in Spain and the expulsion of Muslims five hundred years earlier (ending, ironically, in 1492). Indeed, until the Victorian era, Spain had been greatly influenced by the culture. Its greatest architecture was Islamic in structure and feel. The magnificent Alhambra in the Andalusian city of Granada is emblematic. Indeed, Islam was at the forefront of medicine, art, science, and commerce until the sixteenth century, and the society was tolerant. Malik Ruiz Callejas, the emir of the Islamic community in Spain, told *The New Yorker* magazine, "Back when Paris and London people were being eaten alive by rats, in Cordoba everyone could read and write. The civilization of Al Andalus was probably the most just, most unified and most tolerant in history, providing the greatest level of security and the highest standard of living."

As the investigation of the Madrid bombings proceeded, the Al Qaeda connection became stronger and stronger, and eventually the Spanish courts ruled that the responsibility lay with an Al Qaeda–inspired cell. One of the first acts of the newly elected prime minister was the withdrawal of Spanish troops from Iraq.

At the time of the bombings, I was returning home from one of my rare trips overseas. In Singapore, we had gathered about a dozen American ambassadors to Far Eastern countries. We wanted to enlist their aid to help us in our security efforts. Even those within the top echelon of government in our embassies in Japan, China, Korea, and other key countries in the region were not clear about our mission at DHS and how it fitted with theirs. The State Department, frankly, had not been particularly helpful in this regard, closely guarding, as did so many other cabinet departments, its territory.

Although support from "Main State" as the State Department in Washington is known, was marginal at best, I had arranged a similar event in Amsterdam, attended by U.S. ambassadors to several European countries, and it was quite successful. I assumed that State's reluctance to be helpful was behind the cancellation of a Middle Eastern meeting that I had also planned.

I hoped that by explaining the issues in a personal way I could convince our ambassadors to become partners with us in the effort to create the widest possible perimeter of defense. For example, we needed their help in securing foreign cooperation on the matter of container inspection at distant ports. We needed their help to persuade governments and international airlines to provide passenger information before taking off for the United States. Making our borders the last line of defense, not the first, was always our goal.

Beyond that, I was eager to promote the brand of the newest federal department and to better understand staffing needs in overseas offices. I wasn't operating from a position of power. I needed their help without being able to give much in return. I was also limited in what I could do to solve what they saw as a growing problem with our new visa policies in the wake of 9/11. The reception I got was congenial and positive in every way. And yet there were uncomfortable moments. Questions inevitably came up about the newly restrictive visa policy and the practical effect it was having on our relations overseas. The collective unhappiness about post-9/11 visa policy was so severe during this conversation that the ambassador to Japan, Howard Baker, who had been the majority leader of the U.S. Senate starting in 1981, reminded everyone, "Tom inherited the visa policy from the State Department with a few add-ons from Congress." I appreciated his intervention but I'd also toured enough embassies to know how difficult Congress has made their job. There is no embassy in the world that is equipped to interview everybody who applies for a visa, yet this was the new congressionally imposed policy. Staff shortages resulted in people standing in line for hours, even days. There were insufficient resources available to do expedited background checks on so many applicants. The whole process had come to a standstill and the ambassadors were as frustrated as I was.

A fundamental definition of America had changed. We had gone from the country which welcomed the "huddled masses yearning to breathe free" (as the Emma Lazarus poem proclaims) to being, almost overnight, one of the world's most restrictive countries. We were trying to cut ourselves off from the world at the very time that it was proving both impossible and unwise to do so. The world had become interconnected—its commerce, its sciences, its personalities, its arts, its technology, its cultures. And as in all cases where one circles the wagons, shooting in at a target is easier than shooting out.

Just how close we remained to a potential terror attack was well illustrated by events in Madrid. In the days afterward, Al Qaeda issued a warning to many European countries and to the United States that we were next. The practical effect of the train bombings in Madrid was that the warning hit home immediately.

Within minutes our operations center was in communication with officials of our twenty largest cities, all of whom were concerned about simultaneous attacks on their own mass transit systems. Our job at that point was to tell these officials what we knew about Madrid, which, at the time, was little more than CNN knew, but we promised to keep the lines open and pass along as much information as we could, as quickly as we could.

Congress did its job in what is known, in congressional parlance, as "regular order." Our representatives raced to the microphones to make the strongest and most eloquent case against evil, while committing America's dwindling resources to preventing any such attack on our mass transit systems. The truth was—something members of Congress will not say—there are limits to the security measures we can employ in a mass transit system without affecting its critical use by the community.

We can install more cameras, assign more uniformed police and civilian guards, and so on, but there will never be, in a free society, a fail-safe way to protect mass transit. With tens of thousands descending the subway stairs (or ascending the stairs to an el) and crowding into buses, or even sitting in cars caught in stalled traffic on a bridge or in a tunnel, there is simply no way to guarantee protection without bringing the transportation system to a halt.

Once again it's about taking appropriate action in the context of sustaining the economic value of the system. It's the balance between security and prosperity. It's all about risk management.

That was the lesson of Madrid: At the intersection of prosperity and security, there is a limit on how far a country can go without disrupting the daily lives of its citizens.

This is, of all of the chapters in the brief history of Homeland Security, perhaps the most counterintuitive. It suggests that, if we were ever going to rename the agency, we might call it the Department of Worldwide Security and Prosperity. I understand this would not fly politically—here or overseas. In the United States there is, and has long been, a prevailing America First mentality. And yet the very idea of America First requires a new definition: a worldwide view and a way to look and behave beyond our borders that, privately, might not comport with what the public sees as international relations as usual.

Let me take you back, for a moment, to the early days of DHS, to March 2003, when I held my first meeting with employees in the Ronald Reagan Building about three blocks from the White House but about five miles from the NAC. I intended to deliver to people who had represented twenty-two agencies an idea of what their new employer was trying to accomplish. I knew well what I was up against—a grudging acknowledgment of the new reality with the attendant private, and perhaps some public, grumbling. Every one of the new employees of DHS had been on a different career path a few weeks earlier, and all now wondered where their new path would lead. During the question-and-answer session, I expected to be pummeled with inquiries about seniority, status, benefits, pay, and other obvious concerns of people whose work had changed almost overnight.

Instead, here was the first question from a man in the audience: "Mr. Secretary, what are the international relationships we're going to need to advance homeland security?" It was a stunning question, and one that I didn't answer fully at the time because in March 2003 I hadn't yet figured it out myself. But as time went on, the international aspects of our work became more and more critical, and all of us saw that America's security and prosperity would depend greatly on how we dealt with the rest of the world.

In the immediate aftermath of World War II, the United States was the only nation with a diversified economy. Because of war production, our industrial base was strong and, for all practical purposes, we had no competition. We made the world's widgets and gadgets, and the rest of the world bought them. When our economy sneezed, much of the rest of the world caught a cold.

The last few years have cost us a great deal of international respect and cooperation. That translates to a greater security challenge, lower purchasing power in the international marketplace, the loss of prestige and influence, and more than a few jobs at home. Goodwill is hard to measure, and there are those who kiss it off and say, "We're America. Who cares?" That's a wrong, and dangerous, attitude. Unlike any time in our nation's history, now and forever, more will depend on our global relationships.

For example, the U.S. ambassador to the Netherlands was Cliff Sobel, a close friend of mine. We were having dinner in Washington discussing our roles within the administration. He took his role as America's agent seriously and worked closely with the government, private sector, and even the nonprofits in the Netherlands to advance our interests.

I mentioned that maritime security, ships, crew, and cargo posed an area of vulnerability for America and had to be addressed. We discussed an innovative program called CSI, not the popular television series, *Crime Scene Investigation,* but the Container Security Initiative. We wanted to position DHS employees in foreign ports with the technology necessary to inspect containers. I thought if we could find a major European port to accept this most unusual relationship—using foreign inspectors in their ports—it would be the catalyst we needed for others to embrace it. He noted that Rotterdam might be a launching point for this program and said he would discuss it with the Dutch government.

Within a few days, he was able to convince the Netherlands to become the first nation in the European Union to accept our container security initiative, inspections in foreign ports before goods are loaded onto ships headed to our ports. The result was that other countries in the EU, hostile at first to the plan and angry at the Netherlands for doing what it did, recognized that the Netherlands might obtain a competitive advantage and so suddenly became sympathetic and joined up as well. This would not have happened but for the purposeful intervention of the U.S. ambassador to the Netherlands. Another result of our close work with the Netherlands was a more seamless international antiterrorism effort. The problem with the European Union was that its twenty-five members tended to work independently of each other in terms of their own security, resulting in a paucity of information sharing, something akin to our own interagency issues in Washington.

In the wake of the Madrid bombings, it became clear that no one was safe and that some system had to be worked out that would make it possible to combine individual nations' efforts into one effective operation that looked out for all parties involved. We worked with Gijs de Vries, who served as the Netherlands' deputy interior minister and represented his country in the European Parliament in Brussels. He was able to persuade member states to honor each others' arrest warrants and otherwise get national police forces to work together. All of this was great benefit to us as quietly but steadily we pushed out our international defense perimeter. At a time when many of our traditional allies were balking publicly about Iraq, their intelligence and law enforcement communities were quietly cooperating with ours.

Negotiations with the EU were ongoing and involved several matters. Over time the department's effort to layer defenses around commercial aviation included trained screeners, screening technology, hardened cockpit doors, air marshals, armed pilots, and behavioral observers. The layered approach to some seems redundant. To us it was the only way to avoid a single point of failure.

There remained, however, one critical piece of the security puzzle missing for air travel—prescreening passengers. The EU, very protective of privacy rights, strenuously objected to our initial requests for information about passengers boarding flights to the United States.

While there were several obstacles to overcome to gain their support, there were two that were most pressing initially. The first involved refuting the notion that Americans don't cherish their privacy as much as the Europeans. The department's chief privacy officer, Nuala O'Connor Kelly, was the first congressionally mandated, statutorily defined privacy officer in the entire federal government. She brought her considerable legal and advocacy skills, energy, and commitment to protecting what she often described as every citizen's "penumbral right" within the Constitution. Once we overcame that hurdle, we had a more substantive objection to combat.

And on this issue, I confess to agreeing with my European counterparts. Our initial request for information was extensive and in my judgment exceeded what we needed. We were simply asking for too much information (e.g. food preferences, religion). So we narrowed our requests and ultimately reached an agreement. That provides an important lesson for future policy makers: Do unto others. Don't ask of others what you are unwilling to do or provide yourselves. Double standards just don't work anywhere.

Once the request for information was narrowed and months of continuous negotiation completed, we were successful. There remained one final problem. The EU insisted on providing the information only after their planes embarked. Cat Stevens is a popular pop artist from the late 1960s and '70s and a convert to Islam who took the name Yusuf Islam. He was denied access because his name was on a security watch list. Unfortunately for all the passengers on board his transatlantic flight, the plane was ordered to land in Bangor, Maine; it arrived in Washington six hours later. Over the years, DHS has continued its negotiations with the EU, and now TSA has the information before the flights depart.

We didn't have to look across oceans to engage international friends in our effort to secure America. Our most important economic partners live to our north and south. Trade among the United States, Canada, and Mexico totaled nearly one trillion dollars in 2008 and, according to the magazine *Industry Week*, accounted for a third of all our foreign trade. From the time President Bush summoned me to the Oval Office shortly after 9/11 to discuss the intersection of our security and economy at our land borders through today, all three countries have collaborated to find better ways to enhance both. These lessons we have learned with our neighbors have global application. I believe the Smart Border Agreements we reached with Canada and Mexico in 2003 served as the basis for the Security and Prosperity Partnership of North America announced in March 2005. The joint statement by the leaders of the three countries expresses both the reality and the vision of the twenty-first century: "In a rapidly changing world, we must develop new avenues of cooperation that will make our open societies safer and more secure, our businesses more competitive and our economies more resilient."

We should never forget the important principle embodied in this statement. We cannot, and should not, go it alone!

12

CHRISTMAS ORANGE

"The whole system is designed to catch stupid terrorists." A smart terrorist . . . won't try to bring a knife aboard a plane . . . he'll make his own, in the airport bathroom. "Get some steel epoxy glue at a hardware store. It comes in two tubes, one with steel dust and then a hardener. You make the mold by folding a piece of cardboard in two, and then you mix the two tubes together. You can use a metal spoon for the handle. It hardens in 15 minutes."

—JEFFREY GOLDBERG,
quoting security expert Bruce Schneier, in "The Things He Carried,"
The Atlantic, November 2008

On the morning of July 5, 2002, Los Angeles Mayor James Hahn made a frantic phone call to our Transportation Security Administration (TSA) headquarters in Washington. He needed help right away. Terrorism, or so it certainly seemed, had struck home.

The Los Angeles airport accommodates more than two thousand flights a day at nine freestanding terminals and is the third busiest hub in the world. It attracts the world's top airlines, including El Al. The Israeli carrier is well known for its safety record, its scrutiny of passenger lists, and its all-around security precautions. But it could not thwart the ground attack that occurred on Independence Day.

At the Department of Homeland Security, holidays were always a worry. The media inquired about them all the time. Understandably. Much of the anxiety was self-generated—it seemed that prospective terrorists could strike then, in a moment of heightened vulnerability, just to underscore their point. Picnics, parades, sporting events, high-density air and automobile travel, all led to heightened anxiety and concern. The public needed to be assured that adequate precautions were being taken. But there is so much more to an attack than a date. There was never really any suggestion in the intelligence that holidays had any special appeal to terrorists.

At about 11:30 A.M on July 4, a forty-one-year-old Egyptian-born limousine driver walked into the Tom Bradley Terminal at LAX. He took his place in a line at the El Al ticket counter on the departure level. Suddenly, Hesham Mohamed Hadayet drew three weapons, two handguns and a six-inch hunting knife, and started to lash out at passengers. The attacker was shot by a security guard, but not before two people had been killed and four others seriously wounded.

It was soon determined through Motor Vehicle Department fingerprints that the assailant had lived in California for a decade and, though not a citizen, held a valid green card. City officials didn't label the attack terrorism, but El Al officials felt otherwise, having faced many threats to the airline in countries around the world. At first blush it appeared to be a horrific isolated act. There was rigorous investigation to determine whether the attack was connected to any fundamentalist group. The DHS took a deep dive into all records, working with the FBI. They checked to see if Hadayem's phone number or address led to relationships with anybody we had under investigation; there were plenty of traps that could be run to see if there was a nexus. The Department of Justice, FBI, and ATF did the heavy lifting and quickly determined that Hadayem's act was a personal one, and not motivated by any terrorist organization.

Mayor Hahn, however, knew that the distinctions between terrorism and "ordinary" crime were of no interest to the families and friends of the victims. What had happened was an inhuman event, the Columbine-esque phenomenon that on an ordinary day, when people have ordinary concerns, the bizarre and unthinkable can occur; it was another reminder of widespread and ever-present vulnerability.

The mayor was eager to get help from TSA, and particularly in the person of retired Rear Admiral David Stone, whose tenure as security director for LAX was scheduled to begin in just a few weeks. The mayor, worried that the security at LAX needed vast improvement to prevent more tragedies, wanted him to start immediately.

David Stone had built a perfect résumé for the job by the summer of 2002, except that in all of his world travels, extensive though they were, he could not list LA among the places he had come to know.

When he arrived in LA, he saw an airport full of security holes and needs. Five different companies with no common standards ("little empires" as Stone would eventually refer to them) were in charge of screening, and each did it in its own way. There were many workers who couldn't speak English, and thousands of openings to fill. Meanwhile, there was a strict deadline to work against. Congress had mandated that by the end of December 2002, the new provisions had to be put in place, including the screening of all checked baggage, an enormous task considering that in 2002 LAX handled over 56 million passengers annually and on any one day checked more than 150,000 bags.

Security plans were consolidated, the necessary screeners were hired and trained, and the deadline was met. There were no further incidents at LAX and Stone developed strong relationships with employees and local authorities. Yet he did this under some duress, as he found the federal bureaucracy frustrating in a way the navy had never been.

Admiral Stone's experience as the Federal Security Director (FSD) for the Transportation Security Administration at the airport in many respects was not unique. His colleagues throughout America's commercial aviation system were compelled to build, organize, and lead teams at each of the nation's commercial airports. Because virtually every member of Congress has at least one commercial airport in or near his or her district, the FSDs did so under the relentless scrutiny and frequent criticism of Congress and commentators.

Too little attention was paid to the simple fact that within weeks after the 9/11 attack Congress directed the secretary of transportation, Norman Mineta, to create, organize, staff, and train an entirely new organization, TSA, consisting of nearly 45,000 new hires within the ridiculously compressed time frame of nine months.

Often Congress demands that extremely complex tasks be accomplished in unrealistic time frames without ever acknowledging the scope of the mission. As a former congressman, I can say this without equivocation. Too few members understand, and some may not care, that it is much easier to pass legislation than it is to make it work. Whether the Congress is passing legislation mandating requirements on local governments, states, or the executive branch, they never see the end customers, and more often than not don't appreciate the complexity of the task assigned.

Remember the words uttered by Yul Brynner as Pharaoh in *The Ten Commandments*? "So let it be written: so let it be done." If it were just that easy!

No airport was designed for such a huge security workforce, or the extensive screening measures and equipment for passengers, baggage, and cargo. Screeners didn't have a break room or even a place to store their jackets or the lunches they brought from home. None of the airports were architecturally designed to accept the security measures that were required after 9/11. Congress, and all of America for that matter, expected the highest professional standards to be met by these employees, but they weren't given the most basic of provisions as workers. They had the added discomfort of having to be on their feet all day and generally dealing with unsympathetic, and often angry, passengers who had grown used to arriving at the airport at the last minute and, in essence, diving across the jetbridge as it was being withdrawn from the airplane. Frequent travelers, especially, had a hard time accepting long lines and individual scrutiny. Added to that was the pressure, for the TSA screeners, of knowing that if they made a mistake—if they failed to identify a bag that had a suspicious item in it, for example—lives could be at stake. It made for a difficult job.

All of us were frustrated by the torrent of criticism and rebuke from Congress and its inclination to change the rules in the face of changing political winds in the form of complaints from constitutents. Many only belittled the work of the organization that had been in business less than nine months but, through the work of thousands of dedicated people, had helped restore confidence in air travel. Official Washington had no clue about the level of performance, needs, and dedication of people in the field. Official criticism makes headlines. Official praise is ignored.

When I visited LAX in the spring of 2003 to see the positive changes firsthand, I saw that, in less than a year's time and despite critical issues, security was tighter than it had ever been. Stone himself was ready to move on and did so by becoming deputy chief of staff to Jim Loy, to assist him with Capitol Hill liaison. Jim and his team were spending more and more time shuttling from the NAC to the Hill at the mandatory invitation of dozens of committees and subcommittees. Jim needed someone who could help him sustain his working relationship with Congress, deal with the cacophony of criticism, and support and promote his continuous-improvement agenda.

This matter of endless Congressional testimony is worth noting because it underscores the continued absence of an effective partnership between the new department and the legislative branch. Oversight responsibility was simply diffused among too many committees. Other key agencies of the federal government—the Department of Defense and the Department of Justice and others—had long ago established where the lines of oversight ran with the House and Senate committees, and these were relatively few. The Defense Department, for example, had to answer to only four committees and a handful of subcommittees. By contrast, the Department of Homeland Security, the new kid on the block, about to spend a great deal of new money for security, drew the attention of everyone in Congress. There didn't seem to be a committee on the Hill that considered it off limits. In all, eighty-six congressional entities summoned us to testify. (Indeed, the situation has not improved. In a 2007 letter to the House Committee on Homeland Security, my successor, Michael Chertoff pointed out that, from 2004 to 2007, members of the department participated in 696 hearings and 7,864 congressional briefings.) My senior leadership team and I spent thousands of hours in this process. And while we recognized the legitimacy and importance of congressional oversight, we felt the time could have been more wisely spent.

When we did testify, some of the inquiries and comparisons made us incredulous. It ratified our concern that some of the members, or their staffs, just didn't get the scope of the problem we were dealing with. Often the questions were shockingly simplistic. "Why," a committee member would read from a card prepared by a member of his staff, "can't you just do what they do at El Al?" The Israeli system of security for airline travel is enviable. Any visitor to Israel can see firsthand how security and airline authorities work up profiles of travelers through interviews and background checks. Anyone who's ever flown that airline knows a passenger doesn't get on the plane before facing a pleasant but persistent questioner and several levels of security. Exhibiting more patience than we felt, we would remind the committee members that the El Al system was appropriate for Israel, which has two major hubs and less than three dozen jumbo aircraft. But what they do there—as effective as it has been—hardly translates to a country with more than four hundred major airports and more than ten thousand commercial flights daily. As it is, the security teams at our commercial airports see over two million people a day.

While dealing with these external matters as we were building the department, it was equally clear that we needed to identify and internalize our own vision and goals. To that end, we organized a three-day off-site exercise at a National Transportation Safety Board complex west of the Capitol, to which we invited fifty top staff members. There we hammered out specific missions for ourselves in the same way the FBI, Justice, the CIA, and other long-existing agencies had done long ago.

Until then our employees had only vague notions of how their work—shifted from some other department to DHS—fit into the larger picture. We needed something more than a carefully crafted mission statement. We needed to be able to point to specific responsibilities and tasks that would not only help us explain our work to Congress but make us much more effective and goal-oriented. With Admiral Loy's leadership and everyone's participation, we emerged with specific major areas of responsibility as they pertained to security threats: awareness, prevention, protection, response, and recovery—and all of it with a forward-looking view as the only cabinet department established in the twenty-first century. That is, we were determined not to be locked in by the old ways of doing federal business but to make use of new technologies and a new kind of openness within our own department that would encourage relationships with other agencies.

We were certainly maturing as a department, internalizing our focus, improving our coordination, and building stronger relationships with our state and local partners and across the federal government. Congress began to understand, just as we did, what our specific missions and needs were. Even so, this didn't—and it shouldn't have—made us immune to hard looks.

Notwithstanding our drive to create the perfect system, we made mistakes that became subject to public and congressional scrutiny. Occasionally we had to explain some very embarrassing circumstances.

A twenty-year-old college student, Nathaniel Heatwole, provided one of the worst. He had smuggled box cutters, knives, matches, liquid bleach, and other banned materials aboard a commercial aircraft. He left them in bags in lavatories along with a note signed "Sincerely, 3891925," which represented his date of birth (May 29, 1983), backward. Frustrated that his acts had not apparently been noticed by any central agency, he sent an email to TSA calling attention to all he had done. This only made the situation, and the frustration, more apparent to us. How could a college student single-handedly prove that the new system of air security employing tens of thousands of people outfitted with new technology could be so full of holes? (Heatwole was eventually sentenced to two years of probation and helped produce a training video that showed TSA officials and workers how he smuggled banned items aboard aircraft.)

It's difficult to express the frustration and embarrassment associated with incidents such as this. More training, better technology, and more rigorous oversight are all in play as TSA continues to improve. Yet with thousands of departures and millions of passengers every single day, the goal of eliminating all such incidents and creating a fail-safe system remains, and will probably always remain, elusive. It also underscores the reality that identification of the terrorists before they board the plane is the ultimate deterrent. That, too, is easier said than done.

For every publicized incident there are hundreds known by the Department and subject to review. A security practice was developed in the early days of TSA for that purpose. Every morning, there was an intelligence meeting, in which top managers reviewed incident reports from the country's major airports and from train, bus, and trucking systems. They combed reports of evacuated terminals, unruly passengers, and unattended bags for signs of the next threat.

A watch list was developed. It contained the names of people who had been previously involved in any kind of airport disturbance. It also included names provided by the intelligence and law enforcement communities. In many ways, however, the department was in a no-win position. The more we scrutinized airline passengers, the greater the complaints from those who had been delayed and searched. Gradually, however, citizens were warming to the idea of heightened security, accepting longer lines and delays as a precondition of improved security. We got fewer and fewer complaints, and occasionally the tenor of the complaint was humorous and accommodating, as long as it was somebody else who got pulled in for secondary screening.

One day I took a personal call from Senator Ted Kennedy. He, with one of the most recognizable political faces in the country, had had to wait several times for clearance before boarding the shuttle between Washington and Boston, which he had been taking for decades. He said, "I seem to have trouble when I try to get to the gate." He asked me to look into it for him, and added, in his wry way, "I know some people in your party may think I'm a political terrorist." We both laughed. It was a cordial conversation, but I understood his frustration. I didn't know whether he was on a watch list or perhaps mistaken for someone with the same name who was on it. One call to TSA and the matter was resolved. There were many folks far less prominent who didn't know where to take their complaints. Finally, we established an 800 number and appointed an ombudsman to deal with them. He was extremely busy as we worked to improve the watch list process.

Although our office served as the clearinghouse for such complaints, there came a time toward the end of our first year when intelligence reports seriously tested the organizational maturity of the yet-to-be completed team of this brand-new agency. The intelligence community churns twenty-four hours a day, 365 days a year. There are no holidays and, as we were soon to discover, there would be none for the department during its first Christmas.

There was a significant increase in the sheer volume of threats accumulating after Thanksgiving 2003. The information indicated that the extremists abroad were anticipating near-term attacks that would rival or exceed 9/11. Some of the reports reiterated a continuing interest in the use of airplanes. Others, apart from the method, identified certain urban areas as targets for unspecified attack. As skeptical or uncertain as we may have been, the volume, the unique nature of some of the sources and their connection to commercial flights, and other factors led to grave concern within the administration.

In this time of high anxiety Christmas approached, bringing with it several incidents in New York City. Authorities discovered suspicious packages in and around the city, and as a result several lines of the subway system were closed and the Metropolitan Museum of Art was evacuated of its visitors. Governor George Pataki put state agencies on alert for possible attacks on infrastructure. In our conversations, Pataki asked all the right questions. What did we know about possible terrorist threats against New York City? How specific? How credible? What federal resources were available to help ramp up airport and nuclear power plant security?

Much of the anxiety could be traced to international media. A few days earlier, the Arabic television network Al Jazeera broadcast an audiotaped statement attributed to Dr. Ayman al-Zawahiri, chief deputy to Osama bin Laden, who said, "We are still chasing the Americans and their allies everywhere, even in their homeland."

All of these developments caused the department to embark on unprecedented holiday security preparations, an effort that would eventually be known to all within as Christmas Orange. President Bush called General John Gordon, who had succeeded me as the president's homeland security advisor, and me to the Oval Office the Saturday before Christmas. We talked about the threat and the need for extraordinary vigilance during the season. He knew John and I were committed to remaining in D.C. through the first of the year and extended a hand in appreciation and apology for keeping us from our families.

We had been monitoring a unique source of intelligence and communication that appeared to identify specific flights originating from Great Britain, France, and Mexico that were either targets or carried terrorists. This coupled with other information resulted in discussions for several days in our morning meetings. One morning, after everyone had their say, the president, in a conversational and commonsense manner, asked, "Which one of you, based on this information, would put your family on one of those flights?" No one said they would. The president had made his point. The flights would be canceled.

Asa Hutchinson, former U.S. attorney, congressman, administrator of the Drug Enforcement Agency, brought his extraordinary public service record and considerable leadership skills to the department as Undersecretary of Border and Transportation Security. Hutchinson was asked to call a couple of ambassadors about our decision to cancel several flights originating from their countries. I thought it was the quickest way to give notice. Asa reported back to me that one ambassador initially responded that this was a matter of national pride and sovereignty and no DHS official could prevent the flight from taking off. Asa calmly agreed that we had no authority to control the takeoff, but because we controlled the air space over the United States we could prevent the plane from landing. His counterpart paused and offered that in the interest of comity between nations and our mutual effort against the extremists, the flight would be canceled.

The action we took did not come without criticism. The State Department complained that the notice and action should have been made through the diplomatic corps. The niceties of protocol came in second to immediate and direct communication.

We raised the threat level on December 21. It had been six months since the last alert. We ramped up security at airports; sent teams to the cities where we believed the threat was the greatest; talked to the public on several occasions, running the gauntlet of morning shows; held two daily secure videoconferences with relevant agencies and bureaus; had private conversations with governors, homeland security advisors, mayors, and other local officials; and contacted leaders in the private sector and provided specific measures they were to take at critical locations. We designed a comprehensive plan that engaged our team for two consecutive weeks.

At the NAC, everyone thought the workweek consisted of at least six days and most never understood that staying home on Sunday was an option. General Pat Hughes, Policy Director Sally Canfield, Chief of Staff Duncan Campbell, and countless others never looked at the clock or worried about the calendar. Campbell's cramped office was next to mine and I don't recall any weekend when he wasn't responding to hundreds of e-mail messages or inquiries. His work ethic and sense of accountability mirrored the entire headquarters team. So to most of them, Christmas Orange may have seemed to be the regular order of business. It wasn't!

Many of us slept in our offices during this period. Offices were cramped with discarded pizza boxes, stale pastries on plastic Christmas dishes, coffee cups that looked like biochem experiments. Tired but focused men and women answered the phones, watched the screens, and stayed connected via the Internet. We had opened our doors only nine months before and were still wrestling with all the growing pains associated with pulling this huge enterprise together. We were still working on it, but during those intense weeks I had great confidence in those entrusted with securing the homeland and great pride in their response to Christmas Orange.

13

FEMA AND THE GATHERING STORM

Thou born to match the gale, (thou art all wings),
To cope with heaven and earth and sea and hurricane, . . .

—WALT WHITMAN,
"To the Man-of-War Bird"

Administration critics who mentioned my lack of counterterrorism credentials at the time of my original appointment were correct in their assessment. But there was one major area of the job that made me uniquely qualified for the post. Had the Bush administration taken advantage of what I had learned, and the plan my team had developed, DHS as well as state and local agencies would have produced something other than a pitiful and tragic response to Hurricane Katrina.

I was no longer serving at DHS when the category-four storm breeched the levees and devastated an iconic American city. Like everyone else, I watched the aftermath on television. I didn't know exactly what went wrong, but I had a very strong suspicion, later confirmed, and I seethed about the personal and political maneuvering that had led to such heartbreak and chaos.

My bona fides in dealing with natural disasters go back two decades before Katrina hit, to the late spring of 1985.

May 31 was a day of fitful skies over western Pennsylvania and a lamentable anniversary: It had been ninety-six years since the South Fork Dam failed, water gushed out and flooded the city of Johnstown, Pennsylvania, and left 2,200 dead. A stormy spring day in the modern era could offer its own lessons in Mother Nature's fury, and though the event would kill far fewer, it would remain forever in the memories of those who lived through it, including me.

On this day I was at home in Erie, on a holiday break from my second term as a member of Congress representing the far northwest corner of Pennsylvania. As the storm developed, I became a minor player in the drama, but I was there: Many of those at the heart of it were mentioned in *Tornado Watch Number 211,* an exhaustively researched book by John Grant Fuller. In it, for example, he told the story of the Quay family.

On that morning, Linda Quay, a resident of Albion, a small town of about 1,600 in southwest Erie County, put breakfast on the table for her three children. T-ball was the subject of some of the conversation. Little Michael was to play that night, and the discussion was whether the game would be played as scheduled. His mother had watched the weather forecast on the *Today* show. The weatherman, Willard Scott, mentioned that Texas could be a likely target of violent storms, and one or more of them could spawn tornados. Linda Quay said to her children, "Hey, kids, aren't you glad we don't live in Texas, and we don't have to worry about a tornado?"

Linda Quay was at home on South Farm Avenue that afternoon when she heard that her son's T-ball game was canceled. She was relieved. By then her husband, Charley, the town's assistant fire chief, had interrupted dinners all around town with phone calls ordering every fireman to report for duty. In the Quay house, the family dog began whimpering for no apparent reason. Then the lights went out.

Even so, there was still plenty of natural light, and Linda began serving dinner. She heard a roar outside. Recognizing the sound of a tornado, she yelled to the kids to get to the basement. She crawled to get her little girl who was in a high chair and then to the basement door. She was surprised to see her other children still there.

The suction was too strong for the kids to overcome it. Linda managed to pull the door open, and she and her children slid down the stairs into the basement. The children were crying and asking, "Mommy, what is it? What is it?"

A few minutes later there was silence. Then came a knocking at the door and voices. "Anybody here? Everybody all right?" When the family went outdoors, Linda saw a much different Albion neighborhood than what was there a few minutes earlier. The Quay family had been among the lucky ones. The tornadoes that day hit twenty-eight towns across America, three in my congressional district alone. When the local human tally came in, Albion registered 12 dead and 82 injured; Atlantic, 23 dead, 125 injured; and Wheatland, 7 dead and 60 injured. Scores of homes were reduced to rubble. In Wheatland alone, 95 percent of the industrial buildings were destroyed or damaged. So along with the loss of personal property came the loss of livelihoods. When Pennsylvania governor Richard Thornburg saw the devastation, he described it this way: "The area must be seen to be believed," he said. "We use the word 'awesome' from time to time, but I think there is no other way to describe what the forces of Nature have done. Industrial facilities with structural steel bent out of shape like straw. Whole areas flattened as if they had been carpet-bombed. It's indescribable."

The morning after the storm, I made a tour of the damage in my four-year-old Chevy Caprice. I have always believed that in the wake of any kind of disaster, residents need to see their public officials as soon as possible, even though there may be nothing they can do at that moment except offer hugs or words of comfort. It's rule number one of Response and Recovery 101: Begin the conversation with the citizens you serve as soon as you can. (It was a rule that President George W. Bush ignored in the immediate aftermath of Katrina. Flying over the flooding in New Orleans and the surrounding parishes in Air Force One made him seem imperious and uncaring, which I know he is not.)

From the day the storm reached landfall, it was clear that billions of federal dollars would be needed to recover from nature's fury.

It's not as if there's always sufficient money available or the government will honor all requests. As governor, I once made a request for a disaster declaration when a major winter storm paralyzed Philadelphia and its suburbs. My request for relief was denied. FEMA told me, "No dough for snow." While I didn't agree with the rejection, I had to accept it. As governor, I was sometimes criticized for failure to submit applications for relief, but I knew what the federal standards were, and when we didn't meet them, I didn't apply. No matter the outcome, however, it is imperative that public officials are visible and involved as soon as the storm passes.

On the morning after the storm, I arrived in Atlantic, the small town at the intersection of two state roads. It is known primarily for two things: as the birthplace of playwright author Maxwell Anderson and as one of the many Pennsylvania communities that is home to the Amish, who have lived simply and without the benefit of technology and modern conveniences. No automobiles, no laptops.

By the time I got to town, Amish farmers from Ohio and elsewhere in Pennsylvania were already there, sifting through the wreckage, piling wood that could be used in reconstruction, and otherwise working on behalf of the community. How this happened so fast remains a mystery to me, but that it happened is a marvelous lesson, both in the legendary love-thy-neighbor ethic of the Amish and in the natural order of responding to tragedy. The local authorities were the first to come to the aid of the citizens, followed quickly by the Amish community as a whole. The Red Cross responded quickly, too. In the immediate aftermath of disaster, the federal government was a minor player.

When it was all over, and all the relief efforts were long underway, I sent out a survey from my congressional office in Washington to measure my constituents' attitudes about the response. The Red Cross got high marks, as did the local first responders, and of course the volunteers from religious communities who came from afar at a moment's notice. FEMA, which had established a large presence in the disaster area by setting up disaster assistance centers, was off the charts—the lowest end of the charts, in terms of community attitude. Local residents found it to be bureaucratic and limited in what it could do. If first responders were seen as lifesavers, the federal government was expected to weigh in with life support. In short, cash. People can't begin to comprehend the devastation to spirit and livelihood that such a circumstance brings with it. The federal government is supposed to provide some kind of safety net. It isn't an insurance company, to be sure. But without federal assistance, what is a town like Albion to do when its town hall is rubble? Is the only way to rebuild it to impose a surtax on local residents who have either lost their jobs or homes, or both. It had seemed to me that if there was any purpose at all to FEMA it was to be a significant source of financial support. If necessarily limited in the immediate aftermath of the disaster, certainly thereafter.

I was determined to do something about changing FEMA's mission and capabilities, to rewrite the law, but as a second-term congressman and on all the wrong committees to address that subject (I was on Banking, Veterans Affairs, and Aging), I had to find a way to be effective. So over the next two years, my staff met with staff members of congressmen who were in a better position to address such matters, i.e., they had the right committee assignments. Meanwhile, I talked often with the relevant committee chairmen, Republicans and Democrats, and persuaded them to hold hearings on the subject. My argument was that the real cost of recovery after a major natural disaster is far beyond the capacity of any local district to address, starting with matters as simple (but as daunting) as debris removal. The result of our effort was to get a bill passed in the House of Representatives to widen the scope and responsibilities of FEMA.

But by the end of 1988, with the Congress about to end its session for the year, it seemed that the legislation might die a natural death, because all unfinished bills at the end of a congressional term require that its authors start the process over again. The legislation would expire if the Senate failed to act on it. To those of us who cared about the issue, there was a great deal at stake, for Mother Nature works according to no predictable timetable. She could strike any time. We needed a strong FEMA as soon as possible. So I began one last, almost desperate, push to get this through.

I approached the about-to-retire senator from Vermont, Robert T. Stafford, who was recognized in the emergency community as one of the few people in the House or Senate who gave considerably more than lip service to the problem. I suggested to him that, to address the matter of running out of time, we attach the legislation to beef up FEMA as an amendment to a bill that was going through the Senate in the last couple of weeks of the session. And because he had been working on response to disasters far longer than I had, it would be a fitting gesture to call the legislation the Robert T. Stafford Disaster Relief and Emergency Assistance Act.

This, of course, was a measure of how politics is played. You give up naming rights in exchange for something more important— passage. Because of Stafford's stature, and because his colleagues would want to honor his last congressional request, this was the way to go. The bill was passed just in time. President Reagan quickly signed the Stafford Act into law. Ever since, FEMA's role has been greatly expanded. It participates much more completely and aggressively than the FEMA that existed prior to those northwestern Pennsylvania tornadoes.

I saw the new FEMA in at least a couple of ways. As governor of Pennsylvania following my stint in Congress, the welfare of its sixty-seven counties became my responsibility, and my staff and I were occasionally obliged to respond in the aftermath of natural disasters. We relied primarily during this time on a developing system of state and local partnerships. We knew we also had a federal partnership as well, with FEMA, and we worked to develop it.

I wish I could report that this sort of partnership developed nationally. Much of our effort at DHS was to incorporate FEMA and other agencies into a new plan that would spread the federal presence around the nation. In my view, we needed to be much closer to the communities we served. An exclusive inside-the-beltway presence couldn't possibly develop the kinds of partnerships we needed. From the early days of DHS, we worked on a plan to establish regional offices. The idea was that in each place, federal officials would develop personal relationships with governors, big-city mayors, the leadership of the first responder community, and get to know all of the prominent forces, political and otherwise, in the area. As I saw it, the new Department of Homeland Security was not merely a new cabinet agency but a national mission. We needed to position a portion of this massive bureaucracy closer to the state and local governments if we were to achieve our goals.

We weren't alone in our assessment of the need for this. The National Academy of Public Administration issued a prescient report that concluded, "If the United States fails to modernize federal field machinery and dramatically improve its ability to foster close teamwork among federal state and local leaders around the country in a way that is essential to meet [new challenges] the failure could easily endanger the lives of many thousands of U.S. citizens."

Our plan was ambitious. We knew it would be controversial. Few people or organizations accept change enthusiastically. Every major unit within the new department had multiple regional officers around the country. Thoughtful consolidation of these capabilities and responsibilities at places that made sense for their traditional missions and their newest one—to secure the country—was the only way to build a national network of security.

General Bruce Lawlor, my chief of staff knew as well as I that our first proposal would elicit significant criticism. We were "spot on." We got everyone's attention when the first draft of our proposal gave daily operational control of the assembled units to the regional director. Some saw it as a clear threat to Washington-based authority, which it was. Others were simply comfortable with the way things were. Change was an unwelcome thought. As appropriate, we began to make changes to our scheme that didn't compromise our goals, but satisfied their concerns. The opposition, with a few exceptions, including FEMA, dissipated as the model evolved under the guidance of Bob Stephan my Special Assistant and Director of the Headquarters Integration Team and the extraordinary work of his team.

Thousands of hours. One draft after another. Choosing the best regional centers and alternate locations, defining explicit roles and responsibilities, identifying the specific number of employees from each bureau, writing job descriptions. The massive effort resulted in an integration plan that would make the state and local governments, first responders, communities, and companies in the region part of a national network of communication, information sharing, training, oversight, and collaboration to respond to any crisis, man-made, accidental, or wrought by nature. If we could establish regional headquarters in strategic locations—New York, Philadelphia, Chicago, Miami, New Orleans, Houston, San Francisco, and Seattle—and create smaller units in Juneau and Honolulu, that would position us to respond to any form of crisis in concert with state and local officials and the private sector.

As 2003 became 2004, it looked as if our efforts would succeed. We worked the White House hard. They finally agreed and money was budgeted. But as the effort went on, we lost momentum. Internal critics of the plan had friends on the White House staff and were perpetually degrading the effort. What I thought had been one of the great successes—dealing with one of our nation's biggest needs—turned into my biggest disappointment at DHS. And the events that followed only served to underscore the need for what we had proposed.

I have gotten to know the state of Florida in a number of ways. First, as a tourist. The Ridge family has spent nearly every Easter weekend in Islamorada, in the Florida Keys since 1995. In that informal hideaway, nobody knows or cares what you do for a living and the Washington uniform of dark blue suit would be against the dress code, if there were one. As far as the locals and other tourists are concerned, you are just another guy catching the rays, angling for fish, or perched on a barstool. During that first trip from the Fort Lauderdale Airport to the Keys, the devastation leveled by Hurricane Andrew in Homestead, Florida, three years earlier was still evident. I watched the community struggle to recover throughout the years that followed.

I had other visits to Florida in the unofficial capacity of a golfer who has had the good fortune to tee it up with his friend, Arnold

Palmer. One of the perks of public service is that you get to know many people, occasionally even those who were heroes to you as a boy. I remember watching on our small black-and-white TV when they first started televising golf tournaments. My dad and I loved Palmer, his charisma and that hard-charging mentality. I caddied at a local country club, used my grandfather's clubs, some with wooden shafts, and hoped to develop a respectable game. Hope springs eternal.

Palmer, a native of Latrobe, Pennsylvania, spends winters in Orlando at his course, Bay Hill. I still remember the first time I played golf with him. The first tee, of course, is known to all golfers as a test of nerves, even when no spectators are watching. If I expected that I could quietly slip in a round with Arnie without anybody noticing, I was quickly disabused of the notion. Every time he goes to the first tee he draws a crowd. The careful observer watched Pennsylvania's governor trying to insert a tee into the ground while his right hand was shaking a bit. I felt more nervous than the first time I got shot at in Vietnam. Then, as I later told Arnold, I hit the ground in a rice paddy, hid behind a foot-high earthen dike, and returned fire. On the first tee with the "King," there is no place to hide.

Our round during the spring of 2005 was different from any other. The course had been damaged by a couple of the four major hurricanes that had ripped through the Sunshine State in a period of six weeks, an unprecedented circumstance. As we played, Arnold discussed the extensive damage the course had sustained during the previous hurricane season. Of course, he said, losing a couple of hundred trees is hardly worth noting given the incredible damages inflicted by the storms named Charley, Frances, Ivan, and Jeanne. They had killed 117 people and had damaged or destroyed more than 10 percent of the state's housing stock. In all, property damage exceeded $21 billion.

In my capacity at DHS, I had made several visits to Florida during the hurricane season of 2004, usually via helicopter. Michael D. Brown, the head of FEMA, had asked the White House for a plane and one became available. I should have asked him to second my requests for similar transportation. Michael Brown had served as the deputy director to his friend Joe Albaugh who had served as the first FEMA director under George Bush. Admittedly, his emergency management experience was limited. But his service to our mutual friend Albaugh, along with Joe's recommendation, was good enough for me. He was appointed to succeed Albaugh in 2002. From the very beginning he had made no secret of the fact that he thought FEMA ought to be set apart from the department. It was that attitude and some of the accompanying challenges that led me to recommend to my successor, Michael Chertoff, that he consider replacing him. But considering the heat he took during and after Katrina it's important to note that FEMA and Brown performed well through the hurricane cycle of 2004. Jeb Bush, governor of Florida, and Bob Riley, governor of Alabama, had effectively prepared their states and in collaboration with Brown and FEMA were able to lead timely and successful response and recovery efforts. Perhaps the largely successful response to the four hurricanes in Florida and the great preparation and recovery work of state and local officials in the affected states gave Brown a sense that he could handle whatever Katrina brought.

Brown and I flew in a chopper over the Florida Panhandle and along the coast of Alabama that fall. I noticed that in some areas houses directly next to or across from each other seemed almost untouched but some were down to their foundations. When I asked why, I learned that a new building code had been established in response to dire warnings about lax standards. The recently built houses fared much better than those grandfathered by the code.

In the aftermath of the storms, more than 1.2 million state residents applied via telephone or Internet for state and federal assistance through FEMA offices. When all of the money was accounted for, it was determined that about $5.6 billion had poured into the state through a variety of agencies. That much money going to that many people inevitably comes with controversy.

After any natural disaster, you can count on Congress to send contradictory messages. Message number 1: Give people the money they need to recover from natural disasters as quickly as possible.

Don't just stand there, spend something. Message number 2: We notice, in your haste to help, you're spending money the wrong way and giving it to the wrong people. That, of course, happened in this case, and congressional hearings were held that generated predictable headlines. Haste, after all, does make waste. And so there was a great deal of high-minded debate in the months that followed about situations in which Miami-Dade residents got more assistance than they merited and owners of damaged cars got checks for amounts more than their cars were worth. When you measured it, however, against the bulk of expenditures that were justified, the waste was negligible.

In the wake of the 2004 Florida hurricanes, and the overall effectiveness of the response, it seemed to me that our plan to regionalize DHS made even more sense. We had shown the value of building relationships with local officials. But in the late summer of 2004, we were told to wait until after the elections to push the plan. The administration apparently was afraid that if the plan leaked, those states and cities that weren't chosen to be regional headquarters might become a political problem. Obviously, we differed. It seemed to me that bringing the federal government closer to communities and citizens would be viewed as a positive development within DHS. Our national strategy directed us to build such an organization. Establishing an institutional presence at the regional level to build relationships, share information, and prepare for such emergencies was one of our primary goals from day one! Further, I argued that we were not creating new campuses and new jobs but consolidating existing personnel and agencies in concentrated places. But the argument didn't persuade anybody to set aside their political concerns of the moment. I was assured, let me repeat, *assured,* that we could implement the regional reorganization plan immediately after the election. A line item of fifty million dollars had been included in the budget to accelerate our work the following year. When I went in to coordinate the rollout with Andy Card after the 2004 election, I ran into a brick wall. Card told me, "There are people who have reservations about this." I responded, "Why don't you pull those people together and we can address their concerns and move ahead?" And so we met, but to no avail. The White House, admitting it initially favored our idea, now wanted no part of it. I had not seen an about-face so sharp since my days at the Noncommissioned Officer Academy (they called it the "Shake and Bake Academy") at Fort Benning, Georgia, in the late sixties. After a year's worth of planning and enormous resources applied to the effort—and an explicit and detailed plan produced—it had become a casualty. Card said the plan was to be shelved for review by my successor. Frankly, after all that, I doubted my successor would have much choice, either. No one ever articulated the fatal objections to the plan. How could they? I have every reason to believe that no one even read it, because no one ever asked for it!

One of the eight regional offices would have been in a city that I had grown to enjoy, a place where it's best not to wear dark slacks to the Café du Monde where the consumption of those delicious beignets and all that powdered sugar would be obvious: the Crescent City, New Orleans.

In the days leading up to the devastation of New Orleans, I, like other Americans, was glued to the Weather Channel watching that whirling orange ball that was Katrina proceed on its wayward path. One didn't need to be a meteorologist to know that a category 5 hurricane (ultimately reduced to category 4) moving across a city that sits below sea level could produce massive problems. Very few Americans were aware that FEMA had conducted a previous training exercise with a hypothetical levee breech. There was no way anyone with knowledge of that exercise could imagine a happy ending to the unfolding story.

In late August 2005, as the world knows by now, Michael Brown had gone to Louisiana before the hurricane hit.

He had a major role in the training exercise in July 2004 that anticipated a major storm hitting New Orleans. The training scenario, "Hurricane Pam," was eerily similar to what occurred a year later. Hypothetical Hurricane Pam brought sustained winds up to 120 miles per hour, up to twenty inches of rain in southeast Louisiana, and storm surges that topped levees in the New Orleans area. The exercise included the evacuation of more than one million residents and the destruction of over five hundred thousand buildings.

Now you can understand why I will always wonder what the federal, state, and local officials had been thinking when Katrina reached category four and took aim at the Alabama and Mississippi coastline before bearing down on the Big Easy—and became the costliest ($81.2 billion in damage) and one of the deadliest storms in American history (about 2,500 people killed or missing). In New Orleans, the levee system protecting the city broke in more than fifty places, and St. Bernard Parish was quickly under water, along with many other areas of the city.

Everyone who watched in the aftermath remembers the horror. People seeking refuge in shelters of last resort, the ill-equipped Convention Center and the badly damaged Superdome, both devoid of electricity and sanitary facilities. People holding signs that begged for food and water. And meanwhile, almost no governmental assistance—state, local, or federal—in evidence. It reminded viewers of scenes from third world countries, hapless victims waiting for relief that didn't come.

To be sure, had all gone right—had the federal, state, and local governments done their work—there would still have been great loss of life and property. Hurricane Katrina was more powerful than any measures mere humans could take against it. Even so, there is no doubt that many more people died and many more suffered than would have occurred if the governmental network had been working together in the way that we had planned it.

If we had been able to establish a regional office in New Orleans, it would have instantly engaged Mayor Ray Nagin and Governor Kathleen Blanco, and there would have been mutual support to deal with everything from evacuation to health care to emergency food and water supplies—and attention given to the immense task of dealing with the cleanup, and the even more daunting task of helping recapture the spirit of a city and its environs. For one thing, if things had worked the way we had envisioned, you wouldn't have been able to tune in Mayor Nagin, just four days after the hurricane struck, sitting on the set of *Meet the Press* blaming everyone but himself for the failure to respond.

If this seems like "I told you so," so be it. Had the regional office been established and had the National Response Plan including deployment of the logistical and public communication support team been used in the immediate aftermath of the hurricane, rather than several days later, I believe the results would have been different. The absence of this support team eroded Brown's effectiveness and complicated the department responses effort. His successor effectively used the same team after he was appointed.

And yet, looking back on Katrina and on the bureaucratic disaster that accompanied it, I am compelled to say that there were many heroes who flew under the radar. During and after the storm, the Coast Guard alone rescued more then thirty thousand people, a total that exceeded the number for all of 2004. The leader of this effort was Coast Guard vice-admiral Thad Allen, who was sent to New Orleans to coordinate the federal response days after Katrina landed as Brown's replacement. His leadership, calm public manner, and organizational skills were obvious, necessary, and admired during the crisis. Clearly the president thought so when he later appointed him commandant of the Coast Guard. When we wrote the response plan, we concluded that in the event of a mammoth natural disaster, FEMA's resources could be overwhelmed, and the crisis would require a federal official having unquestioned authority to bring together the requisite national resources. The trouble here was that DHS didn't truly organize around the National Response Plan until after the disaster. So for the first three or four days it didn't look like anybody was in charge. In an after-action report, it was said that the process failed, not people. This, of course, was an exercise in CYA. On the other hand, the leadership of Allen, and of the people who worked with him, should not be lost to history. Confronted with the aftermath of one of the greatest natural disasters in our history, they performed with great distinction.

In the space that I have here, I want to tell the story of a Coast Guard hero in the hope that it will stand for the many selfless acts of official and nonofficial first responders.

By training and experience, Edward Beale was as prepared for Katrina as any mortal could be. Growing up, he was awed by nature's cacophonous power: ice storms, winter's fury, and Hurricane Gloria in 1985, after which his father loaded his three boys onto the pickup and toured the damaged countryside. The oldest of the boys understood, even at age fifteen, that life hangs by a thread. So, on instinct and drive, he took a path that led him through New London's U.S. Coast Guard Academy to the job he treasures: extracting people from desperate circumstance.

In the early morning hours after Katrina struck, Lieutenant Commander Edward Beale, the 3,269th person since 1916 to become a Coast Guard pilot, left his Creole-style home, "a Cape without dormers," which had become a Cape lacking also the prescribed allotment of shingles on the roof. He told his wife, Michelle, that he had no idea when he would come back or when she would hear from him, because all normal communication lines were cut off. Nor could he be sure there would be any place to refuel his short-range craft.

So he put his dog tag on and stuffed the pockets of his helicopter flight suit with a flashlight, a knife, and survival rations, including the "power muffins" that Michelle baked before the power went out. She had loaded them with apricots, walnuts, pecans, and raisins. He called it "breakfast in a bun."

The night was pitch black, winds at fifty knots. That's what the four-man crew of the little HH-65B Dolphin chopper faced as it headed toward Mississippi's coast. All lights below were out, and there was no moon or usual navigational guides to help; there were only night-vision goggles, through which Beale searched for storm victims who needed help.

The crew was amazed by the destruction of houses and property. Beale recalls, "It was as if two giant hands had reached out and grabbed whatever was there and sucked it back into the ocean."

Over the next several hours, Beale's HH-65 lifted people to safety who had taken refuge atop an apartment complex that was disintegrating. It lifted the desperate who clung to tree limbs—a risky maneuver for the chopper in high winds. Several times, Beale's crew lowered the "rescue swimmer" into clusters of survivors to see who needed medical evacuation.

When the craft landed next to a hospital that was without generator power, crew members came across an elderly man and woman whose house had exploded, leaving them with second degree burns over much of their bodies. Though experienced at witnessing serious injury, the Coast Guard personnel were shocked into silence by what they saw—skin red and raw. As the chopper headed back to Mobile to a hospital with a burn unit, they worried about the couple's survival. But Beale recalled that when the orderlies came out to the helipad and wheeled the woman away, "Though she could hardly move, she blew us a kiss. Her husband, all wrapped in gauze, popped us a salute." They were two among the many over the years that Edward Beale has met in this way, never seen again, and never learned their fates.

He gave this account of a part of that day:

> One of the chemical plants and several hotels were on fire, and the smoke plume cut the city in half from east to west. . . . I landed on the roof of the Salvation Army downtown where about 100 people were waiting for evacuation. The metal roof was domed so we landed [in a way that] we wouldn't roll off the edge while all the people loaded. I had a flashback to the History Channel video of the fall of Saigon. . . . I transported 18 people to the middle of Interstate 10 before the helicopter engines began fluctuating [later the craft lost hydraulic fuel]. . . . by that time we had gotten reports on looters and rioters raping, pillaging, and burning everything in sight, and shooting at helicopters. We were quite on edge. . . . Fortunately, all we saw of the mayhem was the burning part. One percent of the people always seem to get 99 percent of the headlines.

Those of us who have had the privilege of working with members of the Coast Guard and other devoted public servants know that there are everyday heroes who never get the attention they deserve.

But that's not the sole impression I want to leave you with.

Here is another scene from New Orleans. Edward Beale's helicopter is being serviced. He watches as victims from the city's poorest neighborhoods are airlifted to the site. Three middle-aged women from the devastated Ninth Ward are among them, and, shaken by all that has happened, console each other. Beale has no idea what their stories are or what they have lost along the way, except that they are from flooded areas. He assumes, correctly, they are hungry and thirsty. He brings them to a bleacher area, and they sit. He gives them bottled water. Then he digs down into a pocket of his flight suit and pulls out three of Michelle's muffins—breakfast in a bun—and gives them to the women. The hurricane victims savor each bite. A few minutes later, without words ever being exchanged amid the din of helicopter blades, one of the women gets up and puts her arms around the Coast Guard pilot and hugs him, and doesn't let go for a good twenty seconds.

I would like to be able to leave it at that, bringing attention to those brave and compassionate souls among the anonymous whose selflessness, resourcefulness, and courage saved lives. But in the aftermath of one of the most devastating natural events in American history, there was much else to learn.

Matthew Broderick, who had stayed on as the operations officer after I left DHS, was in that chair as Hurricane Katrina approached the Gulf Coast. But if Broderick took incoming fire at that point, it was nothing like what he took two years later. In the wake of the devastation in New Orleans and other Gulf Coast communities, congressional hearings were held focusing on the pathetic response of FEMA and the Department of Homeland Security as a whole, and the local and state ineptitude. Much of it had been detailed in a 210-page report by the DHS inspector general, Richard L. Skinner. That report was detailed and, in the practice of such exercises, its language was muted and impersonal in tone. It went so far as to assess the FEMA performance as "insufficient." But if it didn't use purple prose, it was nevertheless damning in its effect. It helped Congress focus on key questions, such as whether the federal government was as committed to actions regarding national disasters as it was to fighting terrorism.

One of the witnesses that the Senate called was Broderick, whose job it had been to be sure everyone had up-to-date and reliable information. Broderick testified, accurately, that he did not pass along reliable information to the White House with catastrophic details of the breaching of the levees and other key developments, though he admitted it was his job to keep people informed. Bob Stephan, seated at the witness table with him, winced at his comments, knowing the full story. As a result of his testimony, he was pilloried in the press. *The Wall Street Journal*'s reconstruction of the federal response to Katrina seemed to single him out for criticism.

If, however, the Senate panel had followed up their question on whether he passed along vital information and asked why, they would have learned something useful about leadership, loyalty, and teamwork.

Where Michael Brown accepted some responsibility, he generally found fault with others during his testimony; Broderick did not. No, he didn't pass along the information about Katrina to the White House. The reason he didn't tell anyone at the White House is because FEMA never gave DHS that information. Brown, indeed, seemed to hint at this in his own Senate testimony. On a previous occasion he had characterized the relationship between FEMA and DHS as a "clash of cultures." DHS was an impediment to his work. He admitted his loyalty and his line of communication went directly to the White House, not to Secretary Chertoff or the department. This seemed to confirm that there had been no special effort to keep anyone in DHS directly apprised of all the information sent from New Orleans to FEMA, including the condition of the levees. Here was a disastrous instance of turf warfare that resulted in many civilian casualties; in Washington, it was a shameless game of pinning the blame on others.

There had been one other gap in coordinating the preparedness and response effort that went unnoticed. Efforts to summon the Interagency Incident Management Group (IIMG) to Nebraska Avenue several days before Katrina hit land were also rejected. The appeal to the deputy secretary fell on deaf ears. The IIMG, a team we created in the early days of DHS, comprised representatives from agencies throughout the government who are literally on one-hour recall to DHS; once summoned, they provide around-the-clock coverage. They become the department's best connections to their counterparts on the ground and provide critical information for decision makers as well as assistance in the response and recovery effort. The IIMG had demonstrated its value to me by providing timely and accurate information during the northeast blackout in August 2003, Christmas Orange, and the 2004 hurricane season.

In the end, the administration blamed the process—the unused-until-too-late response plan that we had devised. While admitting the National Response Plan could be amended based on the Katrina experience, the state and local community did not view the debacle as a process failure and so it's worth reviewing for what might have been. In fact, there was no timely call up of the Interagency Incident Management Group, no regional office, and delayed use of the National Response Plan. The plan didn't fail. People failed the plan.

It remains to me a great frustration that the real heroes of homeland security—those who tried to address issues of natural disaster, terrorism, immigration, transportation, a seemingly endless list—occasionally must battle indifference, ignorance, and arrogance along the way. Then again, and I personally witnessed it dozens of times, the men and women tasked to build and lead this department just bit their lower lip and moved on. The mission was too important and the workload too significant to squander time and energy setting the record straight.

14

THE POLITICS OF
TERRORISM, PART 2

You at *Time,* the rest of the news media, Homeland Security
Chief Tom Ridge, politicians, theorists, commentators, spe-
cialists and so forth—just shut up . . . [Y]ou are doing exactly
what the terrorists want you to do: instill uncertainty in American lives. Enough, already!

—Letter from a reader to *Time* magazine
September 6, 2004

I n all of the Department of Homeland Security, the largest single
bureau was ICE, the Bureau of Immigration and Customs Enforcement. It was ably led by Mike Garcia, later the U.S. attorney for
the Southern District of New York, whose investigation of a prostitu-
tion ring led ultimately to the retirement of the governor at the time.
It also had one of the broadest missions: running the federal air marshals service, investigating money-laundering and other smuggling
crimes, and enforcing immigration laws and detaining illegals.

As we worked on the mission of ICE and addressed outdated
policies and practices that had plagued what pre-DHS had been
the widely discredited Immigration and Naturalization Service, it
occurred to us that it would be helpful to change the name of the
bureau—to reflect more accurately what it actually does—even as
we kept the acronym. And so we settled on the Bureau of Investigations and Criminal Enforcement.

Appropriately, Asa Hutchinson, under secretary for border and
transportation security, and Mike Garcia explained the need for

the change to their counterparts at Justice and the FBI. Protest and objection were immediately forthcoming. The FBI and Justice lobbied the White House in opposition to the name change. They felt that the public and law enforcement communities would confuse the DHS Bureau of Investigations and Criminal Enforcement with the Department of Justice Federal Bureau of Investigation. I have always thought the claim to be frivolous and unfounded, based on turf, not confusion.

After Asa and Mike informed me of their efforts, explained once again the rationale for their decision, and advised that the White House was not supportive, I felt compelled to intervene. I contacted my colleagues, Attorney General Ashcroft and Director Mueller, and discussed the matter thoroughly, but to no avail. While I never felt I needed their permission, as a matter of comity I thought soliciting their support was appropriate.

As we waited for another morning session with the president, I told John and Bob I intended to authorize the name change later that day. A couple of hours later Card called. He claimed he had discussed the matter with the president, who opposed the ICE name change, and then claimed the president told him to remind me, "We are in a war." I didn't respond immediately. My first thought was that he certainly did not take this bureaucratic dustup to the president. And then I thought of saying, "Well, this is my second war, how many have you been in?" But I didn't. Instead, I told Card that when decisions are made about my agency—and there are obviously two sides to the story—I would like to be heard. But, then, as it became clear during the Memorial Day holidays, even when I was heard, there could be complications, and the credibility and effectiveness of the department was once again on the line.

It was standard operating procedure that I would accept media interviews before upcoming holidays. There was a certain routine that developed around all major dates on the calendar. The media would make inquiries about security, intelligence, travel, and the like. And I would agree to radio and television interviews on these subjects. In preparing for the pre-Memorial Day 2003 interviews at the World War II Memorial, the networks had identified the location, because it was to be dedicated the following Monday. We learned that Attorney General Ashcroft had scheduled a press conference for later the same day. In anticipation of two cabinet members speaking on the same day in different locations we thought it best to coordinate our public messages to be certain there was no conflict. We called and e-mailed John's people several times, but never got a response.

The next day, as planned, I did my press conference in front of the memorial. In response to questions about threats and security, I said there was nothing new to report. I noted the same level of intelligence traffic, but concluded there was nothing that would require us to raise the threat level.

Later that afternoon, Ashcroft had a far different message. He went to the airwaves to ask Americans to be on the lookout for Adam Yahiy Gadahn and several of his associates. No doubt Gadahn was a character to fear. Born Adam Pearlman and using the name Abu Suhayb, he appeared on a number of Al Qaeda videos, and was identified on these as "Azzam the American." He was subsequently charged in this country with treason.

But Ashcroft's warning that a plot that Gadahn and others were involved in—by the attorney general's estimation, 90 percent done—a massive attack on the United States, seemed to us at DHS to be overstated, to put it charitably. Pat Hughes, our intelligence chief, and others were convinced of this.

During the next regular morning meeting in the Oval Office, I was told by the president bluntly that I had undermined Ashcroft. I was reminded that counterterrorism is one of the administration's highest priorities, and that a united front had to be presented. No disagreement there. That's why we tried so hard to contact his office the previous evening. My staff and I had done everything possible to avoid precisely the situation that occurred. I felt our credibility was undermined. It was appropriate to ask the country to be on the "look out" for these individuals, but we saw absolutely no reason to suggest an attack was imminent.

No doubt Ashcroft believed he was doing the right thing. His book *Never Again* reveals the passion and commitment he brought

every single day to the counterterrorism mission the president assigned to him after September 11. Nonetheless, it was perfectly legitimate, and I think healthy, for our team to draw its own conclusions.
Competitive intelligence should always be encouraged. And while
we disagreed with the conclusions drawn in that press conference, we never expressed them publicly. There were other occasions
where we were able to communicate to the intelligence community
a difference of opinion. This usually led to private reassessments
and a unified public message.

When the differences between our two departments came to the
attention of the White House, the Department of Justice normally
prevailed. Disagreeing didn't mean I didn't try to understand. The
president believed his constitutional obligation "to provide for the
common defense" compelled him to take aggressive action at home
and abroad to "bring the terrorists to justice." Justice was his domestic counterterrorism agency, and unapologetic about playing
offense. DHS played defense. Advantage DOJ.

Although there were some in the administration who saw potential attacks on every threat matrix, our small intelligence shop
under General Pat Hughes, who rose from the rank of private to
three-star, kept us grounded with thoughtful and compelling analyses. On many occasions when there was interest in raising the
threat level, our department was the least inclined to do so. It wasn't
about threat fatigue. It was a matter of credibility and trust.

In late July 2004, I flew to Florida to meet cruise ship officials
who wanted my thoughts on how they could protect their fleets
from terrorism. This scenario was common: Private industry turned
to the department for advice and reassurance, both of which we
could offer in measured terms. While in the air, I got a call from
Fran Townsend, who had succeeded General Gordon as assistant
to the president for homeland security. Because it was on an unse-
cured line, all she could tell me was that some "interesting information" had turned up and that I should be fully briefed upon my
return. Later that day, I flew back to Washington and assembled

my team at the NAC to get the briefing and determine what, if any, role the department would play. As it turned out, the source was credible, the potential targets identifiable, and we could target our public message and response in a way that we had never been able to do before.

Mohammed Naeem Noor Khan, who was twenty-five years old and thought to be among the next generation of Al Qaeda leaders, had been trying to leave Pakistan. Khan was one of the organization's technology whizzes. He was someone they turned to when they wanted to know the amount of plastic explosives necessary for a specific destructive purpose. He had used Internet cafes to relay coded messages, some of which were intercepted by Pakistani authorities intent on capturing him. After they took him into custody, the Pakistani intelligence service raided a safe house and, in doing so, discovered three laptop computers and fifty-one computer discs. It passed them along to U.S. officials, and they sent them quickly to Washington.

Over the next few days our intelligence team worked with their colleagues in the law enforcement and intelligence communities. They concluded they had discovered critical reconnaissance information that could be a precursor to another attack. The conclusion was remarkable in that it demonstrated a level of detail, a level of patience, and thoroughness of planning. It showed clearly that Al Qaeda was capable of hitting us in places that were not obvious.

The seized computers contained more than five hundred photographs of potential targets and analyses of how these targets had been protected by authorities and how, nevertheless, the attackers could proceed. This was, to us, a visual insight into the seemingly incomprehensible Al Qaeda mind, and, after so many months of rumor and innuendo, hard evidence that operatives were in this country and doing their work. Among the sites on the videos: the headquarters of Prudential Financial in Newark, New Jersey, as well as two sites in Manhattan—the New York Stock Exchange and the Citigroup Building. The videos showed the headquarters of the International Monetary Fund and the World Bank in Washington. The detail of the surveillance was particularly alarming. For example, the visuals showed that the windows behind the six columns on the front of the New York Stock Exchange building made it appear "a little fragile," while it indicated it might be harder to approach the IMF and World Bank because of the heavy security. About the Citigroup Building the terrorists said, "Like the World Trade Center, it is supported on steel, load-bearing walls, not a steel frame." The "usual methods" were recommended by the surveillance operatives: employing a heavy gasoline truck or oil tanker for the attacks. The level of detail demonstrated the kinds of information our enemies sought in order to calculate tactically how they could inflict the most damage.

But there was a catch, as there almost always is in these kinds of intelligence finds, and it's what made determining our course of action so hard. The tapes were three years old, made before the 9/11 attacks. We knew that to many Americans, including political opponents eager to discredit the White House and the DHS, the discoveries would seem irrelevant and dated, or at least could be argued as such. Moreover, if we were to raise the national alert level to orange based on these discoveries, we again risked alert fatigue, as well as the enormous expense faced by state and local officials around the country to whom this specific threat didn't apply. Invariably when we failed to provide specific information that would prompt specific measures being taken, someone would ask some version of "Does it occur to you that every time you go to orange, our budget goes to red? Who's going to pay for this?"

In addition, we were growing weary at DHS of the allegation that on those few occasions when the threat level was changed, it was done solely for political reasons. I often said, "We don't do politics." (And I made good on that by not engaging in any partisan activity during my tenure.) But there were many who thought otherwise, including much of the media and many Democrats, who, in an election year, were not shy about making the charge. Their argument was that the federal government—and specifically the White House with the willful collaboration of the Department of Homeland Security—would do anything it needed to do to scare the hell out of the country in order to keep the Republicans—generally considered to be more vigilant and committed on the issue of security—in power. Not true. The critics consistently ignored the reality of the decision-making process. The role of the White House was to accept or reject the consensus recommendation of the Homeland Security Council.

I knew going in that some people would dismiss the new intelligence as old intelligence. But no one in our department felt that way. One of the CEOs I contacted to discuss the upcoming threat alert had the best perspective: The age of the intelligence was of little concern to him. He took it seriously. Enough said. Our work had shown repeatedly that this new enemy of ours has a different view of the calendar than we do. The 9/11 attack was in the works for years, and so was the attack on the World Trade Center in 1993. The fact that the information we discovered was three years old by the summer of 2004 in no way convinced us that it was outdated or irrelevant.

We decided that the specificity of the information enabled us to use our alert system in a new and limited way. If this was a precursor to a potential attack on the financial sector, meant to be symbolic in the way that passenger jets destroying the White House and Pentagon were, we could be more precise in our warning. We could focus exclusively on the financial community and the region in which the potential targets were located. No need to involve any other sectors or cities. We limited our elevated alert (orange) to areas of New York City, Newark, and Washington, D.C. And in the case of those cities, our information was specific enough to allow local officials to concentrate security forces in limited areas rather than at every subway station and public building. Even so, we knew that being so visible on Wall Street and other economic locations would be alarming to some. There was no other choice. Visible security can be a reassuring sign and a deterrent. It was recorded that the attendance on the floor of the New York Stock Exchange the following day was higher than the same day the previous summer. It was another example of Americans being unwilling to bend to fear, to alter their behavior in the face of the plans of an unknown enemy.

If Khan had been back with his camera in 2004, he would have seen a different picture.

After the threat level was lowered, the reaction around the country to its use was positive. Credibility was always our goal while communicating to the public. Yet, in dealing with these events, I inadvertently appeared to undermine my own.

In the minutes before I was scheduled to appear on national television to announce these plans, the White House called and recommended a few additional words to be included in our announcement. I didn't particularly like the addition. But it seemed pretty harmless, and fighting a battle over it when the assembled media was waiting for a scheduled conference didn't seem worth it. In the context of all I had to say, I concluded, this additional phrase wouldn't really be noticed. After all, the transcript of that afternoon's affair contained thousands of words. Unfortunately, a few of them resonated in the wrong way with critics. It's the age of sound bites. Context and nuance become lost. I should have known better.

My presentation was thorough that Sunday, August 1, 2004. It included the source of the information and an explanation of its relevance. It identified some specific solutions undertaken: buffer zones to secure the perimeter of the buildings from unauthorized cars and trucks; restrictions to affected underground parking; security personnel using identification badges and digital photos to keep track of people entering and exiting buildings; increased law enforcement presence; and more intense screening of vehicles, and packages, and deliveries.

Near the end, I provided the words the White House wanted: "But we must understand that the kind of information available to us today is the result of the president's leadership in the war against terror. The reports that have led to this alert are the result of offensive intelligence and military operations overseas, as well as strong partnerships with our allies around the world, such as Pakistan. Such operations and partnerships give us insight into the enemy so we can better target our defensive measures here and away from home." Little did I realize that one phrase in that paragraph would become press fodder for weeks and make me a target for media criticism that I must admit was justified.

In almost any other situation in government or anywhere else, praising the boss would not be an issue. But in this case, citing "the result of the president's leadership" was loaded with political implication, and this was not lost on our critics. John Kerry had just been nominated for president at the Democratic Party convention. Our announcement, as delivered with the loaded words, was seen by some as a way to divert attention from that event and to reenforce in the minds of Americans that—even as the Democrats enjoyed their hour upon the political stage—only the Republican incumbent could keep America safe.

On November 1, 2007, *The Washington Post* reported that Donald Rumsfeld's "snowflakes," his memos to staff members, had pointed out the need to keep terrorism alive as an issue throughout his tenure as secretary. Terrorism was a legitimate issue, and references to it benefited the administration politically. However, for the next few days after the press conference, I was not dealing with the specifics of the threat but with the meaning of the inserted words.

I am asked, as every public official is eventually asked, whether I have any regrets. I don't harbor many that relate to my time in service to the country. But this was one of them. I should have delivered the threat warning just as we had written it, and apologized later to the White House for my "oversight" in failing to include those congratulatory words. But, at the moment, it all seemed like pointless, throwaway rhetoric. Politics was not on my mind; I had something more important to say. It just goes to show that there's no such thing as throwaway lines in these days of instant replay. There is no media or political tolerance for any mistake of judgment, apparent or otherwise, no matter the extenuating circumstances.

I was not surprised that Vice President Cheney used the self-praise in remarks given two days later . . . and that others were using it. "The president's leadership" was a free-flowing phrase in the administration, as it is in any administration. It was understandable and predictable that the campaign would laud the president.

A new norm was emerging, and I learned a hard lesson. Even so, the politics of terrorism and the lessons learned there intersected one more time before the end of the year.

As we came closer to the election, I knew I should plan to leave after the first of the year. I began to see myself, as we used to say in Vietnam, as a short-timer. But in Vietnam short-timers were often given light duties behind the lines; I knew that until the moment I left the DHS, there would be no such consideration. Vigilance until the final hour was required. I believed, in spite of some of the public missteps and private battles, the department had gained a level of public trust that was significant, but fragile.

A few days before the 2004 presidential election, *The New York Times* reported that national polls showed a virtual dead heat in the race between President Bush and Senator John Kerry. What the *Times* didn't print and didn't know is that an election-eve drama was being played out at the highest levels of our government that speaks to some of the most significant and delicate issues we face as a nation. Had this episode been reported, I can only imagine how the editorial page of the *Times,* never a fan of the Bush administration—or me, for that matter—would have reacted: "The White House has put the country's welfare at risk for blatantly political reasons—so that the president, whose strategy since 9/11 has been to strike fear into the hearts of U.S. citizens, can assure himself a second term." The reality was more complex than that—realities are always more complex than editorials portray them—but I confess that this event, dramatic and inconceivable, proved most troublesome for all of us in the department.

On Friday, October 29, 2004, Osama bin Laden delivered a new videotape message that aired on the Arab language network Al Jazeera. The presidential election scheduled for the following Tuesday was tightening. The most recent polls had Bush leading Kerry by no more than two or three points. Having won my first congressional election by 729 votes and experienced the volatility of the election cycle during several campaigns, this race was literally a dead heat going into the final seventy-two hours.

Late night news, morning show hosts, and probably every

American citizen was wondering what it all meant. The messenger, the message, the timing—was an attack imminent?

Predictably, the message was critical of President Bush. It threatened, "As you spoil our security, we will do so to you. . . . Your security is not in the hands of Kerry or Bush or Al Qaeda. Your security is in your own hands. Any nation that does not attack us will not be attacked." Was it a precursor to another attack?

We huddled that Friday night. Next morning we met early at the department's headquarters. The country was unaware that all levels of government had quietly ramped up security several weeks before the election, although not to the level that would have been required had we actually gone to a higher public threat level (orange). The timing of the tape may have been a surprise; the content was not. Within the department no one felt it necessary to consider additional security measures or to call the Homeland Security Council into session.

Bin Laden had contempt for the president and hated America: This was not news. From September 11, 2001, to this video broadcast, there had been nearly twenty audio and videotapes attributed to either bin Laden or his lieutenant al-Zawahiri. In fact, earlier in October, al-Zawahiri, in an audio recording, again urged Muslims to mount resistance to "crusader America." As was the case after receipt of most of the previous tapes, no one got particularly spun up about al-Zawahiri's remarks. While not a counterterrorism expert, I had drawn some conclusions about these matters along the way. A threatening message, audio or visual, should not be the sole reason to elevate the threat level. Having been schooled by General Pat Hughes, the much larger question had to be answered. Other than the tape, what was the factual basis for taking such a dramatic step?

With internal agreement that the tape should not alter our security posture, my leadership team and I gathered in our makeshift Situation Room at the NAC to participate in a secure videoconference and listening to a discussion focused on that possibility. Participating were representatives from the intelligence community, the FBI, and the Departments of Justice, State, and Defense.

A vigorous, some might say dramatic, discussion ensued. Ashcroft strongly urged an increase in the threat level, and was supported by Rumsfeld. There was absolutely no support for that position within our department. None. I wondered, *"Is this about security or politics?"* Post-election analysis demonstrated a significant increase in the president's approval rating in the days after the raising of the threat level.

There was no consensus reached at that session, and we took it upon ourselves to keep it that way. I was adamantly opposed to raising the threat level and was grateful that Robert Mueller agreed. Absent a consensus, there could be no recommendation for Townsend to present to the president.

There is a cautionary expression that surfaces occasionally during Oval Office or Situation Room briefings and even more frequently in the intelligence and law enforcement communities: "We don't know what we don't know." Let me assure you, it is not expressed as a hedge against future accountability. It is, however, a necessary and painful reminder that total situational awareness in any critical decision-making context is the ideal, never the reality. In the real world of information gathering and analysis, complete and accurate information in the form of actionable intelligence is afforded our leaders about as often as the Chicago Cubs reach the World Series. Assuming we would never have the benefit of a complete picture, we were struggling to understand the proponents' point of view based upon the intelligence we did possess. We certainly didn't believe the tape alone warranted action, and we weren't seeing any additional intelligence that justified it. In fact, we were incredulous.

Admittedly, the notion of an attack during this period had been discussed. Early in the year, we had identified key events at which Al Qaeda might take great glee in dropping something on us: the Democratic convention in Boston, the Republican convention in New York, and the general election were among them. We were all mindful of the impact of an actual attack on the outcome of the Spanish election earlier in the year. But at this point there was nothing to indicate a specific threat and no reason to cause undue public alarm. And as the minutes passed at our video-conference we concluded that others in the administration were operating with the same threat information and didn't know any more than we did, and that the idea was still a bad one. It also seemed possible to me and to others around the table that something could be afoot other than simple concern about the country's safety.

All of us at DHS knew better than our fellow participants of the delicacy of raising the threat level. We had long ago learned the disadvantages of routinely worrying the public, of making people fearful without being able to give them any specific information about the threat. We knew the tremendous cost incurred at local levels whenever the level went up. We could fairly predict the public outcry of a national threat alert without sharing specific and credible information to justify it on the eve of an election. We could not see the justification within the intelligence in our hands. But even then, we knew that there was a widespread suspicion of such motives and tactics, and this could entirely undermine the credibility of not just the department, but the administration.

As the conference concluded, we agreed to talk the next morning. We began immediately to engage in our own intelligence gathering. Without more specific information that could be shared with a suspicious public on the eve of an election, we were moving toward a certain public relations disaster. We had to learn more or put an end to the discussion. We were on the verge of making a huge mistake. Pat Hughes would check around the intelligence community. Jim Loy would reach out to his fellow deputies within the cabinet. Susan Neely would contact Dan Bartlett, the head of public affairs for the White House.

When Neely reached Bartlett, he was aboard Air Force One, which was flying the president to a campaign stop. Bartlett said he had been unaware of the discussion that had taken place earlier that morning. He was strongly advised that DHS was strongly opposed. Neely spoke for all of us when she said, "We think it's a terrible thing to do." It was important to remind the White House that just a few weeks earlier, in August, when there was real, substantial, hard information about the threat to the financial sector, a large segment of the media had nevertheless accused the administration of politicizing the nation's security. And now, with absolutely nothing but the tape to justify raising the level, the administration would certainly take an even bigger hit, and perhaps, from the election point of view, a fatal one. Bartlett told her that he would speak to the president and get back to her. By the next day, the whole idea of raising the level was dropped.

I believe our strong interventions had pulled the "go up" advocates back from the brink. But I consider that episode to be not only a dramatic moment in Washington's recent history, but another illustration of the intersection of politics, fear, credibility, and security.

After that episode, I knew I had to follow through on my plans to leave the federal government. I could reflect with admiration on those with whom I had worked on a number of accomplishments at DHS; accomplishments that will elude history because most of our successes resulted in no visible result and were merely business as usual. I concluded that I had more than fulfilled my duty to serve in a time of need. And so in December I offered my letter of resignation. Even then, though, I knew that the questions of homeland security—what it is and what it should become—would stay with me forever.

My emotions at the time, not surprisingly, were mixed. I was surrounded by talented and dedicated people who had put aside personal goals in order to contribute to the larger effort, a phenomenon that, for anyone who sees it firsthand, will easily banish any deep cynicism about Washington. Yes, people at the top are forever jockeying for advantage. But among those in the ranks, those who labor in a world hidden from public view, there are many heroes whose personal ambitions become secondary to the monumental effort at hand.

I thought about them, of course, when I tendered my letter of resignation. And I thought about the president, too. He had put a great deal of trust in me. And though it hadn't all worked out the way I wanted it to—does it ever for anyone?—I retained a sense of regard and respect. Sure, I was frustrated by many of those around him, and occasionally by him. Even so, with the help of many people we had reached a point in contemporary history of relative security. We had not been attacked from the outside. We had strengthened our efforts at security and at the same time been careful not to trample individual rights. That effort, in itself, is worthy of lengthy documentation. Even in the atmosphere of widespread suspicion and anxiety we were able to get a message across about reasonable measures that needed to be taken on behalf of the public at large. Yes, we had taken our playful hits—what would Leno, Letterman, and O'Brien have done without me?—but it was all for the larger good.

I wasn't burned out by the job. It was just time to move on. It was time to close a chapter and begin writing another one. In a life of public service, I was well aware of the compromises and even treacheries inherent in the system, but felt we had accomplished a great deal. As a former infantry staff sergeant, I had long understood the difference between what you could do something about, what was thrust upon you, what you could ignore, and what you had to do, regardless of the circumstances. You don't run to the commanding general because someone in his chain of command is "busting your chops." You deal with it and move on.

For me, and for many of my colleagues at DHS, it was simply time to go. After years of putting family matters aside, of not watching the clock, of reading intelligence reports until they appeared in my dreams, of constant secret meetings, of running to the Hill every few days to satisfy members of Congress, of bearing a shared responsibility for the country's safety, it was time to let others bring new energy and vision to the effort. Though I had been careful to pick and choose my fights, I had spent my political capital.

At the end, the president invited my family back to the Oval Office for an official send-off. I saw him there in a way most Americans don't. His eyes betrayed his steely countenance. He is a decent, emotional man who doesn't let the public see his softer side, but Michele, Lesley, Tommy, and I were witness to it that day. The president hugged the children and thanked them for putting up with all I had to do that had taken me away from them.

A few nights later, I packed all of my personal mementos at the

NAC, and put them in boxes. There were photographs of me in many settings around the country and around the world, images that I knew I would look at one day and recall what it was like to be the first in an impossible new job.

As I looked around the office one last time, I also thought about the informal games of basketball we held on Wednesday nights in the gym at the NAC. Anybody who showed up could play. I insisted we play zone defense, and for some unknown reason the ball was often passed to me, a circumstance that no amount of limited athletic ability could change. We were just folks in our gym shorts and T-shirts enjoying a little competition and friendship, people trying to have a little fun—an hour of R&R that had nothing to do with Osama bin Laden. It was a welcome relief. We worked hard and never lost our sense of humor. We stayed focused and went to work every day with the goal of making our country a little safer before we went home that night.

As I left the NAC for the last time, a security guard helped me carry my boxes from the office to the parking lot. For the first time in years, I'd be driving myself home, in a family vehicle, a van. As we stuffed the last box in the back, the head of the Secret Service detail said to me, "It's been a pleasure and a privilege working with you, Mr. Secretary." I thanked him. He said, "Good night. And good luck."

I didn't quite understand the "good luck" part until the next morning, when I decided to go out on a couple of errands. There was no way to do it. The kids had taken one of the cars to school, and Michele had taken the other. So there I was. Twenty-four hours earlier I was a man with Secret Service protection and a personal driver, now just another citizen. Later that week, I asked my son, Tommy, for the keys to the car that the kids used. He smiled at my request, tossed me the keys, and instructed me as follows: "Be careful where you park it, and don't forget to fill it up with gas before you come home."

15

E PLURIBUS UNUM

Out of many, one

—Motto on Seal of United States,
adopted by Congress in 1782

M y family never planned, and never took, long vacations during my years of public service. Long weekends were the best they could expect. Yet those years of service gave all of us opportunities to meet people, develop friendships, and enjoy experiences unknown to most citizens. We will always be grateful. Well, *I* will always be grateful. The rest of my family at least understands. I think.

After my tenure at DHS, I had the opportunity to make amends. Head south or west for sun, golf, and beaches? A cruise? Australia's Outback? A return to the paradise I knew as South Vietnam on an old vets' tour—something I've wanted to do for a long time? I settled on a three-day holiday, spent with Pittsburgh friends in the Bahamas. Vacation avoidance is a hard habit to break, and, in those first months after leaving office, I proved the point.

What I quickly learned for myself was that the revolving door of Washington, D.C., led from the inner circles of power to podiums around the land. I was soon a member of the Washington

Speakers Bureau, and, for a year or so, in some demand. Corporations, trade groups, nonprofits, and so on, seemed to be interested in my views on security or leadership. And so I was off to Orlando, Denver, San Diego, Chicago, and many other cities to recount our efforts and enjoy the questions thrown my way.

In those sessions, I tailored my remarks to the needs of the audience, focusing on risk management, the creation of the department, or the daily, inside details of what occurred in Washington. Whatever the message, I could warm the crowd with the news that, in homeland security terms, I was just one of them.

I usually asked how many members of the audience had been selected for secondary screening at airports before boarding flights. Many had been chosen once for special treatment behind the Plexiglas partition. A few had been given this privilege twice, and there were even some three times. Nobody, however, could approach the level of my experience. As a frequent traveler, the former secretary of Homeland Security was singled out more than two dozen times for special scrutiny. It got so that I almost expected it, and was right to do so. Fellow travelers, recognizing me in such compromising circumstance, were often surprised. And many were amused. I remember a suit-clad businessman recovering several items from the tray that had just been scanned catching a quick glimpse of me behind the Plexiglas awaiting "pat down." His initial glances required a second direct confirmation. It was the first secretary of homeland security! He just started laughing. I fit the suspicious profile, apparently, mostly because my travel plans so often changed, and at the last minute—one of the factors used in trying to identify potential terrorists. I suspect even they have figured that out by now.

Whatever the reason, however, the circumstance always managed to connect with my audiences. Here I was, the former security czar, just another face among the usual suspects. In a way, it was perfect. In spite of the inconvenience of it all, I accepted it, and did so in a way that I hoped all Americans would accept a higher level of scrutiny without undue concern about the loss of freedoms. What TSA was doing was not harassment but, as I have often pointed out, engaging in risk management, taking reasonable precautions, but not foolproof ones, under difficult and changing circumstances.

It's true there have been uncomfortable moments. For example, I have witnessed TSA employees being verbally abused by members of the public. But the good news was that this attitude represented a distinct minority. We have come to understand the intangible cost of safer air travel. There is a level of acceptance that would have been hard to imagine in the years prior to 9/11.

In my talks around the country, I found myself echoing themes over and over again through the din of homeland security noise. There is a need for a calm, a reassuring, but also a candid voice. With my public office years behind me, and no longer saddled by the "How will this go down?" concern that people in my position face in public forums, I found myself talking about my work in the way I never had. I would never be, I knew, a kiss-and-tell sort. It was never my intention to blame failures of this policy or that on others. Though politics as usual and stubborn personalities may indeed stand in the way of enlightenment, no one department could lay claim to having been a special victim. I knew that for some failings I had to look no farther than the nearest mirror to find the causes. I also understood that I had the capacity to set the record straight without being gratuitously critical of others. Easy for me to say, of course. But compared to the vitriol of what has become politics as usual, my comments, it seemed to me, were fair and unaffected by political positions and motivations. Any observer could argue that I merely wanted to feather my own historical nest, show what a great job my colleagues and I did against great odds. That is a necessary risk in putting down any personal history. But as time went on, and I faced one curious audience after another, I felt a desire to record our efforts. That led, eventually, to my writing this book.

For example, I was often asked for my view on the too-public feud between the CIA and FBI, and whether the rivalry was as destructive as sometimes painted. When I answered such questions, I could see the need for elucidation—a need to know. From what I saw at my level, George Tenet and Robert Mueller, who headed the agencies, had a cordial and mutually dependent and respectful relationship. Part of that may have been attributed to their levels of experience and personalities. They understood that success depends to a large degree on partnerships. But at the lower levels—the levels where my colleagues at DHS had a great deal of interaction—there had been a deep and historical distrust of outsiders and a legal wall of separation inherited from the Clinton administration, a situation that was impossible to alter without a change in the law.

The Patriot Act has been and will continue to be criticized by political and legal observers. However, lost in the deep (and, to some, offending) resonance were antidotes to interagency conflicts. Not too many newspaper headlines, as far as I could tell, revealed news that among the provisions of the Patriot Act was the removal of an unimaginable legal barrier between the CIA and FBI so that in a post-9/11 environment they could actually talk to one another and share information. The legal authority to talk to one another didn't mean that they *would* share information with each other, much less with DHS or with the states or local governments. The change in that situation would not come through legislative mandate, but through patience, persistence, and pushing.

Much that happened needed some historical amplification or augmentation, or simply setting the record straight. There were other ideas and themes that surfaced directly as a result of this history that seemed to me to be a guide to reliable and appropriate public policy debate and action.

What follows here and in the remaining chapters are views nurtured during my public service career, sharpened during my tenure at Homeland Security, affected in the days and years afterward (Katrina, of course, among those events), and shaped by conversations with colleagues and by international events. You will be able, of course, to find opinions about these issues from anyone with an interest in public policy. These views are unique—even if they are not necessarily original—developed from a perspective that no one else in public office ever had.

That doesn't make me per se correct. Nor does my service in

the Bush administration make me a counterterrorism expert. But I certainly learned more than I could have imagined along the way. I believe the lessons and experience can help inform and hopefully provoke thoughtful discussion about America's future engagement with the rest of the world. America, by design and by desire, has been—and always will be—connected to the rest of the world, intellectually, emotionally, ethnically, and commercially. Our security and prosperity is now and forevermore tied to the security and prosperity of the rest of the world. We must have secure borders and open doors.

Our security depends heavily on our economy. That's not just because a strong economy gives us the resources to build missiles and tanks and to pay the salaries of a first-class military, although we pay private contractors doing similar jobs even more. It is because a strong economy in the twenty-first century by definition gives us the solid international alliances we need in order to provide mutual stakes in prosperity and create partnerships to combat terrorism.

The converse of this hypothesis is also true. Our economy depends on our security. That is, the resources, natural and otherwise, of any country are limited. We need to invest in our technology, in our workforce, and in the education of our young people to spur growth. If we are secure, we can focus more clearly on those priorities.

Much of the intellectual foundation and economic growth in our country's history has been dependent on people coming from around the world to interact with us in many productive ways. In spite of our ever more closely connected world, it is a sad irony that we are less uncomfortable with that notion today than we were before 9/11. America's population looks very much like that of the United Nations, but we are no longer the welcoming nation we were on September 10, 2001. As a result, both our security and our economic interests have suffered.

After World War II, we had a virtual global monopoly as a manufacturing nation and very few competitors. But as the economies of other nations' recovered and matured, and their workforces improved, as their governments invested in their critical infrastructure, markets gradually became global, with global competition. Our heavy industries—steel and automobile manufacturing in particular—learned this the hard way. Yet in spite of the autumn 2008 meltdown on Wall Street, our citizens still consider this country to be the center of the economic universe. If that is true at all, it may remain true only for the near term. We will not be able to sustain our position without a wholesale change in our politics and philosophy as it relates to the rest of the world. As Fareed Zakaria points out in his excellent 2008 book, *The Post-American World,* the tallest buildings in the world are in Taipei and Dubai, the largest publicly traded company is Chinese, the world's largest plane is built in Russia and Ukraine, and the most richly endowed investment fund is owned by citizens of the United Arab Emirates.

In this new world, the global superiority we enjoyed for the decades after World War II is gone. We built a huge economy by manufacturing and selling goods to ourselves and to the populations of emerging but noncompetitive markets overseas. A half century later, we have strong competition in every sector, and America's appetite for goods not Made In America continues to grow.

To stay competitive, we must continue to regain our innovative edge over the rest of the world. Economic advantage is fueled by creative minds in the many disciplines of science, technology, engineering, and mathematics. For decades, thousands of foreign students arrived in America, attended college, became educated in these areas, and remained here. Today, fewer matriculate here, and fewer still remain upon completion of their studies.

We make it difficult for students, tourists, business travelers, and others in non-visa waiver countries to gain admission to the United States. There are thirty-five countries whose citizens can appear at our borders with a passport and gain admission. They do not require a visa. The citizens of the remaining countries, non-visa waiver countries, are obliged to secure a visa from the Department of State before entering with their passport. They are required to appear before a consular officer, after traveling long distances, for an interview and then, assuming their visa request is approved, return days, weeks, or months later to claim it.

The delay, inconvenience, and expense associated with travel to the United States have significantly reduced our interaction with the rest of the world. Recent statistics reveal the extent of this problem. In 2000, overseas travelers, excluding those from Canada and Mexico, numbered 26 million. Yet the U.S. welcomed 2 million fewer in 2007 than in 2000. In the same period the global overseas travel market grew nearly 30 percent, amounting to 35 million new global travelers.

Whether the decline of interest in traveling to the United States is a result of the perception or the reality that the post-9/11 America has become less welcoming, it is in our national interest to turn it around. We can become neither economic protectionists nor political isolationists. With new security measures in place, including extensive information sharing between governments about terrorists, we can manage the risk of a lawful entry for unlawful purposes better than ever. It is an acceptable risk in today's world.

I recall attending a Cisco Systems event at which chairman and CEO John Chambers hoped to recognize some of his best employees from around the world. He delivered his remarks while several seats of honor remained empty because the occupants couldn't get visas. It gets worse. In November 2008 concert-goers in Manhattan, anticipating the joint appearance of an internationally renowned mezzo-soprano and her pianist, were subject to a last-minute change in the program. Seems the pianist of choice was denied a visa at the last moment because, in the estimation of federal employees, he hadn't performed often enough with the soprano to make them a duo. Think of it. As we are issuing, or in this case, not issuing visas, government is in the business of determining the standards of high art.

The policy imperative involves more than travel visas. While secretary, I received several letters from congressmen and senators complaining about the limited number of H-1B visas that were available for their business and industry constituents. The irony is that Congress sets the limits and can therefore adjust them to satisfy the need. But it's not just visa policy that should be addressed in a more complete way, but the broader issue of immigration policy. The tragedy here is that America really doesn't have a policy. The last reform occurred nearly forty years ago and the ad hoc changes grafted onto that outdated system since then have not advanced either our security or economic interests.

Sally Canfield, the policy director at DHS, observed that this byzantine system of rules required a greeting that said, "Welcome to America. Hire a lawyer." America must decide what role we want legal immigration to play in our future and construct an approach that helps us reach the desired outcome.

But we will be unable to establish a twenty-first-century immigration policy that is sustainable if we can't find a way to deal with illegal immigration along our southern border.

I retain many indelible images from my years at DHS. One of them is the view from a helicopter along the United States–Mexican border. I could see below me the arid land the two countries share. And I could see the vastness of it all—stretching along nearly two thousand miles, and understand the pressing need for a better and expanded system of patrol.

Flying west, I glimpsed to my right the city of Nogales, Arizona, the state's largest border town, with a population of about 20,000. I spotted the southern tip of Interstate 19, the superhighway, only a few miles from the border. From this perspective, I could see exactly what happens in the immigration trade. On any given night, many illegal immigrants will sneak over and be picked up by vans on the Interstate. The smuggling operation is very sophisticated, often armed, and always dangerous.

Once, during a helicopter tour, the pilot, hovering over the terrain that separated the fenceless border pointed out a checkpoint manned by the Mexican government that is supposed to stop immigrants before they cross the border. "Worthless," the pilot observed.

During talks with then president Vicente Fox, I suggested it would be hugely helpful if he could take action that demonstrated his government's willingness to protect the integrity of its neighbor's borders. The only formal action was a multicolored brochure that purported to discourage illegal immigration, but actually provided survival guidance to those who chose to make the quest.

It is estimated that remittances back to Mexico from their citizens in the United States legally or illegally, is in excess of $25 billion dollars. The Mexican government is not prepared to turn off the spigot that provides such a massive infusion of dollars into their struggling economy. If we developed a means by which workers could move freely and lawfully across the border, they would likely take their dollars home, rather than send them.

The number of illegals entering this country has grown since amnesty was granted in the mid-1980s to all who had previously entered illegally. Congress failed, until recently, to provide the resources needed to enforce our immigration laws. During that twenty-year interval Congress also failed to design an orderly and humane process that enabled willing workers to enter lawfully from the south.

It is estimated we have anywhere from 10 to 14 million illegal aliens among us. It's impossible to accept the notion that this population, perhaps exceeding that of my home state of Pennsylvania, must be identified and deported before we enact comprehensive immigration legislation.

Since the time I left office, political momentum led to the construction of hugely expensive physical and virtual walls along the border and to the hiring of more agents to track down illegals. I believe an enlightened immigration policy requires enforcement, but we cannot rely on it exclusively. Let's use our dedicated agents to destroy the infrastructure that treats these unsuspecting illegal immigrants like chattel, indentured servants, or slaves. I recall an incident which involved a rival gang that tried to hijack the vehicle of another carrying illegal immigrants which resulted in a gun battle along a ten-mile stretch of Interstate 10 outside of Phoenix. The cargo of illegal immigrants had value if they could be held for ransom.

We should be using agents to apprehend the predators, drug runners, and thieves who are here illegally, while we find a way to legitimize the presence of those who broke our laws to get here, but who have been law-abiding ever since. This does not mean guaranteeing a path to citizenship. Many transitional workers prefer to remain citizens of their home counties. We shouldn't be so arrogant to think that all who would work here would renounce their citizenship for ours. Congress should link strong border enforcement with a biometric-based registration system for foreign workers. A law-abiding worker would submit a digital photo and fingerprints. The employer could only hire from among those that met the requirements. Common sense and technology are required, not amnesty.

Let's assume Congress accepts its responsibility to move swiftly and humanely to fashion a comprehensive twenty-first-century immigration policy. If they were starting with a blank sheet of paper, one of the enforcement tools would surely be an entry-exit system to track all those whom we welcome to our country.

Ironically, that work began in 2002 when Congress created the Department of Homeland Security. As part of its establishment, we were mandated to build such a system, which, by the way, has been discussed since the 1950s. This is evidence that it is not always a virtue for government to move at subglacial speed. The tragedy of 9/11 and circumstances involving two of the hijackers prompted action. A mature monitoring system would have detected their visa violations, and rigorous enforcement might have led to their apprehension. Hani Hanjour and Mohammed Atta had violated the conditions of their visas. They suffered no consequences, but America felt the pain. DHS was mandated by Congress to have an immigration entry system in place at our airports by December 31, 2003.

In April 2003 Jim Williams, a high-ranking official at the Internal Revenue Service, got a call from Under Secretary Asa Hutchinson. Hutchinson asked if Williams would visit the department to explain his implementation and use of new technology at the IRS. Williams was overseeing a project that was providing Internet access for taxpayers and cutting the time between filings and refunds by retiring an antiquated computer system that had been developed during the Kennedy administration. Hutchinson was impressed by the details, but had another agenda in mind. Without announcing it, he was conducting a job interview. The next day, he called Williams and asked to talk to his boss, the acting director of the IRS. Later that day Williams got the news that he would start work at DHS within twenty-four hours, a change that came about so suddenly that, in his hurry, he left the photos of his two children on his old desk.

The federal government has long had an outdated system to record the arrival of visitors in this country, and has had no idea of when or whether they left. The entry system was based on old technology; that is, passport photos and identifications that might, or might not, be accurate. There's an entire industry that produces fake passports worldwide, and it is much more dangerous than a plot point in a spy novel. There was no systematic way to prove that the people arriving at America's doorstep were actually the people they purported to be—except through a visual inspection.

Technology, meanwhile, had been developed that allowed for much more intense scrutiny. A system of biometrics was now possible. And as Williams soon learned, it was my firm goal, drawing upon the congressional mandate, to install a system of biometric checks at every U.S. airport that processes international travelers—more than 150 of them—by the end of the year. Part of the new system would be not only taking biometrics of visitors when they come into the country but recording their departure as well. In that way, authorities could check electronically to see who has overstayed their welcome, as the 9/11 hijackers had done. The task was enormous. Williams pointed out that jaws dropped when my deadline was imposed. As he later said, "There were two stretch goals in my lifetime. One was Kennedy's announcement that by the end of the 1960s we'd have a man on the moon, and the other was Tom Ridge's promise to America that by the end of 2003 we would know for certain who was coming into our country and who was overstaying."

Aside from connecting available technology to the systems at airports, there was another task that involved not science and engineering but sales. Williams knew that foreign visitors could easily be offended by the idea that they would now have their fingerprints checked. Never mind that it wasn't the old-fashioned way, with ink, but with new digital technology. In a matter of a few seconds, a photo of a print could be compared electronically to thousands of FBI or other files of known criminals or terrorists. Yet the very idea seemed intrusive to some. For older Japanese visitors, for example, it brought back memories of the post–World War II era, when General Douglas MacArthur, as the proconsul of the U.S. occupation of Japan, made fingerprinting one of the demeaning requirements of all citizens.

Williams and I, as well as others working on the project, spent a good deal of time explaining why the new system was necessary. I insisted that we call the program something positive—not Exit/ Entry, but US-VISIT. My point was that we should be viewed as a welcoming country—and that perception and reality shouldn't change even in the face of new and hard-to-detect dangers.

Williams, in turn, had several goals that, collectively, would ensure the system would not be unduly invasive. These included enhancing security while, at the same time, making the process of passing through it easier and less time consuming. He also told those working on the project that protecting people's privacy and dignity was paramount.

One of Williams's biggest continuing problems involved the infrastructure needs at international airports. That is, they are physically designed to facilitate people coming into the country. When you land at JFK, for example, a clear process exists through which citizens and noncitizens are obliged to pass. No such system or infrastructure was in place for people leaving the country. Later Williams negotiated to set up kiosks at airports to handle exit processing.

Williams and his team met the "impossible" deadline to install the entry systems at air- and seaports. By the first of January 2004, visitors from non–visa waiver countries (countries like Egypt, Russia, Iraq, etc.) were obliged to have two fingers scanned. (Later, when visitors became more accustomed to the process, the scans included all ten fingers, making it a more accurate test.) In a few seconds, the screen would blink either green (the visitor would proceed) or red (the visitor would be held for secondary screening). "We caught a lot of bad guys," Williams recalls—people who had serious criminal records in other countries and who, in previous years, would have slipped by the system.

Criticism, nevertheless, abounded internationally. We had to calm fears and address the objections of our closest allies, Canada and Mexico, who felt offended by the process. In retaliation, Argentina began fingerprinting (with old-fashioned ink on paper) visitors from the United States. But in short order visitors expected it and grew accustomed to it.

And now, all these years later, we have abandoned placement of the exit system at our airports. Airlines objected to what they viewed as unnecessary complications associated with placing the exit equipment. And though my successor, Michael Chertoff, was generally supportive of US-VISIT, many members of Congress are now, at best, indifferent to it. They have been unwilling to fund it or otherwise address the more complicated matter of entry and exit at our land borders. In some places—near Buffalo, New York, for example—car travelers can leave the country without even slowing down. And yet, there is technology out there—or that can be developed—based on an E-ZPass type system, that could be adopted to meet our needs. It's likely, therefore, that we have people among us who have overstayed their visas. Where are they now, and what are they doing? Whatever happened to that sense of urgency?

16

AN ENLIGHTENED
CONGRESS

Congress seems drugged and inert most of the time. . . . Its
idea of meeting a problem is to hold hearings or, in extreme
cases, to appoint a commission.

—Shirley Chisholm,
Unbought and Unbossed (1970)

In the summer of 2006, retired Coast Guard admiral Jim Loy
(who, at the time was the deputy secretary of the department)
and I went to the Uptown Theater in the very upscale Cleveland
Park district of Washington for the premiere of a new movie, *The
Guardian*. As DHS officials, we were among the special guests with
members of Hollywood's elite, including actor Kevin Costner, caught
the first public glimpse of a film that had our nation's fifth—and
least understood—service at its heart.

For many years, Loy, who had been commandant of the Coast
Guard before retiring in 2001, had tried mightily to raise awareness of what this organization has provided to the country since its
founding in 1790, a service that has chugged along in an aging fleet
under nearly everyone's radar.

The Coast Guard does more with less than any other organization in the federal government. With only about 45,000 members
(the same number as the New York City Police Department) its
total annual budget is what the Pentagon rounds off in its annual
computations. Though greatly underfunded, as Loy points out, it

has a foothold in many areas: law enforcement, the environmental camp, the military, and humanitarian efforts. (In response to Hurricane Katrina alone, the Coast Guard had a hand in rescuing about 33,500 storm victims—a fact that was lost amid the horrifically lame response from other authorities.) In so many ways, it lives up to its Latin motto, Semper Paratus—"always ready."

Because of its multiple missions, the Coast Guard has an ability to adapt and to shift gears in the way no other service can. And yet as Jim Loy and every other officer who ever graduated from the Coast Guard Academy in New London, Connecticut, knows, it has never gotten the attention or the resources it has deserved. This is probably so because it is something of an orphan, or appears to be. The other military services are under the Department of Defense, as was the Coast Guard during World War I and World War II. At all other times, it was felt that because of its diverse missions that it belonged elsewhere. So for most of its existence it found itself in the Department of the Treasury, and then in the last few decades, under the Department of Transportation. Without the—literally—big guns fighting for it, it has suffered.

That's what made the movie premiere so unusual. For decades audiences have been treated to hundreds of films featuring the exploits of the navy, army, air force, and marines. But the Coast Guard? Only a handful. And *The Guardian* was the biggest star-driven effort—the equivalent, in a way, of what *Top Gun* did for the Air Force.

Costner played Ben Randall, a legendary Coast Guard rescue swimmer who is sent to an elite training program to teach others to do what he has done. He turns the program upside down with training methods that are outside the box. One of his charges is Jake Fischer, played by Ashton Kutcher. Ben molds Jake's character, giving him the tools he needs to be a rescue swimmer.

When the screening at the Uptown was over, Loy recalls, there was a touching moment. Admiral Thad Allen took the stage and introduced Costner and Kutcher to the audience. Both men, particularly addressing their remarks to a group of rescue swimmer trainees in the front rows, offered their views on what it was like to do the film. Costner said, "We know now what you do for America day in and day out. . . . What we wanted to do was tell the story to rest of the country."

Loy also remembers leaving the theater and "a lot of mothers seemed to be around me and about half were saying something like, 'I can't wait to encourage my son or daughter to be a rescue swimmer,' and the other half were saying, 'No way I'm going to let my kids on one of those helicopters.'"

I don't know how many members of Congress were there that night, or how many saw the movie at all. And of those who may have seen it, how many were swayed by it—and reminded that, as a body, the Congress is particularly tough on the Coast Guard— unrealistic in its demands and historically underfunding the ser- vice although expanding its mission and praising its performance. When I think of the congressional reform needed to make the homeland security effort stronger, I begin with the Coast Guard.

There is irony and a certain amount of heartbreak when Congress—not surprisingly—was up in arms after certain discov- eries were made about the Coast Guard's Deepwater Project. Deep- water, which began in the late 1990s, was described by the Coast Guard as "a critical multi-year program to modernize and replace the Coast Guard's aging ships and aircraft, and improve command and control and logistics systems."

Loy, and his successor, Admiral Tom Collins, who served so ably as commandant during my tenure, and others had been in- strumental in creating the vision for Deepwater, which began in the late 1990s, was to address a critical need. The service's fleet was sadly and dangerously out of date. I knew this firsthand. I ap- pealed the budget decision after OBM substantially reduced fund- ing for the Deepwater Project in 2004. The final appeal, which is rarely used, is held before several administration officials, includ- ing the vice president. I took a thick steel deck plate from an oper- ating Coast Guard cutter that had a deep crack because of the pounding the ship had taken for nearly thirty-five years. During the same meeting, I also pointed out that Coast Guard rescue helicopters—the very ones used to save so many lives from the rooftops of New Orleans and the Gulf Coast—had an engine failure rate ten times the rate allowed by the FAA for civilian aircraft.

While aboard a Coast Guard helicopter providing an aerial view of the G-8 Summit site above Sea Island, Georgia, in 2004, I asked the pilot about his aircraft. Specifically, I inquired whether the engine propelling us was the type subject to this extreme failure rate. My successor in the White House, General Gordon, sitting in the rear, tapped me on the shoulder and with a wry smile asked if we could change the subject. I thought, if a navy admiral or air force general had delivered similar evidence of neglect and equipment failure, there would be incredulity and outrage in the halls of Congress, and a race to the press gallery to offer support for greater funding.

I did manage to get some sympathy and, eventually, support for Deepwater—or as it was formally known, the Integrated Deepwater Systems Program. The twenty-five-year effort would cost a total of $24 billion and address aircraft and vessel needs as well as command and control systems.

The scale of the program, however, was way beyond anything the Coast Guard had ever attempted, so its leaders knew that there needed to be a public-private partnership. A new private company was formed in June 2002 to manage and oversee the prime contractors, Northrup Grumman and Lockheed Martin. The challenge became, as with many defense contractors, effective oversight. As it turned out, there wasn't enough oversight to prevent significant technical and financial problems, which become a public relations disaster, and so there was hell to pay in Congress when the plan didn't work. There were large cost overruns, the designs for expanded cutters didn't seem to be working; hulls were cracking; and there was a wide array of other engineering and design problems. In the end, the refurbishing plan—including ships already under construction—was scrapped at a great economic and public relations cost. A new plan was developed, but ships would have to be built from scratch. Congress, reluctant to irritate the check-wielding "industrial" half of the "military-industrial complex," held the Coast Guard primarily responsible. It wasn't entirely blameless, but it did not deserve the brunt of the criticism. Congress had failed to recognize the desperate physical needs of the Coast Guard until its fleet was in dire shape. It also found it easier to castigate its leadership than the companies awarded the contract to provide the expertise and oversight needed to replace the worn-out fleet.

On the one hand, I suppose we should have been flattered by all the attention DHS and its components received from Congress. Certainly, we broke the modern record—and perhaps all records— for the number of times people in leadership positions of a federal department were cordially invited to take their seats in front of an array of senators or representatives, pour glasses of water, clear their throats, and testify.

Members of Congress must reform its oversight of DHS. The old, treasured lines of committee authority should have been firmly and permanently reduced when the twenty-two agencies that make up the department were initially combined. There is legislative precedent for this action, but as of now, not the will to act. In 1946, Wisconsin Senator Robert M. La Follette Jr. overcame entrenched interests within Congress and among lobbyists and secured passage of the Legislative Reorganization Act (also known as the Congressional Reorganization Act), which was the most comprehensive reorganization of Congress to date. This measure combined committees with overlapping jurisdiction into an Armed Services Committee, which was given oversight responsibility for what became, in 1947, the Department of Defense. The Department of Homeland Security needs a modern champion to take up their cause.

The Department of Defense, which oversees a budget of half of a trillion dollars, has to prepare for testimony before a handful of committees and a few subcommittees. DHS, pocket change as measured by the size of its budget, answers to eighty-six committees or subcommittees. Yes, this is flattering because, obviously, what DHS is doing is important, but it's also enormously frustrating, and not only because of the incalculable amount of time it takes to prepare for such appearances, sit through them, and then debrief the staff. These committees and subcommittees often work at cross-purposes and send wildly competing messages that lead to even more meetings to try and make sense of it all.

Jim Loy recalls a telling episode. Before he became deputy secretary of DHS, Loy held the high-pressure post of TSA director.

In that position, he was the recipient of certain authorizing committee mandates to alter security at all of the nation's commercial airports in less than a year and half. He identified the requirements imposed by these authorizing committees, calculated the number of employees needed to meet the requirements, and submitted a budget request to support a minimum of 60,000 new employees to undertake the tasks that Congress had demanded. The appropriations committees were not sympathetic. With absolutely no data—other than the budget numbers—to guide them, they cut his request to 45,000. Loy found creative ways to share a few dollars from other accounts to partially meet the higher personnel requirements demanded by the other committees. A better understanding of staffing needs at each airport through actual operations has resulted several years later in a workforce that totals around 43,000.

Occasionally my team and I were summoned to the Hill for a private rebuke. I remember accompanying marine general Frank Libutti, under secretary for information analysis and infrastructure protection, and a member of my management team who had served in the military with great distinction. We were dressed down by a congressman for the slow pace of filling vacancies in his unit. There was no appreciation of the vetting process and security clearances, nor the inherent difficulty of recruiting people when there were attractive employment opportunities (not to mention superior working conditions) in the established agencies. The general demonstrated great restraint during this encounter. On another occasion, a congressional staff member actually threatened to withhold funds unless we answered a certain letter within forty-eight hours. It was just one letter, but it contained over a thousand questions. We answered them all.

I say this not from some ivory tower. I served in Congress for twelve years. Our system of checks and balances demands that Congress oversee the executive branch. No one committee has a full understanding of all that goes on within DHS, and intercommittee collaboration is rare. I believe the strong strategic partnership essential to the continuing development of the department and enhanced security of our country requires a substantial realignment and reduction of the number of committees to which the department reports.

By now you will probably have anticipated what I will say next. I have urged Congress to reorganize itself to strengthen its oversight and effectiveness as it works with the department. Now I encourage Congress to consider the reorganization of the department along regional lines to improve its operational effectiveness and make the country more secure.

The Secret Service has designated areas (4), FEMA has regions (10), TSA has areas (5), Customs and Border Protection has both patrol sectors (20) and management centers (17), the Coast Guard maintains (5) districts, and the Bureau of Immigration and Citizenship Services (3). I believe a single, unified regional structure based upon pre- and post-9/11 responsibilities would greatly improve the department's ability to accomplish its mission.

A regional office and director would provide a single focus for state and local, public and private, interaction with the department. The network of relationships that would be established within the region would be invaluable. Oversight of dollars spent and training exercises would give the department critical knowledge about capacities and needs within the region. Integrating all emerging plans and the development of mutual aid pacts as well as building a seamless information-sharing network would result in the type of collaborative environment necessary to meet the national goals of the department.

In order for the department to accomplish its mission as described in the national strategy published in 2002 and its charge to secure America, it must build and maintain these relationships permanently. The value of this approach cannot be overstated!

There is, I know, a comprehensive regional plan sitting somewhere at the NAC. Someone, I hope, will locate it, dust it off, and examine it carefully for use as the basis of the next most important organizational change within the department. Parochial political resistance to the regional concept will be difficult to overcome in Washington and back home. One can hope that champions of a regional approach will emerge and that the transformative restructuring will be effected. We cannot secure America by working only from inside the Beltway.

The failure of communications on September 11, 2001, was not just a tragedy because so many first responders died and so many victims could not be rescued. The four columns of rising black smoke marked failure after failure in envisioning the need for supplying the best equipment for all who needed it, for training them in its use, and in coordinating its management across agencies.

The 9/11 Commission was created by Congress to discover what went wrong on that day. Its hearings, and its reports, made for painful, distressing reading.

We must change. We must do better. Here is what the commission said:

> The inability to communicate was a critical element at the World Trade Center, Pentagon, and Somerset County, Pennsylvania, crash sites, where multiple agencies and multiple jurisdictions responded. The occurrence of this problem at three very different sites is strong evidence that compatible and adequate communications among public safety organizations at the local, state, and federal levels remains an important problem. Recommendation: Congress should support pending legislation which provides for the expedited and increased assignment of radio spectrum for public safety purposes.

Fast-forward to December 2008. In anticipation of the spending tsunami after the 2009 inaugural, the Public Safety Spectrum Trust (PSST)—the nationwide licensee for the public-safety broadband spectrum in the 700 MHz band—wrote the administration and requested $15 billion to complete a national, wireless broadband network. The request included an excerpt from a November 2008 report from the 9/11 Commission to the FCC which said the commission is "deeply concerned that more than seven years has passed since 9/11 without the implementation of a public-safety network." If the tragedy of 9/11, the specific recommendation of a congressionally created commission and the sustained pleas of police, firemen, and emergency service professionals cannot generate federal support for the network, then what will it take?

Just as the intelligence community, war fighters, and others need as complete a situational awareness as possible, so do these men and women. Broadband would provide the ability to transmit voice, data, and video and add layers of safety for them and security for the people they choose to serve. Praise and gratitude for their service is no substitute for the broadband they need.

In the twenty-first century, the physical and cyber environments are not exclusive domains. When we turn our attention to the protection of critical infrastructure, we conjure up images of physical attacks on bridges, dams, power plants, chemical sites, and brick-and-mortar structures. But there is more: a ubiquitous, generally invisible infrastructure, within walls and underground; it is embedded in our economy and in our daily lives, and it requires at least the same attention—cyberspace.

The physical and cyber worlds are intertwined. Sabotage of one can lead to destruction or disruption of both. Access to the Internet is global, and in spite of attempts to secure critical and sensitive sites, there are dozens of daily reports confirming that our enemies have infiltrated our networks. Consider the impact of crippling computer data on an electric grid that provides life-sustaining power to millions of people in an urban area.

James Gleick, author and Internet pioneer, captured the essence of the cyber world when he observed that "the Internet was built to be an open and cooperative system. That's its strength—and its weakness."

Very few Americans are probably aware of the highly disruptive impact of cyber attacks. But the first and second wars fought in cyberspace showed us that vulnerabilities have spread in new ways and that, when it comes to security, imagination is among our necessary assets.

After Estonian authorities removed a bronze statue of a Soviet soldier in 2007, there were organized protests and, in their wake, the country suffered an attack on its information technology infra-structure. Russia was suspected of being the culprit, though it de-nied responsibility.

The massive hacking shut down banks, newspapers, and many military operations. The country couldn't effectively communicate with the rest of the world, and it was blocked internally. In a thirty-day period, the world saw that a certain kind of invasion—one that kills nobody and brings down no buildings—can bring a country to its knees because vital communications are cut off. Russia employed the same tactic a year later—weapons of mass disruption—blocking Internet communication before sending troops into neighboring Georgia, a tactic that caused considerable chaos among the country's military hierarchy.

We know that terrorists use the Internet to educate, advocate, and recruit. It takes little imagination to conclude malicious incur-sions are part of their long-term plan. The industry that produces the hardware and software that the nation relies upon to support critical systems must continue to develop pre-sale security devices in their products. Users have a responsibility to take precautions as well.

The National Strategy for Cyber Security that Richard A. Clarke, Howard Schmidt, and others drafted for me in 2002 received mod-est attention when introduced, effected some changes in our re-sponse to this challenge, but never received the enthusiastic embrace of the Bush administration or Congress. As recently as December 2008, the Center for Strategic and International Studies helped produce a report, "Securing Cyberspace for the 44th Presidency," that highlighted American vulnerabilities and proposed possible solutions. The recommendations within both documents should receive the attention and action required, and with the support of a tech-savvy president and administration, we can significantly re-duce our cyber vulnerability.

The anthrax attacks in 2001 prompted close scrutiny of our nation's ability to respond effectively to a biological attack. Whether the pathogens are natural or manmade, the potential devastation can-not be ignored. I have never forgotten my first briefing on biopreparedness as assistant to the president for homeland security. We weren't prepared then. On December 2, 2008, the congressionally mandated Commission on the Prevention of Weapons of Mass Destruction Proliferation and Terrorism found that the leading WMD threat to the nation is bioterrorism. We still aren't prepared!

We rely heavily on our public health community to be our early warning system. It was and remains underfunded and lacks the technological infrastructure essential for a modern disease surveillance network.

Surveillance and timely detection should be supported by massive government stockpiles of medical countermeasures and an advanced research, production, and surge capacity that can produce medicines and vaccines rapidly and on a large scale as needed. Now we have neither. We cannot look to the private sector to meet these needs. There is no commercial market to sustain research and development. Consumers, be they individual medical practitioners or hospitals, just are not stockpiling vaccines for Ebola, ricin, or smallpox.

Assuming timely detection and the availability of a medical countermeasure, there remains the challenge of full-scale distribution. The Departments of Health and Human Services and Homeland Security have been trying to solve this problem for several years, including the use of the U.S. Postal Service. The distribution gap has not been closed. Congress needs to champion the trilogy of biodefense—detection, production, and distribution.

I can't think of a single piece of information more critical to our ultimate security and prosperity, both as individuals and as a country, than our personal identity. The ability of an individual to establish identity, to verify "you are who you claim to be," is critical to the many transactions that occur in a single day. As the world becomes more interdependent, as transactions become more global, and as the world embraces identity management and assurance as an element of conducting business, personal identities will become a form of global currency. Whether you are crossing a border, seeking employment, applying for a public benefit, opening a bank account, combating crime, making a purchase, enforcing immigration policy, granting access to public and private spaces, detecting terrorists—identity verification has limitless value.

Much of Europe, Asia, South Africa, and elsewhere are embedding identity management and assurance measures in their economic, social, and security programs. The United States, which is viewed by many as the catalyst for such advances because of the US-VISIT program, is falling farther and farther behind in this effort.

Of course, abuses are easily imagined. The BBC ran a popular series—shown in this country in the Contemporary Masterpiece Theatre series on PBS—that featured something called T.I.A., for total information awareness. In short, Big Brother. The government, knowing every move a citizen or noncitizen makes, uses this information for ill. No doubt, in the wrong hands, such things could happen. It is a matter of trust. And I wouldn't begin to argue that the federal government has earned an unquestioned right to the public trust.

It is curious that Congress implicitly accepts the value of an identification system, but bans the creation of a national one. Congress has approved the use of biometrics (US-VISIT), mandated a transportation worker identification card (TWIC), and supports federal agencies that require them as a condition of employment and access. Social Security cards, driver's licenses, and more traditional forms of identification have outlived their usefulness.

Now is the time for a serious discussion of the benefits of a national identification system that combines both biometric and biographical information. Although there will be concerns legitimately raised about privacy, I believe in the end the proper use of biometrics can serve to protect, not invade it.

We can learn a great deal from other deployments around the globe. These lessons should be part of the dialogue, beginning immediately, with the government, private sector, technology companies, and, of course, privacy and civil rights advocates. We have the technology platform to build a secure system that limits access and use. We must develop the popular will to begin its construction.

There is another reality that our country can no longer afford to ignore. I offer absolutely nothing new with these final thoughts. I seek only to join those who plead with Congress to enact a comprehensive energy policy that includes the appropriate incentives to support nuclear energy, clean coal, natural gas, biofuels, renewables, and conservation.

Energy independence and homeland security are linked. During the past three decades we've gone through several oil crises. Each time, prices shot up, people waited in lines, huge chunks of disposable income went into filling our gas tanks. At the time, we promised ourselves it would never happen again. We promised ourselves we would take immediate and aggressive action to render us less dependent on foreign sources of oil. But every time the price at the pump dropped and the cost of other fuels declined, we lost our ardor and our will to do so.

Unless we embark on a comprehensive approach to energy development, we will find ourselves in the same predicament a fourth and fifth time. We may put our military in harm's way again because we lacked the vision and courage to think and act anew about energy policy. Make no mistake, when we fill up our tanks, some of that money goes to people who want to kill us, undermine our way of life, and replace it with their own.

Imagine the national and international impact if we committed the resources to drive innovation across every potential energy source. The positive environmental, competitive, and economic impact is almost limitless. Jobs, exports, reduced carbon footprints, and, yes, greater security.

17

VICTORY OVER TERRORISM?

Life is the risk we can't refuse.

—MASON COOLEY,
Aphorist and English Professor

On a day during Thanksgiving week 2008, I visited the office of Richard Falkenrath, the former White House official with whom I worked in the early days of my Washington tenure.

As we talked in his New York office—both of us reminiscing about those first days in the White House and the creation of the department—he kept a close eye on his BlackBerry, which seemed to provide new information every few seconds. He also glanced occasionally at the large flat-screen television tuned permanently to CNN. His job is high-profile and high-anxiety. His force of 350 New York police officers is unique on American soil. New York is the only American city to have such a large force devoted totally to counterterrorism. (London is the only international city to do so.)

We talked of how threats against western civilization have changed over the last few years. We agreed that state-based threats were no longer our only national security concern and that the age of traditional wars among great powers was probably behind us. We discussed the progress to date against Al Qaeda and the assortment

of challenges that remain in Afghanistan and Iraq; the risk of political correctness and accommodation in the face of an enemy that
holds a long view; the consequences of unilateralism and the impotence of multilateral organizations. We concluded that the new enemy we face will take advantage of our freedom and openness and
infrastructure. He observed, "We have a system of government that,
by design, is not highly efficient at internal security—that's the way
the founding fathers wanted it."

The practical result of this is a kind of disconnect between
what America generally sees as its responsibility to protect its citizens, and the reality of doing it. As Falkenrath said, "If we had a
terrorist attack in New York today, someone would blame the feds,
but there's nothing they can do to defend the subways."

A couple of hours after I left Falkenrath's office, CNN delivered
the news to him and to the rest of the world that illustrated this
point, showing what open societies are up against. A few men,
armed with AK-47s and grenades, managed to capture worldwide
headlines for three days and to wreak havoc and heartbreak by using the largely unprotected waterways around the city of Mumbai,
India's financial capital. The group was typical of the new kind of
war that we face, and it makes Islamic extremists—not nations—
the force that endangers us, requiring a whole new approach
outside the traditions, enlightened or otherwise, of the military-
industrial complex.

As *Los Angeles Times* columnist Tim Rutten said in the wake
of the Mumbai attack, "There are many facts remaining to be discovered about the atrocities . . . this week, but we already know
what we really need to know. The physical institutions targeted
and the individuals singled out for particular attention by the
killers—Americans, Britons and Jews—are signatures of the fanatic Islamists we've come to know as jihadists. The sites of their
attacks may vary—New York, London, Madrid, Nairobi, Mumbai—
but the object of their quarrel with history remains the same:
modernity."

Indeed, only hours after I left Falkenrath's office, his headquarters was alerted to an FBI report that indicated a possible

threat against New York City during the Thanksgiving holiday period, and thereafter, until the New Year. Described by an internal FBI memo as "plausible but unsubstantiated," it set in motion a number of measures issued from Falkenrath's office and largely ensured that he and his young family would not celebrate the holidays in the way they had planned.

Every day, thousands of men and women like Falkenrath make decisions in the face of new but incomplete information. They must make the right decision every time. The threat is constant, but as we learn more about the enemy, we must be prepared to change our approach and tactics to defeat it.

Do I think America will ever celebrate a Victory over Terrorism Day when we can say with confidence and pride that we vanquished our extremist foes? No.

Do I think there are philosophical and financial limits to the measures we should take to secure ourselves against this threat? Yes.

Do I think America is willing to accept a certain level of risk of future attacks? I'm not certain.

Should we accept some risk and get on with our lives? Yes!

As citizens we are entitled to have expectations of our government relative to our security. Our government must be ever vigilant, share information, use the best technology where it makes sense to do so, and apply diplomatic or even military pressure when required. These expectations are legitimate. Expecting our government to create a fail-safe, risk-free environment is not.

As individuals or as a nation, our lives would be incalculably better if we could avoid tragedy. We cannot. As individuals and as a country, we accept the reality of the moment, deal with it as best we can, and move on. We suffer pain, we acknowledge the loss, and while we can never purge the people or the circumstances from our memories, we do not let those memories sap our strength, our will to live, or our ability to enjoy another, better day. As individuals, we accept the fact that every day does not bring with it success, pleasure, or comfort. So, too, as a country, we must be prepared to accept the fact that some day, no matter how hard we have tried, we may be unable to prevent an attack.

The risk is ever present. It must be managed. It cannot be eliminated. The question for our leaders, our policy makers, and ourselves is "How much security is enough?" At what point does the financial or philosophical cost exceed our willingness or ability to pay for it? Risk management involves making choices—trade-offs.

Do we spend billions defending commercial airlines against shoulder-fired missiles, or do we invest in nuclear detection technology to inspect the 20 million cargo containers shipped to our ports? Do we continue to spend huge amounts on cancer research, or do we divert some of those funds to producing and stockpiling vaccines against bioagents that terrorists might use? Do we appropriate the money to complete the US-VISIT program so we can finally know who has overstayed his or her visa, or do we give the states more money for equipment and training? Do we choose among adding more layers of security at chemical sites, addressing a different security risk in mass transit, or channeling that investment to a national health or energy priority? The list of our national needs and wants seems limitless. Resources are not.

Risk management is a concept that all of us practice in our daily lives, but we don't call it that. People make financial decisions, without ever thinking they're practicing risk management. Do we really need to pay more in order to raise the coverage ceiling on our auto and home insurance policies today? Do we need long-term nursing care insurance to cover our expenses fifteen or twenty years from now? What are the odds we'll have to use it? Do we need a car that has side air bags? Should we bother with our seat belt, or should we make appointments to get a flu shot?

How much risk are you willing to take? Are you prepared to accept the notion that we will never have perfect screening at airports? In a risk-managed world, will you board an airplane full of passengers who have been prescreened because they provided enough biographical and biometric information that the government or a third party has concluded they are probably not terrorists? Will you accept as a trade-off that by providing this information these fliers can arrive later, wear their shoes, and keep their laptop in its case. (They will go through whatever screening devices are deployed at the time.) Will you board?

Consider visa issuance. We need people to feel good about coming to America. We don't want to discourage them with the tedious and time-consuming practices we now use. Would you be prepared to replace mandatory interviews at embassies with character and business references from other Americans, knowing that the ultimate decision to admit won't be made until they arrive? The risk may be slightly greater, but how much greater if our methods of tracking terrorists and their supporters have improved significantly and the database that identifies them is available to the consular officer?

I thought about entitling this chapter "You Can't Kill Them All." We have a great military. We must cherish their service. We must reward their sacrifice. We must also understand their limits. They cannot kill or apprehend all the extremists who would do us harm.

The "War Against Terror" was mislabeled from the outset. Terrorism is a tactic. It has been used for thousands of years by individuals, groups, and sovereigns to advance a cause. We are fighting those who use this tactic and who embrace a theology, a point of view, that the Western world has difficulty reconciling in the context of its own history and value system. The views of these extremists have roots that go far deeper than contemporary history. Never forget the murderous fatwa issued by bin Laden in 1998. "The judgment to kill Americans and their allies, both civilian and military, is the individual duty of every Muslim to do so and in any country when it is possible."

I met the late Benazir Bhutto at a religious symposium in the Ukraine a few months before her assassination. Knowing of her attendance, I read several of her speeches and among the powerful and relevant insights she offered, one especially touched me. She wrote: "You can imprison a man, but not an idea. You can exile a man, but not an idea. You can kill a man, but not an idea."

Assuming we cannot bring them all "to justice" through imprisonment, exile, or death, how do we reduce the threat? How do we make the extremist theology, their murderous tactics, and their anachronistic goals unacceptable to Muslims in our modern world? How do we induce the Muslim world, much of it impoverished, disenfranchised, and angry, to reject this dogma?

In America we seem to poll everything we do, think, or desire. Polling, even with its margin of error, gives us a fleeting glimpse of how people feel about certain matters. From 2001 to 2007, Gallup conducted interviews with thousands of Muslims in thirty-five countries. The results and analyses are provided in the published work *Who Speaks for Islam? What a Billion Muslims Really Think*.

The enormous gulf of perceptions between Muslims and Americans is validated by their research. How wide is that gulf? The authors conclude that many Muslims—both politically radicalized and moderates—admire the West's technology, freedom of speech, and our value system of hard work. Meanwhile, the authors note that Americans who were asked what they know about Muslims predominantly offer two responses: "Nothing" and "I don't know."

The book reveals some startling opinions about the Muslim world's embrace of self-government and free speech. Significant majorities view some form of democracy to be the avenue to progress and a more just society. This suggests a role for Muslim political and religious leaders that cannot be underestimated. They, too, must raise their voices in sustained opposition to the extremists who have hijacked their religion. They, too, must be vocal in their sustained rejection of this ideology of violence, not hope; guns, not butter. They must not allow this extremism to be cloaked in the protection of religious righteousness.

Violence carried out in the name of religion is a false cause. Holy War is an oxymoron. A war that encourages and promotes the violent loss of innocent life cannot be considered the aspiration of any god.

Muslim leaders must eliminate the religious labels the extremists use to define the conflict. If the polling information reflects support for some form of democracy and freedom of speech, then different political, religious, and social views must be tolerated and protected. The more Muslim leaders reject the intolerance of the extremists and their rejection of modernity, the more they will eliminate the false religious cover extremists use to justify their violent cause. Then the extremists will have greater difficulty enticing others to shed blood in the name of religion. Intervention by Muslim public officials and clerics around the world in this fashion is indispensible if the Muslim and non-Muslim world is to be emancipated from this threat.

The book ponders: Is it a clash of civilizations or a clash of ignorance? We know little about each other. The West and most of the Muslim world both repudiate extremism and terrorism. The Muslim repudiation is not surprising since most victims of these attacks are other Muslims. The primary source of Muslim resentment against the West comes from a perception that the West hates them, denigrates their culture, considers it inferior, and is too easily inclined to interfere in the internal affairs of their country.

While it is sadly true that we probably have haters in America, they are a small minority. Of comparable concern is the huge majority that doesn't know much about Muslim religion, history, or culture. As we learn, we must demonstrate to the Muslim world and to its citizens that we have as much interest in them, or more, than we do in their leaders, whom they hold responsible for any number of inadequacies. America led the humanitarian efforts in Southeast Asia after the Indonesian tsunami and the monstrous earthquake in Pakistan. When I walked through the streets of Sarajevo, Bosnia, a few years ago, I saw how the West came to the aid of the Muslim community there and in Kosovo. But our engagement in the Muslim world should not be limited to crises that prompt our humanitarian or military assistance.

We certainly can't expect the media within their world—which is growing in its influence—to help change the perception in spite of any number of good works. We must make substantial investments in public diplomacy messaging with radio and television broadcasts throughout the Muslim world and with developmental assistance, which is rhetorical camouflage for foreign aid.

Until the spring of 2009, foreign aid ranked higher than executive compensation as a target for public and congressional condemnation. Yet if we are to narrow the perception gap, we must be viewed by citizens within the Muslim world as seeking to help them improve their human condition by addressing health, education, and economic needs. I am realistic about the enormous difficulty with this approach. But I do believe this: Whenever a country or organization has invested in improving the lives of the people within another country or region, mutual benefit and a positive impression have resulted. On a grand, humanitarian scale, consider the effect of the Marshall Plan in Europe following World War II. On a lesser, malignant scale, consider the aid that Hezbollah, with Iranian support, provided to the people in southern Lebanon.

I think the most important scene in the popular movie *Charlie Wilson's War,* starring Tom Hanks, comes near the end. Hanks's character pleads for a few million dollars to build schools and roads after the Russians have been vanquished. The same committee that had provided hundreds of millions of dollars of military aid to the mujahideen for weapons to use against Soviet troops rejected his modest request to begin addressing the basic needs of this strife-torn country. His plea is met with ridicule and rejection. The first title card of the movie says: "These things happened. They were glorious and they changed the world . . ." The second title card says, ". . . and then we [messed] up the end game."—Charlie Wilson. Don't you at least wonder what might have been, had we tried?

America and the West must use every possible means to discredit the extremists' view of the world and its complete failure to offer a clear path to a better life for those who embrace it. As Ilan Berman, foreign policy expert and author of the recently published *Winning the Long War: Retaking the Initiative of Radical Islam,* suggests, our job is to address the hundreds of millions of Muslims who can be persuaded that the course of extremism is not in their own interest. Our advocacy, at least initially, is favored by two indisputable facts: First, the primary victims of Al Qaeda attacks have been Muslims; second, bin Laden's aspirations, from killing all infidels to reestablishing the caliphate, have no personal meaning or relevance to most. The globalization of travel and communication has provided Muslims a window into all that is positive in the modern world and how those forces could be used to improve theirs. Extremists reject all of it. Yes, there may be great prejudices against the United States, the result of policy and events over the decades that are repugnant to them. But certainly we can make a powerful case that Al Qaeda and its affiliates have been completely uninterested in the infrastructure or conduct of ordinary life for large Muslim populations.

At the heart of America is a value system that is cherished by us and admired around the world. If America is the product, then that value system is our brand. We cannot tarnish it in our fight against these extremists. Our friends hold us to a higher standard, and we must hold ourselves to the same. Torture and indefinite detention without some form of due process are unacceptable practices. America must continue to lead the global effort against the global scourge of terrorism. We must preserve our moral authority to do so. Our message is flawed and the value of our brand is diminished if we do any less.

America's leadership and credibility depends upon our ability to meet the mission of homeland security. We must protect the tangible (people, places, and things) and the intangible (civil rights, liberties, and the rule of law). Those who doubt our ability to do so don't appreciate the vitality and energy of our democracy. We are our own most vocal critics. We are also our most committed guardians. We are up to the task.

There is no question we were forever changed by the experience of 9/11. In a once inconceivable instant we came face-to-face with a new kind of enemy, a new reality, and perhaps even a permanent condition, international terrorists operating on American soil. While 9/11 may have been this nation's first battle in the war against terror, it will not be the last. Terrorism is a tragic fact, an unwelcome but immutable reality of life in the twenty-first century. Terrorists come in many forms and factions, but they are not deterred by time. They seek to destroy our lives, our liberty, and our economic leadership around the world. In spite of our best—or worst—efforts, we have made great progress in securing our nation. Since 9/11, we have moved from unprecedented grief to unprecedented guard. The late American theatre critic, Brooks Atkinson, wrote, "The most fatal illusion is a settled point of view." This is where danger finds easy sanctuary. That is why America's security must be consistent with changing times. That is why with the passage of every day without incident we get a little smarter, more secure, and closer to that new piece of intelligence or technological discovery that will make us safer yet.

We can never, nor should we ever, guarantee we will be free from another attack. I believe we understand that now. We must understand that every day thousands and thousands of our fellow citizens are at work here and abroad to take us to a new level of readiness and security. For in the end, Americans do not live in fear. We live in freedom. Our ability to maintain our freedom in the face of these new threats is the test of our times.

Acknowledgments

When I was summoned to Washington in the fall of 2001, a period of intense national anxiety, I surely would have failed in my efforts to help secure the American homeland if I had not had the great support, expertise, and commitment of unsung heroes. And when years later, I decided to write a book about the experience, history repeated itself. To the extent that this volume succeeds in providing a reliable history and viable plan for the future, it will be due to the significant contributions of many.

Lisa Gordon-Hagerty, for example, eagerly provided recollections from our earliest—indeed, our instant—challenge, the anthrax attacks. Similarly, Susan K. Neely recalled the particulars of how, in the face of a near panic, we attempted to reassure Americans and prepare them for harsh realities, all the while combating the government's historical resistance to sharing information with the public or, indeed, among its own agencies. General Matt Broderick (ret.), always colorful in his language and candid in his opinions, was among those who could specify in lively detail how politics—even the brand played by the administration that hired us— could complicate our work to an extent that threatened our core mission, revelations that evaded the media but were very real to us. Rob Bonner provided detail and perspective on the crucial matter of U.S. border protection as it changed and developed after September 11, 2001. General Harry Raduege (ret.) and Howard Schmidt provided rich perspective on the profound consequences of cyberterrorism. Bobbie Faye Ferguson told compelling behind-the-scenes stories of how the Department of Homeland Security was finally able to get the entertainment industry to portray the department in a way that would not be misleading and counterproductive. Bob Stephan's recollections of our efforts to try to make Homeland Security a seamless collaboration of federal, state, and local resources show the reader exactly how so much of the heartbreak in the wake of Hurricane Katrina could have been avoided.

Help came from without, too. Several of the international themes were refined over the years through many discussions with Ilan Berman, Vice President of the American Foreign Policy Council. And none of this would have seen the light of day without the contributions of Philippa Brophy of Sterling Lord Literistic, the agent who represents my coauthor and me, and of the book's editor, Rob Kirkpatrick of Thomas Dunne Books of St. Martin's Press. It was a pleasure to work with Lary Bloom. Our collaboration served as a unique path to many a provocative conversation about matters totally unrelated to the book and to a wonderful friendship. We also appreciate the efforts of copy editor Donald J. Davidson, whose suggestions went far beyond word usage to challenge us on accounts of key historical events and conclusions reached. The insights and edits of Pat McGinnis, Rich Galen, and Steve Brill were invaluable, as was the record keeping of my former assistant, Jessica Himanga Miller, and the research provided by Amber Wilkerson Marchand.

There are many others whose recollections enhanced the narration and conclusions that follow. These include General Patrick Hughes (ret.), Admiral James Loy (ret.), Mark Campbell, Colonel Joe Rozek (ret.), Mark Holman, Richard Falkenrath, Asa Hutchinson, Frank Sesno, Randy Beardsworth, Ashley Davis, Barbara Chaffee, Admiral Steve Abbot (ret.), Lieutenant Colonel John Fenzel, General Bruce Lawlor (ret.), Colonel Bill Parrish (ret.), Mike Byrne, Jeff Karonis, Joe Whitley, Josh Filler, Becky Halkias, Admiral David Stone (ret.), Sally Canfield, Duncan Campbell, Wendy Grubbs, and Jim Williams. Advice and support came from Susan Galen, Michele Nix, and Kathleen Landy, my colleagues at Ridge Global and from Richard Calder, Suzanne M. Levine, Jon Joslow, David Coleman, and Bruce Josephy.

Finally, I want to extend special gratitude to all the families, including my wife, Michele, and our children, Lesley and Tommy, whose lives were upended after September 11, 2001. To those who worked and supported me in the White House and in the department and to their spouses and children who also wore the uniform of public service, I say thank you.

Index